Diving Dream to Olympic Team

The Keith Russell Story

Simone Russell

iUniverse, Inc.
New York Bloomington

Diving Dream to Olympic Team
The Keith Russell Story

iUniverse books may be ordered through booksellers or by contacting:

iUniverse
1663 Liberty Drive
Bloomington, IN 47403
www.iuniverse.com
1-800-Authors (1-800-288-4677)

ISBN: 978-1-4401-3577-4 (pbk)
ISBN: 978-1-4401-3578-1 (ebk)
ISBN: 978-1-4401-3579-8 (cloth)

Printed in the United States of America
iUniverse rev. date: 5/11/09

Contents

Acknowledgements

First and foremost, I want to thank Keith's mother, Lurline Russell, for giving birth to and raising this incredible man, for sacrificing so much to support him so fully in his ambitions, for faithfully keeping a journal for him the first twenty-eight years of his life and clipping every newspaper article with his name, even if it was in a foreign language, and trusting me with those precious items. In my thirty-six years, nothing has brought me closer to my Grandma Russell than this history and her faith in me. May you live long (because eighty-seven years isn't long enough). I love you.

Thank you Keith for living your life so well and for letting me tell everyone about it. Thank you for opening your home to me when I started at Brigham Young University and for our talks. You're my hero.

Thank you Aunt Marsha for feeding me delicious Sunday meals and for sharing with me the painful details of Mindy's battle.

Thank you Dianne Tipton-King for doing the first edit. I am so grateful to you for that.

To my BYU professors, Dr. Gerald Haslam, Dr. Richard Kimball, and

Kory Meyerink for encouraging me in this fun and rewarding pursuit and making me work hard for my grades, thank you.

Thank you Benjamin Russell, John Westover, and Alan Allred for taking, scanning, and improving the pictures.

Thank you Sara Larson Johnson for not forgetting me after twenty years and for telling your very personal story. Thank you for answering my questions about the publishing process so that I could realize my own dream.

And thank you to all who contributed to make this story come alive. To Olympians Sammy Lee, Bob Clotworthy, Bernie Wrightson, Micki King, Frank Gorman, Tom Gompf, Rick Gilbert, Janet Ely, Patsy Willard, Barbara Talmage Andrews, Soren Svejstrup, Rachelle Kunkel, and Justin Wilcock, to Keith's divers Julie Cook Egan, Nick Gibbs, Mike Moak, Valerie Hale Blau, Devan Porter, Julie Pothier Parkinson, Justin Beardall, Kristin Reeder Wise, Cristina Conn Hubbard, Kelli Einfeldt Hansen, Spencer Lamoreaux, and Tawni Jones, and to Nancy Turner, Betty Barr Pipes, Barbara Minch, Norris Heckel, Ohio State legend Ron O'Brien, Dartmouth's Ron Keenhold, Stan Curnow at the Air Force Academy, and Jennifer Lowery at USA Diving, thank you.

Preface

Every person deserves to have a biography written, if only for posterity. Every person who has made a meaningful contribution to society deserves to have a biography published. These kinds of people—athletes, entertainers, politicians, philanthropists, etc.—have always intrigued me, along with my own ancestors, whose life histories I began reading when I was six.

Comparatively few have contributed more to the aesthetically pleasing sport of diving than coach Keith Russell. Even fewer have been so directly involved in it as long as he has—nearly five decades, with the last thirty years in coaching. The biggest names in diving the last half-century have wanted Keith, respected Keith, and loved Keith: legendaries like Michigan coach Richard Kimball, Indiana coach Hobie Billingsley, Ohio State coach Ron O'Brien, and Dartmouth coach Ron Keenhold all recruited Keith. Olympic champions like Sammy Lee, Bob Clotworthy, Lesley Bush, Bernie Wrightson, and Micki King have revered him.

When I got the idea to write this biography in October 2006, my last year at BYU, I didn't know that Keith was the guy that everyone in the diving community looked up to. I had just decided to use my Bachelor of Arts degree in family history and genealogy to become a biographer and what better way to start than with my own famous uncle, who at the time lived only three and a half miles from me and practically worked in my backyard (I was a five-minute walk from the center of campus).

The thrill I felt when the idea popped into my head was a double whammy: first, because it was a worthy way to realize my dream and start a career, and second, because now I had a good reason to research the family tradition that Keith had earned a medal at the 1968 Olympics, but the judges gave it to someone else. I wanted to confirm or deny that claim for myself.

I took the first step to writing this biography on Sunday, November 5, 2006 when I went to Keith's house for dinner as I usually did on the first Sunday of every month. I think he thought I was crazy when I asked him permission to do this. But perhaps thinking nothing would really come of it, he granted it. Little did he know that I would pursue this project like it was a full-time job for the next year, then spend another year actively looking for a publisher and polishing it up.

This biography needed to be written for several reasons. First, because Keith does not talk about his accomplishments or contributions. When he received the news that he had been selected as the only American diving judge at the 2008 Beijing Olympics, he didn't tell people. It was like his little secret. Second, his story is incredibly inspirational, like a rags to riches story, only his riches are his friends, his devoted family, his honorable reputation, and his living legacy.

A third reason this biography needed to be written is because Keith's history doubles, to some extent, as a recent history of diving. This is about more than just a world-class athlete, it is a recent account of the world's most exquisite sport. A final reason is the sheer entertainment from reading fascinating stories of royal treatment by famous celebrities, traveling the world, winning surprise national titles, and creating the next generation of world-class athletes.

My objective in writing this biography ended up being not only to celebrate the life of one of the most influential characters in diving, but to commemorate the sport and honor all of its participants at every level. Carry on.

Chapter 1: Ten Meters above Ten Thousand: A Defining Scene

This is it. First dive. Final round. A finely-sculptured young man stands atop a cement slab ten meters above a pool of water. Ten thousand people sit in the stands. Millions more sit at home glued to their television sets to watch the platform finals. This is the 1968 Olympics and he is a top contender for gold. *Sports Illustrated* favors him to be an Olympic champion. And he is close. All is quiet as he prepares for takeoff. Silence is vital to the psychological preparation of the beautiful and intricate movements a diver is about to make. The announcer presents Keith Russell and suddenly the calmness blasts into chaos as ten thousand Mexicans erupt into a jarring display of angry screaming and scoffing. They know the scores. They know where he stands. They know he's good. With an agenda of their own, they break all the rules of respectful diving spectatorship. If they can make him flop, maybe their diver can win. Startled and completely caught off guard, Keith finds himself ten meters above ten thousand people whose intentions are to throw him off his game, do everything in their power to distract and overwhelm him. He finds himself in front of a people who will stop at nothing to win a medal. This is the Olympic Games, an event where athletes perform with power and proficiency and witnesses watch in wonder. It is a contest of athletic ability and agility, not of spectator bias or persuasion. But not this time. So Keith Russell stands before millions, struggling to come to grips with this unexpected bizarre blow.

In disillusionment, he looks down at the Mexican referee. "What is going on? What is this? What am I supposed to do?" his eyes communicate as he searches for some direction from below. The referee just stands there looking back at him with a blank expression, as if to say, "What do you want me to do?" He shrugs his shoulders, unconcerned. Keith isn't competing for *his* country.

Keith's head is spinning. His heart is racing. His body is tightening. This can't be happening. With no help from outside, Keith turns inward for peace. He must regain his composure amidst the deafening noise. He fights to stay focused and confident. He tries to block out the catcalls so he can hear himself think. He battles to keep his mind sharp and his nerves loose. He can't let them get to him.

Despite his efforts, ten thousand people ranting and raving is imposing. And he has no one to turn to for advice. Should he stay? Should he go? Should he back off and hope the crowd does too? He stands alone, at least ten meters from the nearest possible advisor, the center of attention. All eyes are on him. All voices are directed at him. He has trained most of his life to stand in that coveted spot and it has come down to this—uncontainable commotion. Only a handful of family members and friends sit in the stands who appreciate the many years of hard work and sacrifice, frustration, blood, sweat, and tears that Keith has put into this moment, this rare and prestigious opportunity to win gold for his country. Few care.

Confusion fills his mind as he tries to figure out, or better yet, edit out the pandemonium. What the heck are these people doing? Instead of being allowed to display the type of world-class diver he is, he is forced to demonstrate the type of first-class man he is.

The Dive

As he waits for them to settle down, he tries to calm his nerves. Fifteen minutes according to some. Twenty according to others. It's a long lonely wait. It doesn't happen, so finally he just goes for it. With a loss of quiet rhythm, with a lack of natural flow, he forces a forward three-and-a-half tuck somersault. It's beautiful.

The crowd failed to affect his dive. Keith did brilliantly. But the superiority of a dive doesn't determine the winner; the judge's scores do. Keith jumped through the crowd's loophole unscathed; now he had to get through the judges'. Yale University diving editor and later Arizona State University diving coach F. Ward O'Connell stated in his *Swimming World* column that the biased judging, particularly against Keith, left the sport in shambles. He called it "the most controversial of the oddly judged diving."[1] The crowd couldn't get Keith out of the medals, but a few judges did. After three more dives, each accompanied by the same taunting before the dive and a few ridiculously low scores after the dive from judges each favoring their own diver, Keith placed fourth.

Things could have been worse. He could have failed to make finals, like his friend Rick Gilbert. He could have broken a bone, like another friend Micki King. He could have taken an undeserved medal, like the Mexican favorite, Alvaro Gaxiola. But he made finals in both events, didn't sacrifice a body part, and the only thing he took that he didn't deserve were low scores. He did his best and that's what mattered, because that's all he could control. Despite roaring opposition from an aggressive, irrational, and obstinate crowd, this young man kept it together. Yes, he placed fourth, but he placed fourth amidst all that.

Even after everything the crowd did to him. Even after all the poor judging. He had trained his body to take on difficult dives, but no one had trained his mind to take on difficult crowds.

A casual reader scanning the statistics of the 1968 summer Olympics just sees "Keith Russell, sixth place, springboard" or "Keith Russell, fourth place, platform." But there is a story behind the numbers, a big story, because Keith Russell, despite his modest surroundings and demeanor, had many big things: He had a big heart; a larger-than-life, world-famous coach; Olympic medalist teammates and friends; and big-time opportunities and wins. Inside his athletic, sleek GQ frame is a big man, but Olympic statistics don't talk about that, or about how he reached such heights, or about all the adventures along the way. The figures fail to mention the appalling and vicious circumstances in which the Olympian placed fourth, with thousands of spectators sitting before him, intimidating, manipulating, and retaliating.

Only the cold hard facts are given. But things happened along the way that, when told, breathe life into the facts, that bring meaning to the numbers, that made this diver a man. There were walls of financial hardship to tear down, national records to break in one sport and national titles to take in another, a killer tornado to practice in, Olympic champions to beat, top college diving coaches to meet, magazine covers to make, celebrities to dine with and dive for, and more.

Keith Russell never won an Olympic gold medal. So why read his story? Because when devastation could have caused him to throw in the towel, he didn't. He went on to take more national titles, medal in the first World Championships, spot and train future champions and Olympians, and represent the United States again at another Olympics as a judge. He may not have won an Olympic medal, but he won the hearts of non-biased diving fans the world over.

After retiring from competition after his fourth Olympic Trials in 1976, Keith devoted himself to coaching. He founded clubs, coached at universities, and created more national champions and Olympians. Because of how things are calculated and awarded, represented and reported, the significance of his Olympic experience and his subsequent contributions to the sport are missed.

Keith was a phenomenal diver, but he was and is an even more phenomenal man. In 1995, 1956 Olympic champion Bob Clotworthy interviewed Keith. He noted,

> In his remarks about the Mexican spectators at the platform competition, Keith was quite generous. He placed most of the blame on himself, when in fact, he followed Mexican Alvaro Gaxiola in the competition and the spectators booed and jeered [Keith] unmercifully. Their commotion and poor sportsmanship could not have helped him. Ask Keith about the Mexican crowds at the Olympics in 1968, and knowing him, he will be most kind in his remarks.

A true athlete does not make excuses, even when things happen beyond their control. If diving awarded a team medal, as its twin sport of gymnastics does, Keith would have won gold. If it awarded an all-around medal like gymnastics, Keith would have won silver. But fourth place at the Olympics is a triumph for anyone. And fourth place at the Olympics amidst pointed hatred from spectators and abuse of scoring from judges is a fantastic feat.

This is the story of a man who grew up in a large family in a small town with enough determination to make up for what he lacked. In 1968, at twenty, he was the youngest diver ever honored as the world's best by an international poll of coaches.[2] In 1971, he competed in the first international competition on the African continent where he became the second man to ever amass more than 590 points in a single competition.[3] And he did it twice. He started winning international gold in high school and breaking national records before his age reached double digits. This is the inspiring account of a man who started out with nothing but a goal and rose to international success as both a diver and coach, despite many difficult setbacks. More than once, he offered his coaching services for free to talented youngsters whose families could not afford diving lessons, because he cared more about building character than building champions.

Chapter 2: The Genes: His DNA Spells Athleticism

Jon Keith Russell was born January 15, 1948, in Mesa, Arizona, the fourth child of Cyrus and Lurline Ray Russell. Gary was six, Raylene was three, and Judy turned one three days later. Cy supported his family at the time by plastering. He built their home a half mile southeast of downtown Mesa after moving back from Los Angeles in 1942.

Cy was born September 9, 1920, in Mesa, the first child of Frank and Julia Fish Russell. He played varsity football all four years at Mesa High School and earned a football scholarship to Arizona State University.[4] One 1938 Arizona newspaper commented on his playing skills going into his senior year of high school:

> Replacing Norris Enloe, all-state end of '37, Russell has plenty of endurance and agility, requisites for end play. He has completed three years of varsity competition, during which he has improved each year. Speedy in getting down under punts and to receive passes, he also is quick in diagnosing plays being started by opponents.

Cy also lettered in basketball and track in high school. He was Mesa High's number-one man all four years in both the mile and the half-mile.[5] One paragraph of a newspaper article detailed Cy's performance at one track meet:

> Mesa won only one first place in the Class A competition yesterday. Russell scored that victory in the mile when he ran within two strides of McCormick of Phoenix that whole distance and then outlasted him in a stretch sprint to win in the good early season time of 4:45.

When Cy entered high school in the mid-1930s, the world record for the mile was 4:06.7, set by Glenn Cunningham in 1934. This was just 39 seconds faster than Cy.[6]

Keith's mother, Lurline Ray, was born November 21, 1921, in Gilbert, Arizona (Mesa's southern border), to John Alexander and Juanita Stout Ray. The Ray family lived on eighty acres kitty-corner to where Chandler–Gilbert Community College stands. They had a dairy and grew alfalfa and watermelons, but lost it all during the Great Depression.

Lurline attended Gilbert High School her freshman year. After her family lost the farm, they moved to Mesa and she finished up at Mesa High, where she met Cy in English class. When their teacher mentioned he played football, Lurline's ears perked up. She *loved* sports. Perspiration from Cy's helmet turned his white hair orange.

At the football game that night, Lurline paid close attention to Cy on the field and watched him score a spectacular touchdown. They started dating a year later. After a year at Arizona State University, they moved to Los Angeles to find work and get married.

Chapter 3: Exploding onto the Aquatic Scene: America's Fastest Young Swimmer

The day baby Keith came home from the hospital, his aunt Noni and her baby daughter, Suzanne, came to see him. No one knew Suzanne had whooping cough, so he caught it from her. He handled it very well; whenever he woke up coughing at night, he always went back to sleep. According to Keith's doctor, fifty percent of newborns died from the respiratory disease. Keith got over it within a month, but then acquired diarrhea, so for his first year, he subsisted on boiled skim milk and bananas until his mother thought he looked like one.

Keith exhibited an early interest in sports. By age two, Lurline considered him an old hand at ball games. With precision and coordination, he could dropkick anything—from a ball to the family kitten—and hit his mark dead on, which was often his big brother. Consequently, Keith's parents expected him to follow in his father's footsteps as a star football player.

Despite being banned from church for ill behavior at this early age, Cy and Lurline believed Keith had the kind of sweet temperament found only in angels. Lurline kept a journal for each of her children. She wrote in Keith's of his relationship with his father (in his voice), "Dad and me really have fun. The minute he is on the floor, I am on him."

The neighbor girl, Julianne Miller, also noticed Keith's angelic disposition and decided to stake a claim on him. One day when Keith was three, Lurline caught the two walking to the Mormon Temple at the north end of their street. Mormons from all over Arizona went there to get married. Lurline chased them down and asked them where they thought they were going. They informed her they were going to the temple to get married. Lurline suggested they wait a few years.

The Russells spent hot Arizona summer days at the local swimming pool. By age four, Keith's "Fish" genes (his Grandma Russell's maiden name was Fish) had really kicked in. He could swim like a fish on a mission or slice a dive into the water like a veteran. His dad enjoyed acting as Keith's personal springboard, tossing him into the air.

At Fourth of July festivities at the Chandler Water Carnival in 1952, Keith demonstrated his athletic abilities by coming in a close second in a swimming race against older kids and won a free ride on the ponies.

Keith's mother wrote in his journal that summer when he was four,

> We knew Keith was a good swimmer, but we didn't realize how good. Last Saturday—July 26—he told me he wanted to swim across the pool. So we got in the 5 ft. and I swam along beside him. Well he made it all the way across, jumped out of the pool, ran down to the 9 feet, dived in, and swam across again. He can really travel when he is swimming. Altogether he swam across 6 times that afternoon. Mrs. Willard sent someone over to ask how old he was.

Mrs. Willard was the Mesa Aquatic Club swim coach and Patsy Willard's mother. Patsy later competed in the 1960 Rome Olympics, where she placed fourth on springboard, and in the 1964 Tokyo Olympics, where she won bronze. She and Keith later trained together at the Dick Smith Swim Gym.

On March 17, 1953, Keith acquired a fourth sibling when Donetta was born. Keith joined the Mesa Aquatic Club swim team that summer. He also discovered the three-meter springboard. At the Fourth of July Chandler Water Carnival, five-year-old Keith swam against seven- and eight-year-olds and beat them all. In an underwater race, he beat his own eleven-year-old brother by ten feet.

Lurline wrote in the journal she kept for him, "We sure have fun together. I really enjoy having the little guy around. He is so pleasant and easy to get along with."

During the summer of 1954, six-year-old Keith started taking diving lessons. Lurline thought his body was "divine" for a diver and decided to find a good diving coach. Betty Scott, whose son Steve also swam with the Mesa Aquatic Club, told Lurline about the Dick Smith Swim Gym. Betty wanted to get Steve into diving, so the two mothers began taking their sons to Dick's together in north Phoenix.

Dick Smith's gym was eighteen miles northwest of the Russell home. Previously the UCLA swimming and diving coach, Dick Smith had won national titles in intercollegiate and AAU (Amateur Athletic Union) diving championships.

When Dick died in 2006, the *Arizona Republic* recognized his impact on the world of diving in the article "Top Diving Coach Smith Dies at 88":

> With his coaching involvement, the United States stood atop the world's diving platform in the 1960s, and his influence later spread across the globe. The diving world is mourning Smith today. He is a force in the diving world, said Steve McFarland, a former

> international diver and noted coach, who started diving at age 10 at Smith's facility. Nobody before or after him had the impact on the world of diving like Dick Smith had. Smith founded the gym in 1954 and it soon became a launching pad for national and international champions.
>
> [Smith] was an accomplished diver in his own right, but his Olympic success came as the U.S. women's coach in 1964 and men's coach in 1968. His divers included gold medalist Bernie Wrightson, Jeanne Collier, Patsy Willard and Keith Russell. Bronze medalist Tom Gompf also was instructed as a pilot by Smith at Williams Air Force Base. Smith coached Olympic divers from New Zealand, Brazil, Egypt, Finland and South Korea. You can trace back to Smith the success other countries are having in the world.

Keith participated in the State Championship for first-timers in July. He finished third in diving after only twelve lessons and executed a perfect back flip off the one-meter. Cy and Lurline decided to let Keith have twelve more diving lessons. With a growing family of seven living on a schoolteacher's salary, unnecessary expenses were a luxury, but if it taught a child the worth of setting goals, working hard, and making the most of life, the benefit outweighed the cost.

The kindergarten graduate reached new highs and lows that month. His new heights began with diving lessons on the three-meter. But he experienced a new low when he not only fell and fractured his skull on the deck, causing blood to pour from his ear at the Arizona Country Club meet where he was to be the star, but he consequently had to miss the all-important meet for a week-long stay in the hospital. Before being carted off in an ambulance, Keith—not wanting to miss out on any aquatic action—asked his coach if he could still swim in the meet. His very pregnant mother stayed by his side at the hospital. Two weeks later, she gave birth to Keith's fifth sibling, Kathy Jane Russell.

By the time Keith reached first grade, Lurline noticed another talent he had: making friends. She expressed her admiration for him in this journal entry that fall:

> Keith is getting to be a real football player. Jeddy Shumway, Jim Turley, Walter Brown, Larry Harris, Wayne Phelps, David Bowers, and others come over to play and Keith is right there in the middle. They play for hours.
>
> This morning I was acting silly, dancing around, and saying, "Don't you think you have a cute, glamorous mother?" He told me, "Yes, but don't act so sexy." He's always telling me how pretty and sweet I am. How can you help being crazy over a guy like that?

Keith celebrated his seventh birthday in 1955 at a Dick Smith Meet, at Dick's invitation. After only a year and a half of competitive swimming, the first grader matched a national swimming record. The *Phoenix Gazette* reported,

> Keith Russell, 7, isn't exactly dressed for the weather [a swimsuit in January], but swimming at Dick Smith's Swim Gym, he equaled the national novice 25-yard freestyle record of 0:17.4, three seconds faster than the Pacific Coast mark.

Dick told Cy and Lurline that if he kept it up, Keith would be competing at the national level by age twelve and be a national champion by age sixteen. Another coach, Chuck McMahon, predicted Keith would make the 1968 Olympics.

By this time, Keith had to go out of state to find competition. He swam in the Chris Christensen Meet in California that summer against older boys and placed second in his heat (the preliminary contest to determine the finalists). He was last in the twenty-five-yard butterfly, but that was okay because the swimmers finished in one big bunch.

Keith swam it in 0:17.1—not his best, but Dick told him to take it easy, so he did.

When Keith started second grade in 1955, Lurline wrote in his journal,

> He couldn't wait for school to start. For a boy just starting second grade, Keith has had quite an eventful life. Lots of experiences and is an outstanding boy. His diving is really coming along. He really wants to work at it. And he does.

A month after Keith turned eight in 1956, he set a new state record for the boys' fifty-yard freestyle, swimming it in 0:29.4. The state record for the next older age group was over a second slower, at 0:30.8. As of 2005, the national record in the under-ten age group fifty-yard freestyle was less than a second faster, at 0:28.97. Keith also won the fifty-yard backstroke, breaststroke, and butterfly at the Dick Smith Swim Gym meet.

The Russells went to Santa Monica, California in June, where Cy spent summers plastering celebrity pools for his cousin Narvin Peel. Keith competed in the Western States Invitational and took second in both the twenty-five-yard breaststroke and backstroke and third in both the diving and twenty-five-yard freestyle.[7] Keith swam in the first freestyle heat by mistake and won it. Then he swam in his heat and won that. He had his time down to 0:14.9, but swam it in 0:15.3. Jack Heyden won it in 0:15.0.

The Coronado Meet in central Phoenix was the highlight of Keith's summer. He won everything and broke records in both the butterfly (by over two seconds) and the freestyle (by 0.6 of a second). The Sunnyslope Pool Invitational took place a week later in Phoenix. Keith won the backstroke, butterfly, and the individual medley by a length and a half.

At the Fourth of July Chandler Water Carnival that year, Keith, now eight, beat a group of sixteen-year-olds in the butterfly. He also won the freestyle. By summer's end, Keith could do a back one-and-a-half tuck somersault (2.0 degree of difficulty), a reverse dive (1.6 degree of difficulty), and an inward one-and-a-half tuck somersault (2.2 degree of difficulty) off the one-meter. Points awarded on each dive are multiplied by the degree of difficulty of each dive for total score.

In a basic reverse dive, the diver's starting position is the same as a front dive. As he takes off, his legs shoot up over his head. His upper body rotates back toward the board and down into the water in a back dive. In a basic inward dive, the diver's starting position is the same as a back dive. Instead of doing a back dive, he dives forward with a backward motion, so his body moves away from the board while his dive is toward the board. The degree of difficulty goes up to 3.5 for front and inward dives and 3.6 for back and reverse dives. The more flips and twists, the higher the degree of difficulty.

Shortly after Keith turned nine in 1957, he started doing reverse dives off the three-meter. His first one was incredible. Lurline witnessed Keith do a perfect double flip by summer. The future Olympian was coming along nicely.

At the Coronado Meet on June 21, Keith broke state records in both the backstroke and freestyle, defending his titles in those events, and won the breaststroke. He brought the time down in the forty-yard backstroke by over a second, from 0:32.1 to 0:30.5. His sister Judy also broke two state records. She brought the time down in the girl's forty-yard backstroke by over a second (from 0:32.9 to 0:31.6) and in the breaststroke (from 0:31.1 to 30.2). She also won the 120-yard individual medley. The *Arizona Republic* reported on the Russell phenomenon:

Mesa Aquatic Club, led by a pair of young Russells, successfully

> defended its crown last night in the 10 and under AAU swimming and diving championships at Coronado Pool.
>
> The Mesa swim club won both the boys' and girls' division titles for the second straight year. Keith Russell was high point scorer among the boys and sister Judy swam off with girls honors.
>
> Keith, age 9, won the three events he entered and established records in two. Judy matched her brother's performance with three wins and a pair of records.[8]

Keith competed in the Second Annual Junior Olympics Short Course in Tucson and won everything he entered. One newspaper photo covering the event shows him seated front and center among three other relay team members. The caption reads,

> Pictured above is the Mesa Aquatic Club, which reeled off a new [national] record in yesterday's Junior Olympic swim meet at the YMCA. The club's 10-and-under relay team recorded 57.8 in the 100-yard freestyle relay, bettering the old mark of 58.5. From left to right are Jim Passey and Joe Pace. In the front row are: Bill Passey, Keith Russell and the coach, Mrs. Mary Willard.

The Mesa Tribune also featured a photo of the fab four, along with an article stating, "Not only did the [Mesa] Aquatic Club 10-and-under boys set a new national standard, but they won every event in their age division and erased five state records."[9] His sister Judy set a new state record in the twenty-five-yard butterfly.

The Junior Meet in Tempe was also groundbreaking for the fourth-grader. For the first time in three years of competitive diving, he beat thirteen-year-old Ron Onsgard of Tucson, who had beaten him in every previous diving competition. Keith also executed his first two-and-a-half tuck somersault off the one-meter.

The Arizona AAU Junior Olympics Long Course took place on August 2, 1957 in Phoenix. Keith got his picture in the *Phoenix Gazette* for publicity. The same team that broke the national one-hundred-yard freestyle relay record at the Short Course (Joe Pace, Jim and Bill Passey, and Keith) broke the national two-hundred-meter freestyle relay record at the Long Course. Keith also broke the Arizona Junior Olympic record in both the fifty-meter backstroke and breaststroke, swimming the backstroke in 0:41.9 and the breaststroke in 0:46.2.

Another native Arizonan and future Olympian set some state records at the meet as well. Marilyn Ramenofsky won the fifty-meter breaststroke in 48 seconds flat and the fifty-meter butterfly in 42.5. She later set world records in the four-hundred-meter freestyle—including at the 1964 U.S. Olympic Trials—and won Olympic silver in the event. *Sports Illustrated* lists her as the twelfth greatest Arizona sports figure.[10] This is the type of caliber people Keith grew up around, when Arizona dominated the world of aquatic sports.

Keith attended a church dance that fall for children under twelve. This proved a golden opportunity for Lurline to see if he was as successful with girls as he was in the pool. As she put it,

> I took the kids and got a sneak preview of what is in store for Keith. He danced every single dance and on girl's choices, there were three girls who frankly fought over him! Dottie Cox, Carolyn Cummings, and Linda Stradling. Even on the boy's choices, the girls would ask Keith. He wasn't chasing the girls, but he didn't run away from their chasing. He was being cut in on all evening. When they announced the last dance, the three girls made a dash for Keith.

Dancing wasn't the only activity Keith engaged in that night. Apparently, his friend Don did something uncool and got called on it by a group of fifth-grade boys who shoved him outside and pounced on him. As they duked it out, Keith came out and jumped in, knocking off one. Lurline commented on it in Keith's journal: "Richard gave Keith a shove and Keith shoved right back. I was really proud of Keith to stick up for Don; he wasn't scared of those big 5th graders." Keith proved he could hold his own with both girls and boys that night.

A week after Keith's tenth birthday in 1958, he acquired a five-year-old brother. Cy's sister Billie and her husband, James Allred, lived nearby with their five children. One cold night, James and Billie tried to fix their furnace when a gas leak caused an explosion and killed them. Uncle Cy adopted Alan Allred. Other family members adopted the other four children.

Keith competed in the Santa Monica Aqua Fair in California in February and won the twelve-and-under one-meter. Tony Dow, who played Wally Cleaver on the show *Leave It to Beaver*, competed and won his event. Keith's teammate Patsy Willard went to his house afterward. Keith was beginning to fly with the big wigs.

Keith participated in the First Annual Saguaro Invitational in central Phoenix and won the one-meter. He spent that summer diving all day.

The *Arizona Republic* reported on the Coronado Meet in Phoenix on June 20:

> Triple-winners Keith Russell and Bill Passey escorted Mesa boys to victory with a whopping 96 points. Phoenix Country Club swam a distant second with 63, followed by Arizona County Club's 37. Russell, 10, a Mesa fifth grader, broke one record and tied another. After setting four records in age 9 competition last year, Russell continued yesterday by lowering the 50-yard backstroke to 29.3. Later he tied the 50-yard freestyle record of 23.8. Russell also won in 50-yard butterfly.[11]

Arizona's Third Annual AAU Junior Olympics Short Course Swimming Championships took place in Tucson in July. Keith established three new state AAU short course records, winning everything he entered. In the twenty-five-yard freestyle, he was the only swimmer to get under fourteen seconds, with 0:13.7. In the twenty-five-yard butterfly, he was the only swimmer to get under sixteen seconds, with 0:15.4. In the twenty-five-yard backstroke, he was the only swimmer to get under eighteen seconds, with 0:16.7.[12]

The Arizona AAU Junior Olympics Long Course Swimming and Diving Championships took place in Phoenix in August. Several newspaper articles chronicled Keith's record-breaking achievements. One began, "An Arizona swimmer swam his way into the national record books for the third time in three years yesterday." He did that by breaking the National Junior Olympic record for the ten-and-under fifty-meter freestyle.

During the freestyle heats, Keith's 0:33.8 timing took one-tenth of a second off the record set by Bubba Tongay of Miami, Florida, the year before. Keith shaved another one-tenth of a second off in the finals that night.[13] As of 2005, the national record for the boy's ten-and-under fifty-meter freestyle was 0:28.97.

Keith also broke the state fifty-meter butterfly record in the preliminaries and won in the finals with 0:39.8. He swam the fifty-meter backstroke in 0:40.7 for another record, giving him three state records for the meet.[14]

After Keith swam in what the Russells thought was the last meet of the season—the AAU Northern Arizona Open and won the butterfly with a sore throat and a temperature of 102 degrees—Lurline received a phone call from Keith's coach, Mary Willard, who informed her of a Mesa Aquatic Club versus Phoenix YMCA meet right then. The sole purpose was for the other team's Win Young to beat Keith in the breaststroke. Keith hadn't swum the breast all summer and Win had won them all. So Keith went and beat Win by over a second, swimming faster than Win's best time. For the next ten years, Keith and Win rivaled and befriended each other as they rose through the ranks of state, national, and international competition.

Keith competed in the Encino Invitational in California with teammate and future two-time Olympian Patsy Willard and won one-meter in both the ten-and-under and eleven-to-twelve age-groups.[15] His star was rising now, beating out-of-staters. Patsy won both one-meter and three-meter in the women's open.

Keith spent Christmas vacation preparing for the Dick Smith Holiday Diving Festival in January 1959, in which eighty swimmers from Arizona, California, New Mexico, Utah, and the Midwest competed.[16] Lyle and Vicki Draves, both in the International Swimming Hall of Fame, judged. Lyle Draves was America's first great diving coach, beginning an era in which coaches specialized in divers, not coaching swimmers. After the 1948 Olympics, Lyle and Vicki coached at UCLA.[17]

Lyle coached three Olympic champions and two other Olympic divers. Vicki Manalo Draves, his wife, was the first woman to win a gold medal on both platform and springboard at the same Olympics in 1948. Zoe Ann Olsen won Olympic silver in 1948 and Olympic bronze in 1952. Although she retired in 1949 after marrying Jackie Jensen—baseball's Most Valuable Player with the Boston Red Sox—and giving birth a year later, Zoe Ann made the 1952 Olympic team after two weeks of training.[18] Pat McCormick became the first woman to win a gold medal on both platform and springboard in two consecutive Olympics, 1952 and 1956.

Paula Jean Myers won Olympic platform silver in 1952, Olympic platform bronze in 1956, and Olympic springboard and platform silver in 1960. Sue Gossick, the last Draves prodigy, placed fourth on springboard behind Patsy Willard at the 1964 Olympics, then won Olympic gold in 1968.[19]

Keith entered four events at the Dick Smith Meet: the nine-and-ten age group one-meter, which he won; the eleven-and-twelve age group one-meter, which he won; the fourteen-and-under three-meter, which he won; and the men's open three-meter, in which he placed third after Harvey Plant and Chuck McMahon.[20] For the first time in competition, he executed a forward one-and-a-half tuck somersault with a full twist and a forward two-and-a-half tuck somersault.

Lurline offered a peek into Keith's personality and style with this February 1959 journal entry:

> I had a Valentine party for Keith's room at school, as I'm room mother. Keith about had a fit because I made him wear "city slicker clothes," as he calls having to wear both a nice shirt and nice pants at the same time. He is willing to wear either one or the other, but it about kills him to wear both.

In April, Keith did an exhibition at the Desert Water Show at the Ramada Inn in Phoenix. He joined Hollywood stars Tony Dow, Esther Williams, and Buster Crabbe in a benefit for disabled children. Tony Dow was a few years older than Keith.[21]

Esther Williams, Lurline's age, played Mickey Rooney's love interest in her 1942 debut film, *Andy Hardy's Double Life*. She made the 1940 U.S. Olympic swim team but did not compete because World War II caused the cancellation of those Olympic Games. Her movie career played a major role in promoting competitive swimming, which she is credited with popularizing, starting with *Bathing Beauty*, Hollywood's first swimming movie. It was second only to *Gone with the Wind* as the most successful movie of 1944. By World War II's end, Esther was

America's sweetheart for almost twenty years, appearing in twenty-six movies.[22]

Buster Crabbe starred in several Zane Grey westerns, starting with 1933's *The Thunderbird Herd.* Universal Studios gave him the lead in the very successful sci-fi *Buck Rogers* series from 1936 to 1940. He also competed in the 1928 and 1932 Olympics, winning bronze in the 1,500-meter freestyle at the 1928 Amsterdam Olympics and gold in the 400-meter freestyle at the 1932 Los Angeles Olympics.[23]

The Second Annual Saguaro Invitational took place in Phoenix. Keith won both the boy's fourteen-and-under one-meter and three-meter. In the three-meter, he totaled 207.85 points to best the next highest, 139.2, by 68.65 points.[24]

One newspaper article forecasted the final State AAU Meet of the season, where three hundred swimmers and divers from twenty clubs came to compete. It contended, "A threat in diving and swimming is Keith Russell of Mesa. Russell, who holds 11 state AAU records for boys 10 and under, was nationally ranked last season."[25]

Win Young won breaststroke but Keith won everything else, including diving, proving the prediction correct.[26] The Mesa Aquatic Club boy's team scored 173 points thanks in part to Keith—almost three times more than the Phoenix Country Club's second place finish of 65 points.[27]

Keith's sisters, Judy and Donetta, won the most points in their age groups. Future Olympian Marilyn Ramenofsky won the fifty-meter butterfly and Judy Russell won the fifty-meter freestyle, both for twelve-year-olds. She and future world record breaker Marilyn Ramenofsky often split wins in their age group.[28]

Keith participated in the International Water Festival in Phoenix in December, the first "international" swimming meet in the Phoenix Valley. He was the only Arizona boy who qualified for the backstroke and butterfly. He and Win were the only Arizona boys who qualified for the breaststroke. And only one other Arizona boy qualified with him for the freestyle. Keith, by now a local celebrity, got his picture in a newspaper, advertising the event. He is in a beautiful pike dive above the three-meter.

Chapter 4: Cross-Country Competitions of a Grade-Schooler

When Keith turned twelve in January 1960, Lurline talked to him about the dangers of smoking and drinking and asked him to promise her he would never do either. He promised and never did. One Olympic diver disclosed that his drinking and driving, which killed two people and put him behind bars for six years, "destroyed everything [he] ever worked for." He lamented, "I found myself without respect, dignity, purpose, or hope."[29] The father of this Olympic silver medalist later recruited Keith to the University of Michigan, which had one of the top diving programs in the country. Keith saved himself from a possible similar devastating experience with his promise.

At Lowell Elementary School's track and field day that spring, Keith proved his athletic abilities extended beyond swimming pools and diving boards when he won the dash, the broad jump, and the relay. Whatever he did, he liked to do it quickly.

Keith spent that summer mastering a forward somersault with two twists off the one-meter (2.3 degree of difficulty) and a one-and-a-half somersault with two twists off the three-meter (2.5 degree of difficulty). He also started learning triple somersaults and inward two-and-a-half somersaults. Lurline wrote in his journal with high hopes: "I'll bet by next summer he will be doing 3½ [somersaults]."

Keith competed in the Arizona Relays in June against Arizona's two best divers: Hal Easton, twenty, and Ronnie Onsgard, sixteen. His inward one-and-a-half somersault received spectacular sevens. Hal and Keith did the only back one-and-a-half somersaults, for which Keith received the most points. The official rulebook of United States Diving says dives are to be awarded as follows:

Very Good	8.5 to 10 points
Good	6.5 to 8 points
Satisfactory	5 to 6 points
Deficient	2.5 to 4.5 points
Unsatisfactory	.5 to 2 points

Hal Easton won. While only half of Ronnie Onsgard's six dives had a 2.0 degree of difficulty or greater, he took second. Although five of Keith's six dives had a 2.0 degree of difficulty or greater, he took third.

Keith performed even better at the 1960 Tucson Open that month. His best dive, a forward two-and-a-half, received eights. Although Keith's dives had the highest degree of difficulty, Hal Easton won and Keith took second, beating Ronnie Onsgard in third by over eight points. The sixth grader was well on his way to eliminating in-state competition.

At the Junior Meet in Tempe, three years after first beating Ronnie Onsgard, Keith beat the other local diving rival, Hal Easton, on three-meter, which thrilled Lurline. Keith received the only 8.5 in the competition, on his forward two-and-a-half somersault. Besides Hal, no other diver received above a 6. Keith won with 220.75 points, 17.05 more than Hal in second, with 203.70.

The Russell family spent the end of the summer watching the 1960 Rome Olympics. They paid particular attention to Arizona's star diver and their friend, Patsy Willard.

Paula Jean Pope was the favorite to succeed Pat McCormick as Olympic springboard champion. Patsy Willard was expected to be Paula's chief challenge.[30] Patsy led after the first two dives but flopped on her last dive, a reverse one-and-a-half tuck somersault, dropping her to eighth.[31] Ingrid Kramer of East Germany finished the preliminaries in first place, followed by Paula Jean Pope.

August 27 was a historic day in Olympic diving. It was the first time the United States women failed to win the springboard since it was added in the 1920 Olympics. Ingrid Kramer won it in 108-degree heat. Paula Jean Pope won silver, while Patsy got fourth.[32]

Ingrid Kramer also won the platform and Paula Jean Pope took silver again. The other American platform competitor, Juno Stover-Irwin, finished fourth. This was Juno's fourth and last Olympics. At the 1948 Olympics, she placed fifth on platform. At the 1952 Helsinki Olympics, she won bronze on platform while three and a half months pregnant. At the 1956 Melbourne Olympics, she won silver.

Pan-American champion and University of Southern California senior Gary Tobian became the men's Olympic springboard champion. Two-time NCAA champion and Ohio State University student Sam Hall won silver.[33] Juan Botella of Mexico, 1956 Olympic veteran, took bronze. His teammate Alvaro Gaxiola, 1959 Pan-American platform champion, finished fourth.

University of Michigan student Bob Webster became the Olympic platform champion. Gary Tobian took silver. Brian Phelps of Great Britain took bronze, Roberto Madrigal of Mexico finished fourth, Henri Rouquet of France placed sixteenth, John Candler of Great

Britain, also a University of Michigan student, finished seventeenth, and Alvaro Gaxiola finished twentieth. Within a few years, Keith was competing against these Olympians.

The morning Keith started seventh grade at Mesa Junior High, he worked out for the Las Vegas Invitational.[34] He had swim practice at 6:30 every morning at the Mesa Junior High pool three blocks from home. Dick was still at the Olympics with Patsy Willard, so Keith worked alone.

Stephen Scott and Keith's best friend, Stuart Driggs, went with the Russells to Las Vegas, where they stayed at the Blue Angel Motel. [Interesting side note: the first female winner of the reality television show *The Biggest Loser*, Ali Vincent, is Stuart's niece. Ali's mother, Bette Sue, is Stuart's sister.] Keith medalled in every event he entered his first morning at the invitational.

Although Keith got beat for the first time in diving by kids his own age and finished third, he received the highest points awarded in the competition (6.5) on his forward dive. His front double somersault also received the highest total score of 34.65. The score is calculated by multiplying the total points received by the degree of difficulty. For example, if a diver receives three fives on a dive with a 2.0 degree of difficulty, he gets thirty points (3 x 5 = 15 x 2.0 = 30).

Despite that uncharacteristic loss, Keith's diving was ready to be taken to the next level, as Lurline wrote in the twelve-year-old's journal in September 1960: "Dick says he wanted to take Keith to the indoor nationals in Feb." The Olympic coach considered the grade-schooler good enough to compete in the nation's most prestigious meet.

Keith and his dad began playing basketball on a church team. Keith excelled at that too and put in six shots his first game. The Russells, a tight-knit family, worked hard and played hard together.

The Second Annual Optimist Mid-Winter Aquatic Meet took place after Christmas. Divers from California, Nevada, New Mexico,

Texas, Oklahoma, and Illinois competed. One newspaper article, titled "Seventy-five Divers to Compete in Mid-Winter Festival," stated it was fast becoming a major aquatic classic in the West. It predicted intense competition in men's diving between Hal Easton and Keith Russell, whom it called the "thirteen-year-old Dick Smith Swim Gym wizard. The two boys this year split junior AAU championships."

Another newspaper stated that Hal Easton and Keith Russell led Arizona in diving. Other divers included 1959 New Mexico state three-meter champion and University of New Mexico student David David;[35] future Junior National champion Mike Copeland, twenty-six, of California; and Jay Moxley, a former Arizona state champion and future two-time NCAA Division II champion for California State University.[36] So the seventh-grader got some decent outside competition.

Dick Smith claimed that the Optimist Mid-Winter Aquatic Meet attracted more outstanding young divers than any similar meet in the country.[37] Keith won the age-group diving and placed sixth on one-meter and seventh on three-meter in men's diving. Keith also won the backstroke, butterfly, freestyle, and individual medley, proving Keith had outgrown the competition in the western United States. His most difficult dives on one-meter included a back one-and-a-half somersault with a twist, a reverse one-and-a-half somersault, and an inward one-and-a-half somersault with a twist.

Keith went to his first Junior National Three-Meter Competition in Albuquerque a month later. Dick Smith and Betty Moore accompanied her son Rory, Keith, and Stuart Driggs.[38] Keith placed fifth. Only college students placed higher except Steve Norling, who at sixteen was three years older than Keith. He placed third, but Keith had been ahead of both him and Hal Easton going into finals.

Keith then went to the South Texas Open in El Paso with Betty and Rory Moore, where he won both the age-group and men's open diving.[39] He took second in the backstroke, third in the butterfly, and fourth in the freestyle against future Olympians Charles Hickcox and Bill Mettler. Keith and Bill later competed together on Mesa High's swim team. Lurline wrote about his first visit to a foreign country (Mexico) afterward: "They had gone over the border into Old Mexico and that was a thrill to him. He tried to 'Jew' them down in their prices etc."

Keith competed in the Fourth Annual Saguaro Invitational in Phoenix and won the three-meter in his age group. Lurline, by now a veteran of diving meets, showed her true colors at this one. As usual, she recorded the points each judge awarded each diver. At the end of the meet, she circled the points Glen Jones gave Keith. In each case, Glen gave Keith the lowest points.

Lurline approached Glen and showed him her record of the judges' scores and told him she did not agree with his judging. He responded by offering to film Keith's dives and show them to her. She said she did film Keith's dives and would he like to see them? She informed him that his scoring hadn't been low for the other divers, just Keith. She used Mike Lewis as an example. Mike received a 6 (satisfactory dive) from Glen and a 3.5 (inferior dive) from another judge on the same dive. Lurline told Glen that had it been Keith, the 2.5-point difference would have been the other way around.

She cited specific examples:

- Glen gave Keith a 4 on his front dive. The other judges gave him 6s and a 6.5.
- Glen gave Keith a 5 on his back dive. The other judges gave him three 6.5s and a 7.
- Glen gave Keith a 4.5 on his inward. The other judges gave him two 6s, a 6.5, and a 7.
- Glen gave Keith a 5 on his back one-and-a-half pike. The other judges gave up to a 7.

- Glen gave Keith a 4.5 on his back one-and-a-half somersault with one-and-a-half twist. The other judges awarded him up to a 6.5.

Regardless of Glen's poor judging, Keith won with 326. Win Young followed twenty-three points behind in second with 303. Mike Lewis got fifth with 172.75.

Win Young, Keith's Dick Smith teammate and future Olympic teammate, was one year older. He became the University of Arizona diving coach, where he coached Michelle Mitchell from 1979 to 1983. Michelle won silver on platform at both the 1984 Los Angeles Olympics and the 1988 Seoul Olympics. She became the University of Arizona diving coach after Win, who passed away in 2006. He is ranked Arizona's twenty-fifth greatest sports figure. Michelle Mitchell is ranked fourth.

At the Second Annual Arizona AAU Swimming Relays in June at Arizona State, Keith won the three-meter. This was significant, because it marked the first time Keith beat both Hal and Ronnie at the same time. Keith received the only nine awarded in the competition, on his forward one-and-a-half with two twists (2.4 degree of difficulty), which also received eights. Ronnie Onsgard received the only other eight, on his forward two-and-a-half somersault.

Of the five judges there, three had daughters who medalled in diving at the next Olympics in 1964. Don Bush's daughter Lesley won gold, Bob Collier's daughter Jeanne won silver, and Mercier Willard's daughter Patsy won bronze.

By August, Lurline noted that Keith "made the decision that diving was to come first." He spent all day, every day "working like the dickens," as she put it.

The *Deseret News* published an article on Keith that summer:

> Keith is only 13 but recently defeated the three-meter diving champion of the state of Arizona at University of Arizona. He started his diving career at the age of six and since then has competed in diving meets in Arizona, California, Nevada, New Mexico, and Texas. Keith comes from a swimming family. His sister, Judy, 14, is the Arizona Women's backstroke champion. Kathy, 6, and Donetta, 8, hold state swimming records also for their age bracket. Before specializing in diving, Keith held three national records in freestyle.[40]

After winning the boys' thirteen-to-fourteen age-group three-meter at the Arizona Age-Group Championships in August, Keith lost to Win Young at the Arizona Senior Meet. This got the better of Lurline and she "certainly let Keith know [her] feelings on the subject." Keith responded, "I have beat both Ronnie and Hal at one time or another, haven't I?" Lurline agreed. Then he asked, "How do you think they felt when someone a lot younger beat them? Did it make them quit? No, it didn't. It made them work harder and now they are beating me again. Mom, that is what I'm going to do. I'm going to work harder and beat Win." Keith wanted to turn the lemons of losing into the lemonade of greater motivation and effort to win.

He told Lurline by nationals he'd have a back two-and-a-half tuck somersault. She noted in the journal she kept for him, "With all the bad times I gave Keith, he never lost his temper at me; he just reasoned with me, told me that he wouldn't quit, that he would work harder, and he would beat Win."

The 1961 National Senior AAU Outdoor Championships took place in Los Angeles. Keith and Lurline went with their friends the Driggs: Cordon the dad, Florence the mom, and Stuart, Keith's best friend. Dick had a seven-meter platform recently erected at his gym, but Keith didn't start learning dives off it until after the Junior Olympics two weeks earlier. When he left for his first Nationals, he only knew four dives off platform: a front dive, back dive, reverse, and forward one-and-a-half somersault. After arriving in California, he had six more to learn in order to compete.

Keith competed on three-meter against such former and future Olympians as:

1956 springboard silver medalist Donald Harper

1960 and 1964 Mexican Olympian Roberto Madrigal

1964 Olympic champion Ken Sitzberger

1964 springboard bronze medalist Larry Andreason

1964 platform bronze medalist Tom Gompf

1964 Olympian Lou Vitucci

1968 platform silver medalist Alvaro Gaxiola of Mexico

Other significant divers included:

1956 NCAA champion Frank Fraunfelter

Purdue's NCAA All-American John Vogel.

Keith's first dive off three-meter was a jackknife, "right on the nose." He had a beautiful hurdle and lots of height, for which he received high points and a compliment from Olympic champion Gary Tobian. Keith's next dive was a back dive, "the best he [had] ever done," according to his mother.

Keith's first optional was a front one-and-a-half somersault with two twists. Lurline commented in Keith's journal on this particularly stunning dive:

> He got such terrific height and went in really vertical. We have it on film to prove it! At that moment, I didn't care where Keith came in … he was a diver! He could take the heat under the

stiffest competition. All this time Dick had faith in Keith. And Keith had faith in himself.

Keith executed a better forward two-and-a-half somersault, which took sixes and sevens, than Olympic silver medalist Don Harper, who received straight sixes. Win's best dive, his front dive, took straight fives.

When the results came in, the announcer listed the top sixteen divers who qualified for semifinals.

1st Alvaro Gaxiola

2nd Tom Gompf

3rd Lou Vitucci

4th John Vogel

5th Larry Andreasen

6th Don Harper

7th Ken Sitzberger

8th Fred Schlichting

9th Kim Pearman

10th Nat Smith

11th Frank Fraunfelter

12th Steve Norling

13th Roberto Madrigal

14th Jack Fury

15th Bill Theuriet

16th Keith Russell

Lurline wrote of her profound enthusiasm: "Cordon had just bought me a lemonade and I almost dropped it. Florence grabbed it. I was so happy. So was Dick. He had me call the [*Arizona*] *Republic*." Keith was the youngest to make semi-finals by two years—two other boys were fifteen.

Lurline wrote about the three-meter semi-finals in Keith's journal:

> The next round, Keith followed the former Olympian. He did an inward, a back dive, and then a two-and-a-half pike [2.4 degree of difficulty]. All of them to the very best of his ability. The best I have ever seen him do. And the highest points he has ever received.
>
> At the end of this round, he had come up to 13th. Poor Win and Hal didn't hit their dives at all. Ronnie [Onsgard] got 30th, Hal [Easton] 31st, and Win [Young] 32nd. So maybe Dick wasn't so far off when his vote for all-state diver went to Keith. And in this case he proved he really is the best diver!

Lurline learned at the last minute that Keith had entered the ten-meter competition. He'd never even been on one before. Lurline commented on her first view of the ten-meter: "When we first saw the thing, we all about fainted. I'd never seen anything so high in my whole life." Keith's first dive off platform was a handstand dive, which he'd just learned there. He didn't stay up on it, so he missed it. His second dive was also a handstand dive, but successful.

Keith and Win each executed a forward two-and-a-half somersault on platform, for which Keith received straight sixes and Win took straight fives. Lurline thought if Keith had done his inward one-and-a-half somersault instead of that first handstand dive, he would have made the semifinals.

Keith decided after his first Nationals, after rating so high among America's best—thirteenth in the nation at age thirteen—that diving was his life. No grade school boy came close to him. Now he wanted to go for the big time: the Olympics. He understood what a big deal it was to place so well at such a young age at such a major national competition. Now he wanted to see what he could accomplish if he really set his mind to it. How far could he go?

Keith had a write-up in the *Phoenix Gazette* for his head-smashing and record-slashing at the Arizona AAU Championships in Phoenix that month:

> Keith Russell, Mesa's water wizard, today boasts three state titles, three gold medals, two records, a bump on the noggin, and one bruised finger after completing one of the busiest nights encountered by any Valley 13-year-old last night.
>
> Earlier in the evening, Keith commenced his versatile tank performance by winning the 3-meter diving title, completely out-classing his opponents while racking up 372.50. After a rest following his collision, Keith went back into action and shattered the 100-yard freestyle record with a 1:00.7 clocking.[41]

Another local newspaper article on the dash and crash, titled "Mesa's Russell, Tucson Y Star in State Aquatic Meet," stated,

> The versatile Russell continued his domination of the boys 13–14 [year-old] 3-meter diving and came back in the swimming to set two meet records. Russell splashed to his first record in the 100-yard backstroke, lowering the mark by five-tenths of a second to 1:11.1. He smashed his head against the end of the pool in his driving finish and had to be assisted from the water. After first aid treatment, Russell returned to chop four tenths off [future

Olympian] Bill Mettler's record time for the 100-yard freestyle with a 1:00.7 clocking.

Bill Mettler grabbed three titles for himself in the fourteen-year-old age group. He took the one-hundred-yard freestyle, two-hundred-yard freestyle, and one-hundred-yard butterfly. After swimming with Keith at Mesa High, he attended Yale on a swimming scholarship, and made the 1964 Olympic Team as a member of the eight-hundred-meter freestyle relay team.[42]

Keith and Win received the only eights awarded on three-meter at the championships. Keith took straight 7.5s on his forward one-and-a-half somersault with two twists for 54.0. Keith won with 372.20. Win followed 21.65 points behind in second with 350.55.

Judy Russell made a big splash at the championships as a four-time winner. She won the one-hundred-yard backstroke, one-hundred-yard butterfly, two-hundred-yard freestyle relay, and two-hundred-yard medley relay. She took second in the one-hundred-yard freestyle.

Future Olympian and world record breaker Marilyn Ramenofsky, whose father attended to Keith after his poolside collision, tied with Judy for high-point honors in their age group. Marilyn won both the one-hundred-yard freestyle and two-hundred-yard freestyle. She'd just learned that she'd been selected as one of eight girls to compete on the U.S. swim team at the Maccabiah Games in Tel Aviv, Israel later that month.[43] The Maccabiah Games started in 1932 in Tel Aviv. Since 1953, they have been held every four years. The Maccabi World Union is an "Organization of Olympic Standing."[44]

Future Olympic champion Charles Hickcox also competed in the Arizona Championships and won the fourteen-year-old age group one-hundred-yard backstroke.[45] Keith was second to him all summer in that event. At the 1968 Olympics, Charles Hickcox won the two-hundred-meter individual medley, four-hundred-meter individual medley, and the 4x100-meter medley relay and took silver in the one-hundred-meter backstroke. He was "World Swimmer of the Year" in 1968 and inducted into the International Swimming Hall of Fame in 1976. He is ranked second on the list of "Fifty Greatest Arizona Sports Figures."[46]

As Keith entered eighth grade, his relationship with his dad continued to develop. They enjoyed planting a vegetable garden together with beets, carrots, onions, radishes, and turnips. His relationship with his sisters was a different story. One day while Cy and Lurline were gone, the girls locked Keith out of the house. Fortunately he had his trusty BB gun, so he just shot Judy in the butt a few times. That's the last time he remembers seeing his gun.

Keith dominated the third annual Midwinter Aquatic Festival the day after Christmas 1961. He won both the boys' thirteen-and-fourteen one-meter and three-meter and the men's open three-meter. One newspaper journalist called Keith "the star of the meet."[47] For the first time in competition, Keith executed a back two-and-a-half tuck somersault off three-meter (2.8 degree of difficulty).

One article, "Mesa's Russell Wins Two Diving Events in Meet," began,

> Keith Russell of Mesa scored heavily on both required and optional dives and won the men's open 3-meter yesterday at the Mid-Winter Aquatic Meet.
>
> Russell's victory in the senior open 3-meter competition was the result of consistency in the five required dives and brilliance in a number of optionals. He gained highest laurels with his optional forward 1½ somersault double twist.[48]

Two weeks after Keith turned fourteen in 1962, Lurline wrote in his journal about his typical boyish reaction to motherly love and her feelings on the subject:

> Last night I was kissing all the kids good-night. Keith at this age thinks kissing is for the birds, and his mom is something below that. He agrees that when he gets a little older he will appreciate his mother again. Well, he didn't want a kiss. So teasing him I told him I didn't want him to feel left out—all the others received a kiss and I wanted him to feel loved and secure. He buried his head under the covers to escape security. He showers all his love and affection on Silver Chief. Sometimes I envy that dog!

Dick raised his coaching rates that year from ten dollars a month to twenty-five. Since Keith's parents could not afford the new rates on a schoolteacher's salary with seven children, he stopped going. After a couple weeks, Dick called to find out where he was. When they told him their situation, Dick insisted they pay the old rate.

Lurline wrote about one of Keith's diving lessons in March:

> I took Keith to Dick's last night. I don't do it often as I work two days a week. [Win] was doing triple-twisters which are in the book for the first time this year. Then Dick announced the lesson was over. But Keith kept right on diving. He kept going for a forward 1½ with a double [twist off the three-meter]. And he made an almost perfect one.
>
> Then he went for a 2½ [pike somersault]. It was a beauty. That put us a little late. A few weeks ago someone stole the tail lights right out of the back of our [Chevrolet] Corvair. So we can't drive after dark. So we were hurrying home, watching every car, hoping not to meet up with a cop.

Cy took Keith, Win Young, and Rory Moore to the Junior National Three-Meter Championships in San Francisco in April. Not only did each gain national rankings, but Keith finished second. Mike

Copeland, twice Keith's age at twenty-eight, won the title. Keith had led in first until the last two dives. Future Olympian Rick Early took third and Win finished fourth. Rory Moore made finals for the first time in a national meet, finishing seventh.[51] Keith received the only eight awarded in the competition on his forward two-and-a-half pike.

One journalist offered valid explanations for the successes of all three young Arizona divers: They were in the right place at the right time, with the right coach, and all worked hard. In his words,

> Entering five national championship events with 30 national ranking spots to be decided, all the [Dick] Smith troupe did was win 15 of the rankings—exactly half—and two national titles. Smith [mused], "Nothing like it ever happened before." The fact is that last month's championship payoff was the result of an immense amount of determination, enthusiasm and plain hard work.

The journalist pointed out that the previous fall, two of the nation's top women divers, 1961 ten-meter champion Barbara McAlister of California and All-American Bette Barr of New York, moved to Phoenix to be coached by Dick Smith. The champion-creator considered Barbara McAlister and Arizona native Patsy Willard "two of the top three divers in the world." The journalist added, "Then during last month's competition, Phoenician Nancy Poulsen, who has been training with Smith about a year, won the junior national 1-meter title."[52] With the right inner force (desire and determination) and the right outer force (Dick Smith), Keith had sufficient drive in the right direction to successfully land a spot on the U.S. Olympic Team.

The Saguaro Invitational took place in May in Phoenix. Keith didn't perform at peak, but he did gain some impressive publicity. The *Phoenix Gazette* featured three consecutive photos of him in a textbook-perfect dive. The caption read,

Keith Russell displays his aerial twist prowess and smooth water-entry form during a practice dive from a 3-meter springboard. He's one of the Valley's top entries in the men's open diving competitions at the fifth annual Saguaro Invitational Aquatic Meet.

The article that followed proved just as flattering:

Main hope among Arizonans in men's diving is Mesa's Keith Russell, who has perfected some difficult routines for his optionals. He's a brilliant performer in somersaults with varying twists. Another top Valley contender is Phoenix's Win Young.[53]

Jay Moxley of California built up an early lead and "held off strong finishes by teammate Mike Copeland [who placed second] and Keith Russell" for a victory in the men's one-meter.[54] Win took third. A crew of dominant divers paced the Dick Smith Swim Gym into first place. California, Mexico, and Texas teams claimed the rest of the top five spots. Patsy Willard won the women's open one-meter. Barbara McAlister took second, Nancy Poulson took third, and Jeanne Collier took fourth—all Dick's divers, three of whom were future Olympians.

Excitement is felt in one summer journal entry Lurline wrote about the Third Annual Arizona AAU Swimming Relays at Arizona State University: "I just had to sit down and write this today on June 9th. But after not having worked out for ten months, [Keith] qualified first in a fast time of 57.8 in the 100 yards short course freestyle at the Arizona relays." Others had "all been working like mad" for the event.

Keith's achievements continued in the men's open three-meter at the Arizona Relays when the soon-to-be high school freshman beat defending champion Hal Easton of the University of Arizona with his forward one-and-a-half somersault with two twists, which took 7.5s for 52.8 points.[55] The college kid claimed second.

The Sunnyslope Pool Invitational, a sixty-eight-event AAU meet, took place that month in Phoenix. The chairman of the Arizona AAU Association's swim committee called it "a key meet for all Valley swimmers."[56]

In the age-group one-meter, Keith received the highest points on all ten dives and won by 76 points, with 387.5. For both Keith and Win, their back one-and-a-half with a twist was their worst. Keith received straight fives (not bad) for 35.2, and Win took 18.7. Keith's inward one-and-a-half received his highest points, two 7.5s and an 8.

Keith shined on three-meter where he averaged sevens to Win's fives. Keith received his highest points, two 8.5s and an 8, on his reverse. His forward two-and-a-half somersault took an 8 and two 7.5s. The fourteen-year-old could now successfully execute a forward one-and-a-half somersault with three twists (2.9 degree of difficulty), for which he received straight fives. This became his signature dive. Keith won with an impressive 430.95 points.

Lurline wrote about a typical summer day in 1962 for Keith:

> He has really taken [diving] seriously and worked so hard. Sometimes I feel sorry for him. For the most part, his schedule is up at 6 a.m. and diving by 7. Then he doesn't get home until 8:30 to 10 p.m. So we don't see him at all.

The Russells met future Olympic champion Bernie Wrightson that summer, who moved to Arizona like other top divers to train with Dick Smith. Lurline wrote her thoughts on him: "There is a new diver who will enter ASU. Bernie someone. He is really good. Sometimes he can dive the socks off Keith, but other times Keith is better."

The International Swimming Hall of Fame inducted Bernie Wrightson in 1984. According to his ISHOF profile, Bernie Wrightson was the best springboard diver by gold medal count from 1964 to 1968. He won eight U.S. AAU and two NCAA titles, including a platform. In 1966, he won every major United States springboard title.

Keith competed in the Fourth Annual Los Angeles Invitational at the Olympic Stadium, "the biggest aquatic extravaganza west of the Mississippi" in July.[57] Bernie won the three-meter with 495.55, followed by future Olympic bronze medalist Larry Andreason, who had 479.15. Keith took third with 472.35 and future Olympic bronze medalist Win Young finished fifth.[58]

Dick Smith's girls did even better. Future Olympic silver medalist Jeannie Collier won, future Olympic bronze medalist Patsy Willard was second, and Nancy Poulson took fourth.[59] Barbara McAlister, "the top woman diver in the country,"[60] missed Los Angeles to compete in the Japanese National Championships, where she won two titles, three-meter and platform.[61] She was the cover girl that week, July 23, 1962, for *Sports Illustrated*.[62]

Keith left by train on August 2 with Win and Win's mother for two weeks of national competitions. First was the Junior National AAU Three-Meter Championships in Albuquerque. While Jay Moxley won the three-meter title, Dick Smith's team took everything else.[63] Win took second, Keith third, and Bernie Wrightson fourth.[64] Keith's best dive, his reverse, took eights. He'd just beat Jay Moxley in L.A.

From Albuquerque, the divers went to the 1962 National Senior AAU Outdoor Championships in Philadelphia.[65] Although Dick Smith named Keith, Win, Rory, and Bernie to bid for the national champion title,[66] Keith placed eighteenth, five spots below the year before. Win Young finished twenty-first, up eleven spots from the year before. With seventy-one divers in the springboard competition from as far away as Japan and West Germany, this was the largest National Championship ever.[67]

Although Win Young made All-State diver that year, Dick Smith felt Keith was by far the better diver. Win rarely beat Keith, but there were no hard feelings. Win and Keith remained friends.

The day Keith started ninth grade, he arrived home at one in the morning from a meet in El Paso, where he won both the men's open one-meter and three-meter as well as the age-group three-meter. He began high school a winner.

On November 19, 1962, two days before Lurline's forty-first birthday, Keith got another brother. His parents let him name the baby, so he named him Rory, after his friend Rory Moore.

The Fourth Annual Optimist Mid-Winter Aquatic Meet took place just before Christmas. With sixty-one divers, including five from the 1962 All-America team, and hundreds of swimmers, the meet became the largest aquatic event in the Southwest, with entries from as far away as Canada, Mexico, and Venezuela.[68] It also attracted the world's best diving coaches as judges: Hobie Billingsley and Dick Kimball.

Hobie Billingsley was NCAA champion on both boards in 1945 his first year at Ohio State University. He was the second college diving coach ever hired when he started in 1959 at Indiana University, where he coached for thirty years.[69] He served as the U.S. women's diving coach at the 1968 Olympics, the U.S. men's diving coach at the 1972 Munich Olympics, the Austrian diving coach at the 1976 Montreal Olympics, and the Austrian-Danish diving coach at the 1980 Moscow Olympics.

Hobie was voted U.S. Diving Coach of the Year seven consecutive years between 1964 and 1970 and was the first "NCAA Coach of the Year" in 1982.[70] His Olympic champions include Ken Sitzberger (1964) and Lesley Bush (1964). His Olympic bronze medalists include Win Young (platform, 1968); Jim Henry (springboard, 1968); and Cynthia Potter (1976). Other Olympians he coached include Luis

Nino of Mexico (1964 and 1968); Tom Dinsley of Canada (1964); Rick Gilbert (1968); and Rick Early (1972).

Dick Kimball was the 1957 NCAA champion on both boards.[71] He began coaching at the University of Michigan (his alma mater) in 1959 and didn't stop until his retirement in 2002.[72] He was the U.S. men's diving coach at the 1964 Tokyo Olympics with three divers on the team. One, Bob Webster, won platform.[73] Dick also served as the 1984 and 1988 U.S. Olympic diving coach.[74] His son, Bruce Kimball, won Olympic silver on platform in 1984.[75] Both Dick Kimball and Hobie Billingsley actively began recruiting Keith in the next few years.

On three-meter, future Olympic bronze medalist Larry Andreasen was "pressed all the way by Keith" according to one newspaper account.[76] Bernie Wrightson led all the way to win. Keith received sevens on his inward two-and-a-half somersault with a twist for fifty-two points and his reverse two-and-a-half somersault for fifty-six.

Keith won the age-group one-meter.[77] His worst dives, his back one-and-a-half somersault and his reverse one-and-a-half somersault, took straight fives. He received straight sevens on his forward two-and-a-half somersault. His best dive, his forward somersault with two twists, received two 7s and a 7.5 for 47.3.

Keith won the fourteen-and-under three-meter by 58.10 points with 390.25. His worst dive, his reverse two-and-a-half somersault, received straight fives for a fairly good 42 points. Don McAlister took second with 322.15 ahead of future Olympic silver medalist Dick Rydze in third with 317.55.

Bernie Wrightson, Larry Andreasen, Keith Russell, and Dick Rydze were only half the future Olympians in the Midwinter meet. Future Olympic silver medalist Jeanne Collier won both boards in the girls' fifteen-to-seventeen age group and future Olympic bronze medalist Patsy Willard won both boards in the women's open. Barbara

McAlister (Barbara Talmage at the 1964 Olympics) took second and Jeanne Collier took third in the women's open three-meter.

Jose Robinson of Mexico (future three-time Olympian) won the boy's fifteen-to-seventeen three-meter, and future Olympic bronze medalist Larry Andreasen won that age-group one-meter. Future Olympic silver medalist Dick Rydze won the eleven-and-twelve one-meter. As a high school freshman, Keith competed against the world's greatest up-and-coming divers.

Chapter 5: First Olympic Trials: America's Best High School Diver

Keith spent the beginning of the year preparing for the National Senior AAU Indoor Championships at Yale in March. His parents spent that time trying to figure out how they could afford it. Sometimes sponsors donated money. This time, Dick said if they could put up a hundred dollars, he'd put up the rest. Although the high school freshman was now a veteran of Senior National Championships, this meet was significant because it was the first one he flew to. He'd never flown on a plane before. He flew with teammates Bill Mettler, Earl Beatty, Win Young, and Rory Moore. The flight from Phoenix to New York on American Airlines cost $165.

On March 18, Lurline spared no detail of the big day of his departure:

> Today I saw my 15-year-old boy board an astro-jet plane and take off for New Haven, Conn. via New York City. He was excited

about this trip because of the flying. He had oatmeal mush and toast for breakfast.

I tried to get him to wear his new shoes, but he wouldn't. I about flipped when he didn't object to Cy trimming his hair. The kids were all tickled to death to hear that Nancy Poulson had gotten 2nd on the platform and will get to go to the Pan Am Games. Patsy [Willard] got 3rd and Barbara [McAlister] 5th.

The National one-meter competition was not memorable for the Dick Smith divers. Only future Olympic bronze medalist Tom Gompf, who began training with Dick Smith while stationed at Williams Air Force Base, made finals. Win Young was next best in twenty-fifth. Bernie Wrightson followed in twenty-sixth. Keith hit his foot on his forward two-and-a-half pike and finished thirty-sixth out of fifty-three divers. All but four in the top twenty-four came from the northeast:

1. Rick Gilbert, Indiana University (Keith's future Olympic teammate)
2. Tom Gompf, Air Force
3. Lou Vitucci, Boston, Massachusetts (1964 Olympian)
4. Stanley Cox, Ann Arbor, Michigan
5. John Vogel, Bloomington, Indiana (1961 AAU champion)
6. Ken Sitzberger, Oak Park, Illinois (1964 Olympic champion)
7. John Walker, Indiana University
8. Juan Botella, Columbus, Ohio (1960 Olympic bronze)
9. Robert Bramble, Bloomington, Indiana
10. Frank Gorman, New York (1964 Olympic silver)
11. Charles Neel, Bloomington, Indiana
12. Larry Andreasen, City of Commerce, California (1964 Olympic bronze)
13. Bruce Brown, Ann Arbor, Michigan
14. Tadao Tosa, Japan (1964 Olympian)
15. Fritz Fisher, Bloomington, Indiana
16. Daniel Garteiz, Cincinnati, Ohio

17. Randy Larson, Akron, Ohio (1964 NCAA champion)
18. Shunsuke Kaneto, Japan (two-time Olympian)
19. William Glueck, Columbus, Ohio
20. Roy Nichols, New Brunswick, New Jersey
21. Ronald Squiers, College Park, Maryland
22. Bob Webster, Army (two-time Olympic champion)
23. Richard Flynn, Columbus, Ohio
24. Glen Whitten, Army

Jay Moxley, winner of the 1962 Los Angeles Invitational, Saguaro Invitational, and Junior Nationals, placed two spots below Keith in thirty-eighth.

Indiana University sophomore Rick Gilbert also won the three-meter national title followed by:

2. Ken Sitzberger (married Keith's friend Jeanne Collier)
3. Bernie Wrightston, 1968 Olympic champion
4. Juan Botella, Ohio State University senior
5. Lou Vitucci, Ohio State University junior
6. Bob Webster, University of Michigan alumni
7. Lt. Frank Gorman, Harvard alumni
8. John Vogel, Purdue alumni
9. Lt. Tom Gompf, Ohio State University alumni
10. Edward Boothman, Royal Oak, Michigan
11. Estel Mills, Princeton, New Jersey
12. Frank Fraunfelter, 1956 NCAA champion
13. Rick Earley, 1972 Olympian
14. John Walker
15. Keith Russell (the youngest diver in the semi-finals)[78]

Lurline's report on those Nationals in New Haven, via Keith, offered insight into Keith's modest personality, Lurline's hopeful observation, and their relationship:

> Keith didn't say too much about his diving, but he was satisfied, which satisfied me. He said his back dive was his best. He got

> 7½'s on it. He didn't do too well on his triple twister and his first optional dive, his inward 2½ tuck. He didn't get the lift he usually gets. He can really hit that dive. Well, maybe in another 5 years he will be more ready for the Olympics than next year.

Keith was almost homeless his first night at his first Indoor Nationals. Bernie Wrightson originally planned to stay in the Yale dorms and Keith originally planned to stay at the YMCA, but they decided to switch. When Keith and his teammate Earl Beatty arrived at Bernie's dorm, Coach Schlueter told them they couldn't stay there, so they went to the YMCA. But when they got there, they were told they couldn't stay there either because they were under eighteen.

By that time, it was almost midnight, so they went to look for Coach Schlueter and ran into the new national one-meter bronze medalist Lou Vitucci. He let them stay with him, where they found Bernie, but they stayed the rest of the time at a Yale dorm.

Lurline began an April 1963 journal entry with "Keith is in the living room making life almost unlivable for Alan and the little girls [Donetta, ten, and Kathy, eight]." With all his astonishing diving achievements, Keith apparently found a rare moment to be a normal boy and do what big brothers do, torment younger siblings.

By the end of his freshman year of high school, Keith started pursuing another interest. Her name was Marsha Lofgreen and she gladly reciprocated. Lurline had this to say about it:

> He is growing up and has started liking the girls. I should say one girl in particular. Marsha Lofgreen. Before every dance I tell him to dance with all the girls. But he doesn't mind so good. He was real thrilled when Marsha got the trophy for outstanding musician at East [Mesa] Jr.

Keith met Marsha at a ninth-grade party at the end of the school year. He was attracted to her from the start. She was cultured, mature, and smart in school. She also excelled in ballet.

The AAU Junior National Championships took place in July in San Lorenzo, California, south of San Francisco. Future Olympian Larry Andreasen of Los Alamitos, California, won the title with 469.65 points. Julian Krug of San Jose, future University of Pittsburgh diving coach and the first person to successfully execute a forward five-and-a-half somersault from ten meters, took second with 440.70 points.[79] Vic Laughlin of the famed Santa Clara Swim Club followed 0.05 of a point behind in third with 440.65.[80]

The next three spots went to current or past Dick Smith divers: Keith finished 3.35 points behind in fourth with 437.30; Earl Beatty was fifth with 431.20; and Win Young took sixth with 428.70. Keith bombed his first dive, taking straight fours, but received pretty good sevens on the rest.

The Arizona Association Senior AAU Championships took place in Phoenix that month as well.[81] One newspaper article offered raving reviews of Keith's stellar one-meter performance:

> Keith Russell of Mesa turned in the best performance of the meet. Russell compiled an overwhelming total in the one-meter competition with 445.85 points to capture the gold medal and upset defending champion Steve Sinclair of Phoenix YMCA.
>
> Russell turned in a sparkling performance, probably his best of the season. He drew an almost perfect score on the last of his 11 dives—a forward double somersault from the pike position. The near-perfect dive drew scores of 8½, 8, and 9 from the judges and accounted for 56.10 points of his total.[82]

Another article complimented Keith's beautiful three-meter work: "Keith Russell of Mesa swept both men's springboard crowns with another sterling performance for 450.25 in the 3-meter."[83] His friend and teammate, future Olympic silver medalist Jeanne Collier, won the women's one-meter.

The Fifth Annual Los Angeles Invitational took place in July. Future Olympic silver medalist Sharon Finneran, sixteen, broke a world record and became the second woman to swim the mile in under nineteen minutes, taking seven seconds off the previous record.[84] Her brother, Mike, also excelled in aquatic sports. The 1971 national champion and NCAA champion competed in the 1972 Olympics, where he placed fifth on springboard. He later coached diving at Alabama, South Carolina, and North Carolina State.

While future Olympic bronze medalist Larry Andreasen won the three-meter, Keith and his teammates took half the top six spots with Win Young second, Keith third, future Olympian Rick Early fourth, and future Olympic champion Bernie Wrightson fifth.

Keith's forward one-and-a-half somersault with two twists received the only 8.5 awarded at the LA meet.

The 1963 National AAU Outdoor Championships took place in north Chicago the following week in August.[87] The Phoenix Thunderbirds, a committee of the Phoenix Chamber of Commerce, donated $75 for Keith to go.

Keith's teammate, Tom Gompf, twenty-four, was the surprise platform winner. The 1961 Ohio State University graduate had moved to Phoenix that winter to be coached by Dick Smith. He'd never placed higher than second in Big Ten Conference diving, which had the best diving programs in the world, including Indiana University, coached by Hobie Billingsley and the University of Michigan, coached by Dick Kimball.

Larry Andreasen of Anaheim, California finished second; Win Young, third, Lou Vitucci, fourth; and Bernie Wrightson sixth. Keith finished sixteenth in his first ten-meter competition. He'd only competed on five-meter before.

Future Olympic bronze medalist Larry Andreasen won the national three-meter title. National indoor champion Rick Gilbert took second. Tom Gompf followed in third and Keith's one-time roommate, defending champion Lou Vitucci, finished fourth.[89]

Lurline wrote in Keith's journal about his experience, feelings, and surprise platform performance:

> Keith got 12th in the springboard which is the best he has done. [He took thirteenth at his first Outdoor Nationals]. But Win was 10th so Keith wasn't satisfied at all. Keith got brave and, at the last minute, entered [platform] and, what do you know, he got 16th.

The cost of the trip was manageable, since Keith paid only four dollars a night for hotel, he drove home with teammate Earl Beatty, and Bernie Wrightson's parents took them out to eat a couple times.

Both Keith's mother and coach commented on his impressive improvements his sophomore year of high school. Lurline wrote about one workout she went to in November 1963: "He put in some 3½ [somersault]s he could have piked out of easily, and some beautiful triple twisters." One newspaper article that month quoted Dick Smith: "Keith Russell at 15 is capable of doing a 1½ [somersault] with a quadruple twist [off the charts with a 3.3 degree of difficulty]. With that kind of ability, he's headed for a championship future."

At every chance he got, Keith found himself with Marsha Lofgreen. They went to the Saturday night dances together. He walked her to sixth period. And once, when his parents took him to a game, "he was nowhere to be found upon its completion. And we guessed right … we picked him up at Marsha's house."

At an exhibition in north Phoenix in December, Earl Beatty and Keith demonstrated the lighter side of diving called clown diving. That's when Lurline saw him do it for the first time. She didn't know he had it in him. She thought he had on "the funniest hat you ever saw with a flappy brim all the way around."

Earl Beatty, acting as announcer on one board, asked Keith about his first dive. Keith said his first dive was dedicated to his girlfriend. Earl replied, "Yeah! I'm going to dedicate it to my girlfriend too!" Then he jumped off the diving board straddling a broom and added, "The old witch!" as he executed a most uncoordinated dive. His comment, coming unexpectedly as it did, elicited laughter from the crowd.

Keith announced his last dive was his favorite. When Earl asked which one that was, Keith answered, "Well, you just wait and see!" He proceeded to make a big fancy production out of it. He performed a high hurdle, as if to do some fantastic dive, only to miss the end of the board "on accident" and just fell in. Whereas traditional diving requires grace, precision, and skill, clown diving just requires skill so the clown doesn't hurt himself on his flying stunts, which could include riding motorcycles off the high board.

Keith enjoyed the high school football games his sophomore year at Mesa High. The 1963–1964 season proved especially exciting, because Mesa High went unbeaten and won their sixth state championship.[90] Plus Marsha Lofgreen sat with him.

Keith participated in the Fifth Annual Mid-Winter Aquatic Festival in Phoenix. Future Olympian Luis Nino de Rivera of Mexico won the men's open three-meter. Future Olympic bronze medalist Larry Andreasen followed in second, Keith took third, future Olympic champion Bernie Wrightson took fourth,[91] and future Olympic bronze medalist Win Young placed fifth.[92]

Keith started out in first place after his first dive received two 7.5s and a 7 on his forward dive. His forward three-and-a-half earned straight 7.5s for 65.25, the highest score of the winter competition. His forward one-and-a-half with three twists garnered straight 6.5s for 56.55. It was the best triple twister he'd ever performed in competition.

After the three-meter competition, a judge told Lurline that Keith had every dive made, his takeoff and lift were brilliant, he just needed to finish his dives. This probably meant he needed a clean finish, a vertical entry with no splash.

Keith won the boys' one-meter by 45.2 points with 417.20. Win Young took second with 372 and Luis Nino de Rivera followed in third.[93] Keith received his highest points on one-meter, an 8 and two 7.5s for 52.9, on his reverse one-and-a-half somersault. His next highest points, an 8, a 7.5, and a 7 (plus a dropped 9), came on his inward one-and-a-half somersault for 54 points. He took his lowest points, two 5.5s and a 5, on his forward one-and-a-half somersault with two twists.

This was the first time Marsha Lofgreen attended a diving meet. Lurline recounted how good and relaxed Keith felt in the boys' one-meter competition:

> He had plenty of [confidence] on the low board because he didn't worry about how it came out. He did all his difficult dives, 2½ pike and a double-twisting 1½ and didn't blow a dive. [Luis Nino] De Rivera was using his high degree difficulty dives and crashed three. Jerry Van Dyke (Dick's brother) awarded the open trophies.

Jerry Van Dyke had just landed his first television role on *The Dick Van Dyke Show*, where he played the lead character's brother (his real-life brother). He has more recently guest starred on such shows as *Yes,*

Dear (2000) and *Coach*, for which he received four consecutive Emmy nominations for Outstanding Supporting Actor in a Comedy Series.

Keith was playing football in PE the day after he turned sixteen in mid-January 1964. As he was running with the ball, he slipped on the grass when he turned to escape a tackle and broke his ankle. Although that prevented him from diving the rest of the school year, it didn't stop him from swimming on Mesa High's first swim team and winning every backstroke competition.

The success of Mesa High School's first swim team made one newspaper:

> When anyone ventures into something new, he is not expected to be at the top from the start. Generally, it takes a while to rise up to meet the competition. But not so with Mesa High School. The Jackrabbits have taken up the sport of swimming for the first time in the history of the school and already they are among the top teams in the state.
>
> Coach Wibby Koski's swimmers have recorded a 4-1 dual meet record, and have even avenged that one loss. Scottsdale defeated Mesa by one point early in the season when the rabbits were yet unorganized, but last week Mesa clobbered Scottsdale, 52-34. No team yet has been a fair match for Mesa.
>
> Besides [future Olympian Bill] Mettler, Koski lists good underclassmen who are overshadowed. These are Stephen Leathers, Keith Russell, Franklin Laneback, Stuart Driggs, Steve Scott, Mike Elliott and Mike Grant.[94]

Mesa High first competed against Coronado and won each of the ten events for a 61-24 finish. Some of the more spectacular races included Bill Mettler's win by over two minutes in the four-hundred-meter freestyle with 4:41.3; Stephen Leathers' win by nearly thirty seconds in the two-hundred-meter individual medley with a time of 2:37.1 over teammate Steve Scott, who finished second with 3:06.9; Stephen Leathers' one-hundred-meter butterfly win with 1:13.8, almost forty seconds faster than second place at 1:52.3; and Stuart Driggs' win in the one-hundred-meter breaststroke with 1:26.1, twenty seconds faster than second place at 1:46.8.[95]

Mesa High won all but the fifty-meter freestyle for a 52-34 margin against Scottsdale.[96] Mesa High won all but the two-hundred-meter medley relay for 56-30 against Westwood.[97] Then Mesa High won again against Coronado, 66-20.[98]

Coach Koski made predictions for the state meet at the University of Arizona in Tucson that proved fairly accurate: Palo Verde, predicted to defend its title with sixty-seven points, won with sixty-three,[99] and Mesa High finished third, as predicted.[100] Future Olympian and Yale swimmer Bill Mettler won the two-hundred-yard freestyle and the one-hundred-yard butterfly at state. His teammate Stephen Leathers placed third in the butterfly. Keith won the diving by over eighty-five points, with 376.4.

Keith had a good measuring stick in teammate Bernie Wrightson to see what it took to win. The future Olympic champion racked up wins in that year's Saguaro Invitational, Los Angeles Invitational, Las Vegas Invitational, Mexican Nationals, and Canadian Nationals, as well as the regional qualifying meet for the Indoor Nationals.[101]

The U.S. Junior National Diving Meet was the first competition at the new Olympic Diving Complex in Mesa the day of its dedication, June 13, 1964.[102] To spark interest, one newspaper article informed its readers, "Patsy Willard and Keith Russell of Mesa will be among the more than 80 entries" in the meet.[103]

The Olympic Diving Complex, known as "the hole" to locals, housed Arizona's first ten-meter platform. Termed "the greatest diving complex in the world," the $100,000 structure was built with voluntary contributions of land, labor, and materials.[104] C. H. Turner, because of his great interest in amateur athletics, especially diving, offered his land. He piped in 108-degree water from his well to fill the pool.[105] Dick Smith's brother, Marion, a pool builder, built the pool and served as project chairman.[106] Keith's dad plastered the pool. Unfortunately, the century-long housing boom in Mesa brought about its demise in 1973 when the nine-year-old complex was torn down for the new retirement community of Leisure World.

Bernie Wrightson won the junior national one-meter. His best dive, his back dive, got an 8 and two 7.5s. Pat Lane of Commerce, California, took second with 461. Keith followed 4.75 points behind in third with 456.25. Pat Lane's teammate, future two-time Olympian Luis Nino de Rivera, followed a distant 55.5 points behind in fourth with 400.75.

Keith finished fifth on three-meter at the Junior Nationals. Since he'd only trained for two months after taking a few months off for his broken ankle, his placings against the other future Olympians was brilliant.

On Saturday, July 25, 1964, the *Phoenix Gazette* featured a photograph of Keith preparing to do a back dive off the one-meter as it announced the up-coming Nationals. The caption read, "Russell, three-time member of *The Phoenix Gazette*'s All-State aquatic team, is a qualifier for National AAU senior championships at Los Angeles. Watching instruction are Bernie Wrightson, Frank Gorman, and Tom Gompf." The Nationals served as tryouts for the Olympic trials. If a diver made finals in Nationals, he qualified for the Olympic trials.

One Arizona newspaper article basked in its plethora of world-class athletes:

> Arizona divers climaxed an amazing domination of the National AAU championships yesterday when Bernie Wrightson and Patsy

Willard won gold medals. The Arizonans [Barbara Talmage, Bernie Wrightson, Patsy Willard] won six of eight events.

The Arizonans' coach, Dick Smith, called his team's domination of yesterday's final events "the greatest performance ever in a national diving meet." DSSG divers captured four of the top five places in the men's three-meter.

Smith protégés Tom Gompf, Keith Russell, and Frank Gorman were second, third, and fifth, respectively, in the Arizona sweep. One of the meet's features was the lofty finish of Russell, 16.

Bernie Wrightson won two senior national titles, the one-meter and three-meter, as well as the junior ten-meter title. Patsy Willard won both the woman's one-meter and ten-meter titles, and their teammate, another future Olympian, Barbara Talmage, won the national three-meter. Keith placed third in both the national one-meter and three-meter.[113] Reigning Olympic champion Bob Webster finished second to Bernie, while future Olympians Luis Nino de Rivera of Mexico took sixth and Lou Vitucci took seventh behind Keith.[114]

Lurline expressed her exhilaration at Keith's exceptional performance at Nationals:

> Keith called us the night of the 1 meter competition. He had come in 3rd! Imagine our elation at that. We just could hardly believe it. He told us it was because John Vogel wasn't there nor Lou Vitucci.
>
> He didn't enter either tower competition. Bernie got 1st on the Jr. tower, 1st on the 1 me. and 1st on the 3 meter so he had a good day. Well, Vitucci and Vogel turned up for the 3 m. And do you know what! Keith got 3rd on the 3 meter too. I called up the paper to see if they had any reports on the meet and when they said Keith Russell got 3rd I had him repeat it about 4 times.

> Now Keith is eligible to go to New York and try out for the Olympics. You had to get in the top 8 to qualify and I would have been thrilled with an 8th. I can still hardly believe he made 3rd. Mercier Willard, Patsy [Willard], Pete Igoe [father of Keith's teammate Kathy Igoe], Bob Collier [father of Olympic champion Jeanne Collier], all said Keith dived superbly and was giving Bernie a real battle for 1st place.
>
> Going into finals Keith was 2nd. He did a poor back 2½ [tuck somersault] which put him back into 4th place. Then did a superb reverse 2½ tuck somersault that brought him back to 3rd. We got to see it over ABC *Wide World of Sports*. What a thrill that was to see Keith dive. The day before, he was on T.V. with the girl divers for an interview.

Arizona added seven divers to its already impressive list of five qualifiers for the Olympic trials: Bernie Wrightson, Keith Russell, Win Young, Earl Beatty, Rory Moore, Bette Barr, and Nancy Poulson.[115] Jeanne Collier (1964 Olympic silver), Tom Gompf (1964 Olympic bronze), Frank Gorman (1964 Olympic silver medalist), Patsy Willard (1964 Olympic bronze), and future two-time Olympian Barbara Talmage previously qualified for the Olympic trials.[116]

Lurline offered a humorous glimpse into Keith's personality in August:

> Keith is working [out] 5 hours daily. Today they had a practice meet. [Lou] Vitucci has come to work out with Chuck [McMahon], Bernie, Frank, Keith, and Tom. Keith said he never knew who won, only that he did lousy.
>
> One night I came home at 10 p.m. and Keith wasn't here. Patsy or Dick had called and he had to go to Phoenix to record some interviews. It was for the Olympic Fund raising deal. Keith never knows quite who things are for or why.

> Also last night, Keith had to go to Phoenix to have pictures taken. He thought this might be for the [*Arizona*] *Republic* or [*Phoenix*] *Gazette*. We can say this much. He is as modest as ever, and nothing has gone to his head at all.

Lou Vitucci, the latest addition to the Dick Smith Swim Gym, came from Cincinnati. He'd recently graduated from Ohio State University, where he won three Big Ten titles and five NCAA titles. He was also a two-time national champion, a 1963 Pan-American Team member, and a member of the 1964 U.S. Olympic Team a few months later.

Keith took off for the 1964 Olympic Trials in New York City in August. One newspaper celebrated the historic trip with a large picture in its sports section of Keith, Dick Smith, and nine other Phoenix divers bound for the trials: Patsy Willard, Barbara Talmage, Nancy Poulson, Jeanne Collier, Bernie Wrightson, Win Young, Frank Gorman, Rory Moore, and Tom Gompf posed outside on the TWA airplane steps. Keith received a hundred dollars from the Phoenix Thunderbirds for the trip.

Astoria Pool in Astoria Park in northwest Queens hosted the 1964 Olympic Trials.

Opened in 1936, it is New York City's oldest and largest pool. Built by the Works Progress Administration, an organization the U.S. government created to give people work during the Great Depression, it also hosted the 1936 Olympic Trials.[117]

Astoria Park is across the East River from Manhattan's Upper East Side. The long diagonal northwest side of the park is on the east side of the river. The Triborough Bridge takes I-278 over the southwest end of the park. Hell Gate Bridge is the slanted northeastern border of the sixty-five-acre park.

Keith had friends in the U.S. Olympic Swimming Trials as well: Marilyn Ramenofsky, Charles Hickcox, Bill Mettler, and Rory's sister

Kendis Moore. Forty female and sixty-five male divers vied for a spot on the 1964 U.S. Olympic diving team.[118]

A few days after arriving in New York and a few days before the trials, Keith wrote his family of his various experiences:

> How is everybody? I am okay but a little discouraged because I can't do back 2½ and back lifts the right way. So far I've had a nice stay. Today we checked out of our motel. And you'll never guess where I'm staying. I'm staying at Buster Crabbe's apartment in Rye, New York! It's right by a huge country club with lots of the prettiest countryside I've seen in all my life! I think we'll be staying here another night.
>
> While staying in Manhasset we drove by the [World] Fair every day. They're giving free passes to the competitors. Love you all Keith

Manhasset, where Keith first stayed, is northeast of Queens, seventeen miles east of Astoria. Keith finished eleventh in the springboard competition, but his friends placed:

1. Frank Gorman
2. Larry Andreasen
3. Ken Sitzberger
4. Bernie Wrightson
5. Tom Gompf
6. Rick Gilbert
7. John Vogel
8. Lou Vitucci[119]

In the women's springboard tryouts, Keith's teammates and friends took four of the top five spots:

1. Jeanne Collier

2. Sue Gossick
3. Patsy Willard
4. Lesley Bush
5. Barbara Talmage[120]

Keith went to the World Fair twice and saw the play *Around the World in Eighty Days* at the Jones Beach Marine Theatre in Wantagh, south Long Island, thirty miles east of Astoria. Many of its stage sets were mounted on barges that moved in and out of the lagoon.

Lurline wrote about Keith's trip at and driving home from the 1964 Olympic Trials:

> Keith got 11th in New York. Frank Gorman won and Keith has been beating him every meet. Keith was gone two weeks and spent only $80.00. This included his transportation, lodging, food, and entertainment. He ate at several [at least five] Chinese restaurants. He felt bad because he hadn't done well. Just the day before, all his dives were going great.
>
> He came home with Mrs. Willard and Earl [Beatty]. They stopped only one night coming back from New York, in Joplin, Missouri. Keith drove thru St. Louis. He said Mrs. Willard is "Crazy." She speeds up to a sign, slams on the brakes, and asks: "What does it say, What does it say!?" What a ride it must have been.

With so many friends and teammates at the 1964 Tokyo Olympics, like Tom Gompf, Frank Gorman, Lou Vitucci, Lesley Bush, Barbara Talmage, Jeanne Collier, Patsy Willard, Kendis Moore, Marilyn Ramenofsky, and Bill Mettler, Keith intensely watched the games to see how they all did.

Ingrid Kramer, East Germany's 1960 Olympic champion, finished the springboard preliminaries in first place with Patsy Willard second, Jeanne Collier third, and Sue Gossick fourth.

In finals, Ingrid Kramer, who had kept such a large distance ahead of the silver medalists in 1960 on both events, claimed when she won springboard this time by almost seven points, "Few medals have cost more toil than this one." The women who caused her that toil were Jeanne Collier, silver medalist, with 138.36, and Patsy Willard, bronze medalist, with 138.18, both Keith's Arizona teammates. Sue Gossick finished fourth. Ingrid's points came more from exactness than elegance. She dove with precision. She didn't make mistakes, but according to one commentator,

> Ingrid Engel's final jumps are not too breathtaking because of the presence of the young Jeanne Collier. She risks two dives whose degree of difficulty is valued at 2.6 and receives the most points. Her daring has paid off. Jeanne Collier takes the second place away from her teammate, Patsy Willard, who is usually more valued than Jeanne.[121]

Keith wanted Frank to win the men's springboard. Frank led from the start with a near perfect forward two-and-a-half somersault and finished the first round in first place with 105.99. Larry Andreasen followed in second with 100.31. But the next day, Ken Sitzberger rose from third to gold. Frank Gorman ended up silver medalist after over-rotating a dive.[122] Larry Andreasen, who died in 1990 after diving from Los Angeles' 385-foot Vincent Thomas Bridge, won bronze for a complete American sweep of the springboard.

The Italian greats and Mexico's finest failed to make finals. Here's how they placed:

10th: Franco Cagnotto, Italy (first of five Olympics)

12th: Luis Nino de Rivera, Mexico (first of two Olympics)

13th: Klaus Dibiasi, Italy (first of four Olympics)

15th: Alvaro Gaxiola, Mexico (second of three Olympics)

19th: Jose Robinson, Mexico (first of three Olympics)

The women's platform preliminaries proved both delightful and devastating for the Americans. Lesley Bush was the delight, finishing the first round in first place with 53.78 points. The Russian women claimed three of the top five spots, with Germany's Ingrid Kramer less than a point away from first in third with 52.98. Pan-American champion Linda Cooper was eighth with 47.80 and Barbara Talmage followed less than a point away with 47.28 in eleventh.

Lesley Bush became Olympic champion with 99.80 points. Ingrid Kramer overtook Russian Galeena Alekseeva for silver with 98.45, leaving Galeena with bronze. Linda Cooper moved up four spots to finish fourth with 96.30. Barbara Talmage moved up three spots to finish eighth.

The phenomenal thing about this Olympic competition is that Keith's friend Lesley Bush, at nineteen and with only three years of platform diving experience, beat out a three-time Olympic champion.[123] Lurline expressed her surprise at Lesley's brilliance in a journal entry: "Lesley won the platform. That really floored us."

Bob Webster became a two-time Olympic champion on platform. Klaus Dibiasi won silver, and Tom Gompf, 0.97 of a point behind, won bronze. Lurline wrote about Lou Vitucci, "Poor Lou came in very badly. He missed his handstand dive and was in last place for a while." Vitucci finished nineteenth.

While the U.S. women won half the medals, one gold, one silver, and one bronze, the U.S. men scored all but one—two gold, one silver, and two bronze. The United States men have since failed to duplicate that medal count (five medals of six awarded) in Olympic diving, and the United States has failed to generate that many champions (three of four possible) in one Olympics. Keith must have felt a sense of satisfaction in the women's diving, as three friends and teammates medaled.

Patsy Willard sent Keith a postcard from the Olympic Games, in which she revealed the struggles amidst which she won her bronze medal:

> Hi, the games end[ed] two days ago and I'll get to come home [Oct.] 27th.
>
> It has been a lot of fun but I'm looking forward to Mesa. I've been sick the whole time I've been here, and the weather is horrible. Tell you all about it when I get home. Patsy.

College diving coaches noticed Keith, an incoming high school junior, after his remarkable placing at the Olympic trials. He received a recruiting letter from Jerry Darda, the new University of Wisconsin diving coach in Madison, as early as October. He informed Keith that at the Big Ten Conference school, "We have an excellent combination of academic offerings and diving program."

Jerry Darda coached at Wisconsin from 1964 to 1994. His star pupil was the new Olympic champion Ken Sitzberger, who he coached from the time Ken was six through high school.

Keith took a few months off from diving after the Olympic trials. When he started back in December, he received a letter from the Florida Association of the AAU inviting him to compete in their state diving meet on January 3, 1965, in Brandon, Florida, a southern suburb of Tampa on Florida's west coast.

Keith worked hard to get back into shape for the Florida AAU Meet. In the meantime, he competed in the Sixth Annual Mid-Winter Meet after Christmas. As America's best high school diver, he won his age-group one-meter and placed second on three-meter to Bernie Wrightson.

Lurline commented in a journal entry on the competition between Keith and future Olympic bronze medalist Win Young: "In both competitions Win was diving right behind Keith and Keith sure did outdive him. And Win has been back on the board longer than Keith."

Brigham Young University coach Walt Cryer attended the Mid-Winter meet to recruit Keith. He talked to Lurline, then visited with Keith and his parents at their house. He said that Keith wasn't yet eligible for a scholarship, but when he was, it was there for him.

On their way to the Florida meet in January 1965, Bernie Wrightson and Keith stopped in New Orleans to pick up Olympic bronze medalist Larry Andreasen. The night Keith arrived in Florida, he went on a double date, arranged by a boy he stayed with (and yet he got jealous if Marsha even looked at another boy). They went to a drive-in. At first, the boys sat in the front and the girls sat in the back, but the other boy's date eventually starting feeling very neglected. She decided she'd feel better if she mixed some vodka in with her Seven-Up. This loosened her up a bit and she then decided she'd like to make out. The other boy wasted no time hopping in the back seat.

Keith's date moved up front and came up with a scheme of her own for attention. She was "sleepy" and she "just might go to sleep any place." Keith, not wishing to dishonor himself or cheat on his girlfriend, told her there was the door, she could sleep against it. So she did.

Olympic champion Ken Sitzberger won the Florida meet and Bernie took second. Olympic platform bronze medalist Tom Gompf took third. John Vogel finished fourth, Olympic springboard bronze medalist Larry Andreasen took fifth, and Keith was sixth—one point behind Andreasen. Keith also scored a tour of the University of South Florida in north Tampa with its diving coach.

Barely halfway through high school, Keith was making things happen.

Chapter 6: First International Competitions: The World's Best High School Diver

Keith played church basketball his junior year of high school. That spring, Lurline wrote about a particular game that demonstrated athletic talent and passion for physical exertion that extended beyond the pool:

> Keith has had a cold for some time, and it finally got him down. But they had a basketball game that night. He was going to play only if they needed him. And did they ever. He played one of his best games with a temp and a bad ankle. Keith made 15 points, 5 out of 11 field goals, and 5 of 7 free throws. And can he ever jump.

The Senior National Indoor Diving Championships took place at Yale in April. Lack of money again almost prevented Keith from going, but Dick went to the Mesa Chamber of Commerce and they provided $300. He only had to pay for food, which nearly broke his family. Fellow Jackrabbit and future Olympian Bill Mettler, a Yale swimmer, invited Keith to stay with him, which saved on expenses. Bill had recently broken national records in both the two-hundred-meter butterfly and freestyle. Princeton and Southern California also offered Bill swimming scholarships, but Yale placed third in NCAA rankings.[124]

From JFK, Keith took a limousine the seventy-five miles to Yale University. Reigning Olympic champion Ken Sitzberger won the one-meter with 519.65. Defending champion and Keith's future Olympic teammate Rick Gilbert followed .15 of a point behind in second with 519.50.[125] Future Olympic champion Bernie Wrightson took third and Keith finished eighth.

Keith was as high as fourth in the three-meter preliminaries, until he missed his reverse two-and-a-half somersault, which dropped him to ninth going into finals. Rick Gilbert grabbed the national title. Ken Sitzberger took second, Ohio State freshman Charles Knorr finished third, Bernie Wrightson was fourth, future Southern California diving coach Rick Earley was fifth, and Keith took sixth.

The highlight of the 1965 Indoor Nationals occurred in swimming when Yale student Steve Clark, who swam on all three 1964 Olympic champion relay teams, became the first to break forty-six seconds in the one-hundred-yard freestyle, when he swam it in 45.6 seconds. Swimming experts rated this equivalent to breaking the four-minute mile in track.[126]

Lurline briefly analyzed and summarized the key points of the national championships:

> He got 8th on 1 meter and 6th on 3 m. Had no excuses. The judging was fine. It was his diving. But we felt pretty good about the 6th place. He was the only high school student who made finals. The fact is we thought Keith didn't do so well on 1 m. but

Larry Andreasen got 16th and he had gone to the Olympics. Keith also beat him on 3 m.

The Russells saw Keith dive on national television. ABC's *Wide World of Sports* showed the top six divers on their final dive. Lurline thoroughly recounted the thrill of seeing her son's dive broadcast nationwide:

> He stood on the board for some time, then they showed his dive, then a good long shot afterwards. His muscles showed up really good, better than most. He gets so embarrassed when we talk about it. But it is true. His dive was his back 2½ and he got 7 and 7½ on it, which was good and we were thrilled with his performance.

Hobie Billingsley from Indiana University and Jerry Darda from Wisconsin visited with Keith about his college plans. Hobie said he'd very much like to have him at Indiana if he decided against Arizona State University. Lurline speculated that Keith's friend, future Olympian Rick Earley, even tried recruiting him when he gave Keith an Indiana University sweatshirt.

Keith received a recruiting letter from University of Michigan diving coach Dick Kimball that month, who, after pointing out that his diver, future Olympic champion Micki King, had just won the national platform title, said, "I would like to encourage you to continue your diving and education at the University of Michigan. We can give you a scholarship that will cover all your college expenses." Dick Kimball offered to fly Keith in so he could check out the campus and catch a football game.

The Russells received the final addition to their family of ten on May 15, 1965. His name was Darren Eric Russell. Keith now had four brothers and four sisters, but the larger family and tighter budget didn't faze Keith. Money issues didn't interfere with his goals. He never gave much thought to that aspect of diving. For some reason, the money was always there. He just focused on preparing himself for the next big meet.

The National AAU Junior Championship took place in May at the almost one-year-old Olympic Diving Complex in Mesa. The *Phoenix Gazette* raved about Keith's dazzling three-meter performance:

> Keith Russell completely dominated the National AAU junior championship. Russell went far into the lead after the third dive and steadily increased his victory spread through six optional dives to close with 518.15, more than 100 points ahead of runner-up John Andrews of Albuquerque (405.15).[127]

Future Olympian and North Carolina State coach Mike Finneran placed third with 392.15, and Jack Deschowueur of Bordeaux, France followed 48.60 points behind in fourth with 343.55.[128]

Keith's beautiful forward one-and-a-half with three twists garnered a 9 and two 8.5s, for 75.80. Two more near-perfect dives, a back two-and-a-half somersault and an inward two-and-a-half somersault, contributed to his incredible win.[129]

Keith got his picture and a write-up in the May 31, 1965 issue of *Sports Illustrated* for his junior national win.

Keith competed at the Seventh Annual Los Angeles Invitational in July and defeated defending champion Bernie Wrightson 508.15 to 502.65. Keith managed a thirty-point lead ahead of the future Olympic champion going into the final three dives, but he finished 5.5 points ahead of the runner-up.

Two other world-famous Phoenicians who trained with Keith at the Dick Smith Gym, Kendis Moore and Marilyn Ramenofsky, broke world records at the Los Angeles Invitational. Kendis broke the two-hundred-meter butterfly record and Marilyn broke the four-hundred-meter freestyle record.[130] That month, the *Arizona Republic* featured the athletic achievements of the Moore family, including Kendis' accidental transformation from one of the top female divers in the country into one of the top swimmers in the world. It was an amazing story:

> Next month, three of the Moores—Rory, 17; Kendis, 16; and Kerry, 15—will compete in the National AAU outdoor championships in Toledo, Ohio.
>
> All four seemed destined to be divers until a 1963 swimming and diving meet in Las Vegas. "Kendis was diving in the meet," began Mr. Ken Moore. "One of the girl swimmers became sick and Kendis was asked to swim in her place on the 13–14 medley relay team. They broke the national record with Kendis swimming the freestyle leg."
>
> Kendis since has become one of the nation's brightest prospects in the butterfly and backstroke. She is ranked No. 3 in the world for the 200-meter butterfly, [and] No. 2 in the United States for the 200-meter backstroke. She enjoyed her greatest moment when she defeated world record holder Sharon Stouder, of Calif., in the Saguaro Invitational. Kendis, at 13, was the youngest performer on the tower in the 1962 AAU National diving championships in Chicago.[131]

On August 8, 1965, Keith and Bernie arrived in Maumee, Ohio, a southern suburb of Toledo, for the National AAU Diving Championships. Keith decided it was time to win.

Defending champion Bernie Wrightson staged a phenomenal finish to take the three-meter title. Seventh after a poor performance in the preliminaries, he got mad and put that negative energy to positive use, working his way to first after the semifinals. He continued his winning streak to score his third consecutive national championship.

Keith placed second with 533.65, putting on the best display of his career, according to Dick Smith. Olympic champion Ken Sitzberger came 0.9 of a point behind in third. Future Olympic bronze medalist Win Young, an Indiana University freshman, took fourth with 525.50. Olympic bronze medalist Tom Gompf finished sixth with 514.15, Rick Gilbert was seventh and Olympic bronze medalist Larry Andreasen took eighth.[132]

At age seventeen, Keith had just beat the world's best springboard diver. His national silver medal put him on the map, showing the world he was ready for international competition. Less than one year after winning an Olympic gold medal, Ken Sitzberger lost to America's top high school diver, Keith Russell.

One newspaper discussed Bernie Wrightson's battle with Keith to defend his title:

> Wrightson amassed 550.56 points relying on high degree of difficulty dives in the finals to beat off a threat by Russell, who surprised the gallery by edging Olympic gold medalist Ken Sitzberger by a fraction of one point for second place.[133]

Bernie Wrightson won the national one-meter title by scoring 66.3 points on his last dive. Ken Sitzberger finished second after scoring 67.50 on his last dive. Rick Gilbert finished third. Tom Gompf finished fourth, while two of Keith's future Olympic teammates, Jim Henry and Win Young, took sixth and seventh. Keith finished tenth.[134]

Dick Smith said Bernie Wrightson was "as strong as any male diver in the country and possibly the best diver the United States ever had." He also noted that if Wrightson could add the ten-meter title to his triumphs in the three-meter and one-meter, he would become the first man to sweep all three national titles.[135]

Keith wrote his family about his feelings and frustrations at Nationals: "It's been an awful long week but it's been worth it. I was a little discouraged after diving low board. Tenth really isn't as good as it should be."[136] Keith didn't feel a national rating of tenth-best diver in the United States on one-meter reflected his talent or effort.

Bernie completed an unprecedented triple victory by winning the national ten-meter title.[137] Rick Gilbert followed 23.75 points behind in second while Japanese Olympian Toshio Ohtsubo finished third. Tom Gompf took fourth again and Larry Andreason followed in fifth. Keith finished sixth, again beating Olympic champion Ken Sitzberger, in fourteenth.[138]

Keith filled his family in on his decent platform performance: "Sixth off tower I cannot complain about. I was third after the prelims, seventh after the semis, and then finished sixth. You will probably see a dive or two on TV."

Keith wrote his family about the next day, about all the cool things he scored, and how his female friends had fared in the women's Nationals out of sixty-one divers.[139] His letter proved he was as enthusiastic about their successes as his own.

> We went to get our uniforms fitted [for international competitions in Europe]. We get shoes, socks, shirts, and a bag. That's pretty good besides getting our food and lodging. I cannot wait till we get going.
>
> Patsy [Willard] got 2nd off tower and so she is qualified to go to the Mexico trip. Theresa [Brookbank] got 12th off tower. That's pretty good for a 12 yr. old getting in the finals. I saw Kendis [Moore] win the 200 mtr. [butter]fly, breaking the world record. She's going on the trip.

> I'm rooming with [Lyle] Draves. He's the diving coach for the Western Europe trip. We'll compete in Cardiff, Whales [*sic*]. It is suppose to be an indoor heated pool. This is something completely new to me.

Between 1948 and 1956, Lyle's female divers completely dominated the sport, winning every Olympic gold medal awarded in that time.

Lurline discussed the Russell family's thrilled reaction to Keith's national placings in the journal she kept for him.

> He was second in the nation on 3 m. board and we were the happiest family in the entire world. The girls [Donetta and Kathy] and I were in Albuquerque at a swim meet, but I called the TV station and got the results from them. It was fabulous. He had films of the 3 m.
>
> But on the tower is where we got our biggest thrill and surprise—6th place. And just last May he didn't enter the tower because he didn't have a complete list [of dives]. Add the points from both boards and Keith rated 2nd in the nation. He got the trip he wanted—the Western European tour. Lesley Bush and Miki King were the girl divers and Tom Gompf the other man diver. It was on this trip in London that Keith beat Tom for the 1st time in tower diving!

Three of the four divers who won the upcoming international competitions dove for world-renowned diving coach Dick Smith: future Olympic champion Lesley Bush, Olympic bronze medalist Tom Gompf, and Keith. The other diver, future Olympic champion Micki King, dove for Dick Kimball at the University of Michigan. Keith's mother could not have been more proud of these divers had they been her own children. She clipped and saved every newspaper article on them.

Keith's next stop was the United States–Great Britain dual swimming meet.[140] The team took TWA to JFK, arriving that night. Two hours later, they took off for London, arriving the next morning. They stopped at Oxford for lunch and a tour of Oxford University on their way to Cardiff, Wales.

Cardiff is in south Wales, on the Irish Sea, directly west of London. The team arrived in Cardiff that afternoon and checked into the elegant Angel Hotel across the street from Cardiff Castle. The Beatles, Marlene Dietrich, and Oscar winner Gregory Peck are a few notables who had stayed at Cardiff's most famous hotel.

The next morning, the team attended a reception given by the Lord Mayor of Cardiff. Then they toured Cardiff Castle, Llandaff Cathedral, and St. Fagan's Museum, before they got to Keith's favorite part, lunch. Cardiff Castle is just east of the River Taff. By 1860, it's owner, John Bute, was reportedly the world's wealthiest man.[141] The medieval castle was everything Keith imagined, creaky, stony, intricate, topped with towers and surrounded by a mossy moat. Llandaff Cathedral is northwest of it. St. Fagan's Museum, further west, is Wales' most popular heritage attraction. The one-hundred-acre park is on the St. Fagan's Castle grounds, donated to the Welsh people by the Earl of Plymouth.[142]

The men dove platform and the women dove springboard in their first meet that night.

Keith wrote his family of the outcome and his fascinating experiences:

> Just got through diving here in Cardiff on high board (tower [in] our language). I got second to Dave Priestly [28th at the 1968 Olympics]. Tom [Gompf] was third and John Miles (British) was fourth. Tom and I both missed our gainer 2½, which caused our loss. David really dived well. It's an indoor pool—first indoor tower I've ever seen—but the temp. and water and equipment

were just great! Tomorrow we'll dive springboard. David will not dive because he only dives tower.

The people here are very pleasant. Their talk is really hard to understand.

The weather—except for this evening—has been great.

The money in Whales [*sic*] is the neatest thing. It's fun to figure out how much a shilling is or how much a half-crown is worth. Another thing is the traffic. They drive on the wrong side of the road and drive on the wrong side of the car. Very hard to get accustomed to. It's really great here!

Love, Keith

An Arizona newspaper article titled "Keith Russell Gets Springboard Title" (with an ad for a *new* GMC pickup priced at just $1,679) notified local residents of the outcome: "Keith Russell amassed 469.5 points in winning for the first time in international competition. Tom Gompf, an Air Force pilot who trains with Russell under Dick Smith, was a close second at 467.5." Keith's teammate, future Olympic champion Lesley Bush, won platform.

The Americans each received a formal dinner invitation card that night:

EUROPE V. U.S.A. INTERNATIONAL SWIMMERS
City of Cardiff
THE LORD MAYOR
on behalf of the Cardiff City Council
requests the pleasure of the company of
Mr. Keith Russell
at Dinner at the Castle
on SATURDAY, 21st AUGUST, 1965.
at 6.00 p.m. for 6.30. p.m.

Anyone who knows Keith knows he has a hearty appreciation for food. He's not picky, but he is selective about what he drinks and avoids anything alcoholic. So having to make a toast at a formal affair in a fancy castle posed a challenge. He wrote his family about how he managed to overcome the situation:

> They set the table with glasses [of] dry wine. At the close of the dinner, a guy with the makings of a perfect butler hit the table with his little hammer about three times. Everyone quit talking and listened. He prayed silence that we listen to the Lord Mayor of Cardiff.
>
> L&M stood up and told everyone to arise and make a toast to the Queen! All arose and said "To the Queen." I was game on standing up—but not drinking. We sat down but the L&M wanted to make a toast to the Pres. of the United States [Lyndon B. Johnson]. A girl on the opposite side of me slipped her ¾ empty cup to my side and took my full cup. Then they made the toast. Here's a picture of me in Whales [*sic*] national newspaper.
>
> P.S. I won the springboard.

Monday morning the American tour took off for London. There they checked into the Queensway Hotel next to Hyde Park in London's northwest borough of Paddington, bordered by Westminster to the east and Kensington and Notting Hill to the west. The crew toured London and the East End that afternoon. The tour included a drive along the Thames Embankment, a visit to the Tower of London—British government seat and the living quarters of monarchs—and St. Paul's Cathedral.

Tuesday brought more sightseeing and fun. This time, they visited the West End. They drove to Trafalgar Square, watched the changing of the guard at Buckingham Palace, and passed the 350-acre Hyde Park to the Kensington Museums.

The tour ended with a visit to Westminster Abbey, where the Royal Tombs are located. Since the coronations in 1066 of both King Harold and William the Conqueror, all but three British monarchs have been crowned in the abbey. They flew to Paris, where they spent that night.

Keith wrote his family about his day in London and his trip to France: "This morning I went shopping in London. Well, here I am in Paris, France! This is one place I've always wanted to go. Tonite I hope to go to the Eiffel Tower. The French money is really neat too."

Wednesday, the Americans toured historic Paris, starting with a drive along the Left Bank of the River Seine in the heart of Paris. They saw the Jardin du Luxembourg (Garden of Luxembourg), the largest public park in Paris, and Palais du Luxembourg (Luxembourg Palace). Built for King Louis XIII's mother, Marie de' Medici, they were completed in 1627.

The crew went to Notre Dame Cathedral and Montmarte in north Paris, where they visited the Sacred Heart Church and enjoyed the panoramic view of Paris spread below. They then left for Nice, where they were transported to Hotel Metropole in Monaco. France borders Monaco on all sides except its east coast, which is on the Mediterranean Sea. Monaco covers only two square miles.

Lurline sent Keith a letter, telling him of the buzz over him:

> Donetta, Kathy and Alan are expecting a present from you when you come home, so don't forget them. We [were] sure thrilled to hear about your win and 2nd place in Cardiff. Everyone in Mesa seems to have heard about it. Zelma Miller [neighbor] said she and Ed heard about it on the radio coming home from Utah.
>
> Lamar Pond, Shirley's husband [Lurline's oldest sister's oldest daughter], went out to tell Verda [Lurline's oldest sister] about you being on T.V. Sat. on *Wide World*. They gave only one dive—

off tower. But it was your reverse 2½ and you got 7 and 7½ and it was very good.

Cy wrote Keith a heartfelt letter of fatherly praise as well:

> Want to congratulate you on your diving. I often wondered if I would have a boy who would excel in [sports]. I certainly have my answer. I have a boy who far excelled me and I'm happy for you. This is far beyond my fondest dreams. This is a trip of a lifetime Keith. Before you forget the details you better write them down. Your family (dad) will want to know everything.
>
> Just used one of Donetta's pens up. (Should I tell her?) I pray every day that our Father will bless you every minute you are away.
>
> Love Dad.

On Thursday, the Americans worked out, shopped, and went sightseeing. That night, the U.S. women competed against the French women in Monaco Harbor. Keith wrote his family about his incredible experiences there:

> Wed. we arrived in Monaco. And ever since, we've had a riot. This place is neater than any other. Yesterday I went diving in the Mediterranean Sea! Not only did we go diving but we dived off a restaurant situated above the sea. It was really great.
>
> Last night we gave an exhibition. I didn't do too bad. We also did clown diving, that really set the house on fire. Princess Grace was there too. I'm having fun though!

Princess Grace of Monaco was born Grace Kelly in Philadelphia in 1929. She debuted on Broadway in 1949 and on the big screen in

1951. She became a star in Alfred Hitchcock's *Dial M for Murder*. She won her first Golden Globe in 1954 and an Oscar in 1955. She came from a sports-oriented family. Her father was a three-time Olympic champion rower, her mother became the first woman to head the Physical Education Department at the University of Pennsylvania, and her brother was a four-time Olympic rower. The princess died in 1982 in a car accident.

Olympic champion Micki King fondly recalled the magical trip to Europe, particularly the visit to the princess's castle:

> Jack Kelly, Olympic Bronze medal Rower, and brother of Actress Grace Kelly, arranged a European tour for US Swimmers and Divers who won a national title the summer of 1965. Keith and I had little in common. I was 21 years old and he was 16! This "difference" brought us together. I became Keith's "big sister" on the road. When he forgot his towel, I loaned him mine, when he lost his camera, I found it, when Tom Gompf teased him, I smacked Tom. I made sure Keith didn't miss team meetings or the bus. The only thing I never worried about was Keith missing breakfast, lunch or dinner. Keith knew his way around at mealtime. He told me once; dinner with his (big) family taught him to be quick!!
>
> We traveled to England, Wales, France, Spain, and Portugal doing exhibitions at each city and getting royal treatment at every stop. But, it was our visit to Monaco on the French Riviera, where the "ROYAL" treatment became real.
>
> Jack Kelly arranged for our team to visit the Royal Palace of Monaco as guests of Princess Grace and Prince Rainier. As we entered the gate, there SHE was to greet us. Princess Grace was everything we envisioned. This very special woman, famous actress, more beautiful in person than on the screen, and PRINCESS, welcomed us in person to HER palace. We were in awe as she personally escorted us to the Royal

Pool. Then, something happened that left a lasting impression on all of us. The famous Princess of Monaco lined us up around the pool—then, SHE pulled out a camera and took pictures of US!! Princess Grace made the US national swimmers and divers the celebrities that day.

We spent an unbelievable afternoon in her Royal Garden. The Royal pool was a bit shallow for a diving board, but the four divers improvised. We had a blast "playing" on that board. Keith and Tom were the daring ones who did back flips and front doubles (yikes) off the lower-than-one meter plank. Princess Grace kept her movie camera on us all the while. It wasn't long before Prince Albert, a little tyke back then, wanted to do flips, too. Wisely, Keith and Tom taught the Prince his first flip by tossing him safely into a back somersault while they stood waist deep in the shallow end. But, Princess Grace, who quickly turned into the Mom, almost flipped herself when she saw the Royal son airborne in tuck position!

On Sunday, the American entourage flew to Lisbon on Portugal's west coast. Keith wrote his family about his latest excursions and plans:

We arrived here (at hotel) about 4 PM and was surprised to have a letter. It took 4 days from Mesa to Lisbon. Yesterday we went sight-seeing. We went to this little shop that made perfume. I practically bought the store out. I hope I got some good buys for my money—I sure hate spending this hard earned money!

Tomorrow I think I will have time to do some shopping. I don't want to buy much here because I think it's cheaper in Spain. Then Tues, we get to go to the beach!

P.S. Mom, slow down a little on your letters.

On Tuesday, they went to the westernmost point in Europe. The ocean water was cold, so Keith contented himself in building sand castles. After a ride on the coast, they journeyed to their favorite destination—bed.

On September 1, the entourage left Portugal for Madrid in central Spain, which they toured a few hours before leaving for Bilbao in northern Spain.

The rest of the week, they competed in the Spanish National Championships. Keith won his second international competition when he took the springboard with 184.53.[143] Tom Gompf followed 15.23 points behind in second, with 169.30, then won the Spanish national platform title, followed by Keith in second.[144]

Tuesday, the Americans toured more of Madrid, where they saw España Square, the Royal Palace built in 1764, and the Prado Museum, Spain's main art gallery, then flew home.

Several top universities recruited Keith. University of Michigan coach Dick Kimball flew Keith to Detroit that month. After visiting the diving facilities and touring the campus, the legendary coach treated Keith to a Michigan-Georgia football game. Then Keith hung out with his European tour friend and future Olympic champion Micki King, who treated him to dinner and a movie with other Michigan divers.

Dartmouth College came calling in October. The smallest Ivy League school regularly ranks in the top ten "Best National Universities."[145] Coach Ronald L. Keenhold wrote Keith that he hoped he would have an open mind in regard to choosing a college. Coach Keenhold competed in the 1956 Olympic Trials and judged the 1964 Olympic Trials. In twenty-five years, Dartmouth had only one losing season in swimming. Varsity swim coach Karl B. Michael served as U.S. men's diving coach at the 1956 Melbourne Olympics.

A week later, Brigham Young University shot off a letter of introduction enticing Keith with their spectacular new facilities: "This is considered one of the finest swimming facilities in the United States.

We hope you folks will have an opportunity to visit our campus and look this new swimming facility over."

A few days after that, Michigan State University attempted to tempt Keith with the marvels of their facilities and personal compliments:

> I have watched you perform in national competition often. Keith, we at Michigan State University are most interested in you. Your abilities in diving have already been proven, and everyone I speak to about you says you are a fine gentleman. We have one friend in common who speaks very highly of you. I am speaking of Betty Barr. I have just written her recently, and she did nothing but praise you as a person and a diver.
>
> Michigan State, being a Big Ten University, can offer you one of the more outstanding academic schools in the country. Our diving program is just beginning, and with our fine facilities it should not take long to compete with the best in the country. Immediately adjacent to our indoor pool is our outdoor pool, with four springboards and a one, three, five, seven, and ten meter tower.
>
> Last year was the first year Michigan State recruited for diving, and this year is the first year Michigan State has a diving coach.
>
> Keith, I believe with the facilities Michigan State has and a lot of hard work, we can accomplish our goal. Our goal is to dominate the diving picture in the United States. I say this fully realizing that Michigan, Indiana, Ohio State, and Arizona are strong diving powers.

All four universities Coach Charles McCaffree mentioned were actively recruiting Keith. Keith's next letter arrived a few days later from Indiana University's legendary diving coach Hobie Billingsley, who expressed his wish to have Keith visit Indiana. Olympic champion Ken Sitzberger also wrote and encouraged Keith to come.

Usually, it's the regular person who sends mail to the stars, but in Keith's case, it was the star's brother who sent mail to the regular kid when Princess Grace's brother, John Kelly sent Keith pictures of them in Monaco.

Ohio State University diving coach Ron O'Brien jumped on the bandwagon before the year's end and informed Keith that he'd have no problem being admitted to the Big Ten school. Another legendary diving coach, he later said of Keith, "I have known Keith for over forty years and have always admired and marveled at how kind and peaceful he is and at the same time, intensely competitive. I've never heard Keith say a bad word about anyone!"

Keith received heavy publicity for his record-breaking achievements at the Seventh Annual Mid-Winter Aquatic Meet in Phoenix. One article explained it best:

> Keith Russell, 17, scored a grand slam in the Mid-Winter Aquatic Meet by winning four diving titles. During more than eight hours of competition, Russell won the men's open one-meter and boys' 15–17 three-meter titles yesterday.
>
> On Monday he won the men's open three-meter and boys' one-meter. It marked the first grand slam in the seven year history of the event.[146]

A photo showed a dive with the caption: "Here's the end of a perfect dive—Russell cleanly slices into water." The *Phoenix Gazette* featured a four-photo sequence of him doing a forward three-and-a-half somersault from three-meter. Journalist Jim Dobkins dubbed him "the official hit of the Mid-Winter Aquatic Meet."[147]

Keith's best dive was a forward three-and-a-half somersault.[148] Thus ended his childhood and began his adulthood as one of the world's greatest divers.

Chapter 7: America's Number Two Male Diver by Eighteen

Keith visited Indiana University in Bloomington in early 1966. Claiming two of the last three Olympic champions, Ken Sitzberger and Lesley Bush, it boasted the world's best diving program under legendary coach Hobie Billingsley. Keith stayed with his friend, fellow Phoenician and future Olympic champion Charles Hickcox.

Since Dick Smith had always allowed Keith's parents to pay what they could for his services, ten dollars a month, Keith wanted to remain loyal to him by attending Arizona State University, where Dick coached. But Keith also wanted to see what other opportunities were out there. Because Indiana was the place to go for diving, he wanted to cover his bases by feeling it out before he made his decision.

Keith flew to Tampa for the 1966 Senior National AAU Indoor Championships in April. The next morning, Dick Smith picked Keith up at the YMCA in the deadliest tornado in central Florida history. The F-4 tornado, with winds between 210 and 260 miles per hour, killed three in the Tampa Bay area alone.[149] The fastest tornado on record in

Florida, it traveled from Tampa 130 miles east across the state to Cape Canaveral, killing eleven more.[150]

Keith wrote his family about his intense experience among the devastation: "After stops at Tucson, El Paso, Houston, San Antonio, and New Orleans, the plane finally stopped in Tampa. By the way, a tornado destroyed people, buildings, etc. I worked out that windy, rainy Monday afternoon."

Dick Smith and Big Ten divers dominated the national meet. Results for three-meter:

1. Bernie Wrightson, Arizona State University senior
2. Ken Sitzberger, Indiana University junior
3. Rick Gilbert, Indiana University graduate
4. Chuck Knorr, Ohio State University freshman
5. Randy Larson, Ohio State University senior
6. Bruce Brown, Michigan
7. Win Young, Indiana University freshman
8. Keith Russell, Mesa High School senior

The one-meter results had the same top five, but with a couple switches.

1. Chuck Knorr, 1968 U.S. Olympic men's alternate
2. Ken Sitzberger, 1966 NCAA one-meter champion
3. Rick Gilbert, 1964 NCAA one-meter champion
4. Bernie Wrightson, 1966 NCAA three-meter champion
5. Randy Larson, 1964 NCAA three-meter champion
6. Win Young
7. Dick Morse
8. Bruce Brown
9. Keith Russell

The platform competition was Keith's best, while Rick Gilbert, who had a 1.60-point lead going into finals, apparently decided he really liked bronze medals and collected his third one. The finals results:

1. Chuck Knorr 456.80
2. Bernie Wrightson 427.35
3. Rick Gilbert 425.80
4. Bruce Brown 404.85
5. Gordon Creed 394.80
6. Jose Robinson 390.70
7. Keith Russell 385.75
8. Dick Rydze 341.80
9. Peter Rhodes 325.55
10. Mike Finneran 318.65

Keith finished 43.95 points ahead of future Olympic silver medalist Dick Rydze and 67.10 points ahead of Dick's future Olympic teammate Mike Finneran.[151]

Seven Arizona athletes, five of whom were friends and teammates of Keith, were named to the 1965 AAU All-America swimming team: Bernie Wrightson, Olympic bronze medalist Tom Gompf, and Olympic bronze medalist Patsy Willard for diving, and Kendis Moore and Marilyn Ramenofsky for swimming.[152] Keith and Tracey Gilmore were the other two Arizona AAU All-Americans.

Bernie Wrightson, Patsy Willard, and Ken Sitzberger received an honorable invitation to accompany President Lyndon B. Johnson and Mrs. Lady Bird Johnson to Mexico, where they put on an exhibition at the American embassy at the birthday party of the president of Mexico.[153] Since Bernie had a previous but less distinguished commitment to do exhibitions in Oklahoma, he asked Keith to fill in for him. Keith accepted and accompanied Rick Gilbert to Bartlesville.

While Keith dove in Oklahoma, he missed watching his female friends dive in the AAU Women's Nationals in Mesa. Two friends, Olympic champion Lesley Bush from New Jersey and future Olympic champion Micki King from Michigan, stayed at his house. Dick Kimball, who brought Micki King, stopped by Keith's house on recruiting business. Knowing Keith belonged to the Mormon Church and planned to serve a customary two-year church mission in the middle of his college career, he promised Keith's parents he could go on his mission and keep his scholarship, if that's what it took to get him to sign with Michigan.

Keith also missed an honored visit from Lyle Draves while in Oklahoma. Lyle's diver, future Olympic champion Sue Gossick, won the national three-meter title. Lurline wrote in Keith's journal about the rich experience of the privileged visit:

> Lyle was the European tour diving coach [last summer] and had taken reels of moving flicks. He called us up and said he would come here to the house and run them for us. It was absolutely fabulous. And much of Keith and his diving which was very good. He spent over two hours with us visiting and showing the pictures.

After deciding against Michigan, Dartmouth, and Indiana University, Keith flew to Columbus to check out Ohio State University, which has also turned out many Olympic divers. Most noteworthy are Olympic champions Bruce Harlan and Bob Clotworthy, silver medalists Donald Harper and Samuel Hall, and bronze medalists Juan Botella and his friend, Tom Gompf. The Big Ten school boasted the longest tradition in collegiate diving.

On June 1, 1966, Keith graduated from Mesa High School in a class of 370. He went to the Los Angeles Invitational with his family that summer, where he stood out, winning the platform title by thirty-one points, with 576.25. His buddy, Win Young, took second.

Keith took tens on his two best dives, his forward three-and-a-half somersault and his reverse two-and-a-half somersault. His triple twister received three near-perfect nines for a seventy-three-point total. He messed up a little on his worst dive, an inward two-and-a-half tuck. Otherwise, that dive was one of his most consistent ones. All his other dives were "good [receiving scores between 6.5 and 8] or excellent [8.5 to 10]" Lurline wrote in his journal. She also recorded what top coaches and athletes said about Keith's phenomenal diving:

> Jack Roth [coach of Olympic bronze medalist Larry Andreasen and 1964 Olympic diver and Pan-American Games champion Linda Cooper] said that was the best tower diving he had ever seen. Several others said the same thing, including Dr. Gossick [father and coach of future Olympic champion Sue Gossick].
>
> [Olympic champion] Donna [de Varona] and Barbara [Talmage] were there. They couldn't get over how well Keith did on platform. Because when they were here, Keith was still very timid about his high diving. Barbara thought he had the best kick off on his reverse dives and back dives she had ever seen. We were real happy to see them and they were impressed with Keith's diving.

Two-time Olympian Donna de Varona became the first female sportscaster when she signed on with ABC in 1965.

Keith competed at the U.S. Junior National Outdoor Championships in Litchfield Park, Arizona, thirty-five miles west of the Russells, in July. The *Arizona Republic* reported on the stunning competition:

> No. 2 ranked senior Keith Russell provided excitement as he came out on top in a close battle in the men's open 3-meter with Arizona State University's Bernie Wrightson, No. 1 ranked senior in the country.
>
> Russell carried a small margin into the finals but drew enthusiastic applause and high scores on his final three dives. He left spectators awed with his final dive, a forward 1½ somersault with three twists. It was of the highest degree (2.9) of difficulty in junior diving.

Keith spun through the air and sliced the water in perfect form. All five judges awarded eights for the title. Keith finished sixteen points ahead of Bernie in second, with 532.[154]

Theresa Brookbank, thirteen, won both the women's open three-meter and ten-meter. The Dick Smith diver, ranked sixth nationally in senior diving, provided excitement in the women's diving when she won her national ten-meter title by over ninety points.

Although Keith continued a powerful performance on ten-meter, Bernie Wrightson won. Keith's worst dive, his inward two-and-a-half, wasn't that bad at all, taking two 5.5s and a 6, for 40.8. He received straight 8.5s on his stunning forward one-and-a-half with three twists, for 73.95. His exquisite reverse two-and-a-half received two 8.5s, a 9, and a dropped 10, for 70.2, and his near-perfect forward three-and-a-half took straight nines (and another dropped ten) for another 70.2.

Keith took second with 484.65 points, 76.4 points ahead of Olympic bronze medalist Larry Andreasen, in third, with 408.25.[155] The impressive panel of judges included four-time Olympic champion Pat McCormick; her coach, Lyle Draves; Olympic champion Gary Tobian; and future Arizona State coach Ward O'Connell.

Keith gave an exhibition in August at the West Texas Invitational in Midland. Afterward, J. H. Hartley, president of the Midland "Y" Swim Team, wrote Keith's coach this complimentary letter on his diving:

> Keith did a first class job and executed his dives in championship form, both from the 1-M and 3-M boards. His appearance was the highlight of our meet and afforded people in this area their first opportunity to witness the performance of a champion diver. We feel Keith's performance greatly enhanced and furthered the interest in springboard diving for this area as numerous coaches and competitive divers made a special effort to be here for his exhibition.

The big event of the year for Keith was the Sixteenth Annual National AAU Outdoor Championships in August in Lincoln, Nebraska. The Thunderbirds gave Keith $121 for the meet. Lurline wrote about Keith's highs and lows at the nation's most prestigious diving meet:

> Keith did his all-time best in 1 meter. Came in third! We were thrilled about that. Then disaster hit! He was in first place on the [three-meter] springboard and he tipped his toes on the back 2½ [tuck], got threes on the dive and ended up 4th.

Another account of the national meet added a few more details:

> Bad luck prevented what early in the [three-meter] looked like a 1-2 finish for Keith Russell of Mesa and defender Bernie Wrightson of Phoenix.
>
> Midway in the event, Russell picked up a 2½ back somersault beautifully, but ticked toes on the board on the way down. The impact flipped him over and he scored only 3's on the dive—yet finished strongly to take fourth.[156]

Bernie Wrightson defended his national one-meter title by coming up from behind to beat and defeat Ken Sitzberger, who finished second.

As national Olympic diving chairman, Keith's coach Dick Smith commented, "This has been the strongest American showing in history."[157] One article agreed, "At the midway point, the meet showed promise of becoming the best ever held in America."

The three-meter was a fierce competition between the next generation of Olympians. Bernie Wrightson failed to defend his national title and finished third behind his future Olympic teammate

Rick Gilbert and Olympic champion Ken Sitzberger. Keith followed in fourth, and Win Young finished fifth. Of the top five, three competed for Indiana University (Rick Gilbert, Ken Sitzberger, and Win Young), and three had been coached by Dick Smith (Keith Russell, Bernie Wrightson, and Win Young).

Keith also came in a painful but delightful fourth place on platform. The pain came from hitting it with his left foot and breaking his metatarsal on his inward two-and-a-half somersault.[159] The delight came from it being his highest placing on platform at nationals.

Lurline discussed her thoughts on the platform competition in Keith's journal: "There were no results in the morning paper, so we didn't know if he had gone ahead and dived or not [after breaking his foot]. He had gone from 1st to 6th place on his failed dive. So he must have had a good lead to stay that high."

When Olympic champion Ken Sitzberger married Olympic silver medalist Jeanne Collier that month in Phoenix, the Russells received an invitation. They were like diving royalty. Ken died tragically eighteen years later in Southern California from a traumatic head injury at a 1984 New Year's Eve party, according to the *New York Times*.[160]

That fall, Keith started college at Arizona State University, where Dick Smith coached. The best college freshman diver in the country had polished his techniques to the extent that he had his pick of colleges with the best diving programs, as they all wanted him to dive for them. These skills stemmed from passion and experimenting with ideas and methods, like visualizing. Because diving gave him so much satisfaction, he always wanted to test ways to improve it, so he could get the most enjoyment and success out of it. He found that imagining himself diving, which he did when he went to bed, improved his sport. He would feel it in his body and see it in his mind, every move, every hurdle, every flip, every twist, every entry, from head to toe.

Another technique he mastered was positive thinking. To do his best, he had to eliminate worry and doubt. His mind-set at meets was "I'm going to do my best. I know what to do. I will do what I know how to do." He credited ninety percent of his good dives to this effective effort. Competitions were about attitude. Consequently, he considered his thoughts a powerful force. Without the weight of worry, Keith was free to soar to great heights, literally and figuratively. His mother played a big part in this sports psychology. She was a smart woman and wanted her son to be happy more than anything. Diving made him happy, but losing could have made him sad if only winning mattered. So she counseled him simply to do his best and not worry about issues beyond his control, like subjective judging.

Goal setting was another progressional technique. In high school, his goal was to get a diving scholarship. He did. Now his goal was to make the Olympics. This was important, because having those games on his resume would be advantageous for any coaching position. Setting his sights on a bigger picture, a monumental purpose, was essential, because practice could be brutal and make anyone without drive and direction opt out. Every day, Dick bombarded Keith with orders and commands:

"You're not doing it right!" "You should've done that!" "Why didn't you do it this way?" "You need to do it that way!" "Swing your arms up like this!" "Jump your hips like that!" "Your hurdle is too high!" "Your hurdle is not high enough!" "Your approach needs to be like this!" "Your entry needs to be like that!" "Clean up your entry!" "Go more vertical!"

But Keith was determined to do whatever it took to reach his goals, to put up with whatever he had to, to turn his dreams into reality, including scorching hot Arizona summers. The excitement for Keith lay in seeing how far he could go with this. Where could this take him? It had already taken him to Paris, London, New York, and a princess's castle, which doubled as a famous actress's exotic home.

Because he didn't allow his coach's criticism get the best of him, he got the best of it by learning from his mistakes and developing the inner strength to sustain the positive energy he needed to achieve his best. And when things didn't go the way he planned, if it was beyond his control, he took it like a man and moved on. And this system served him well. He found a great deal of happiness and fulfillment in diving.

Keith went to Mexico City in October to compete in the "Little Olympics," an experimental test on the high altitude's effect on athletes.[161] He placed second on springboard, less than half a point behind Bernie Wrightson.[162] Charles Hickcox, "the brightest star in America's swimming future," won six gold medals in a preview of the world's greatest international meet.[163] Lurline relayed what she heard about Keith's spectacular performance:

> He dived beautifully. Bernie told us! And got 4th on the tower. But Bernie said there was no way for him to get any higher. It was pre-determined that the Russian [Mikhail Safonov][164] would get first. Bernie said Keith never dived better, but they wouldn't give him higher than 7½ on a dive.
>
> The Mexican diver was bound to get a medal and he got 3rd, so Keith came up with a 4th. Bernie said the Mexican diver couldn't have made our semifinals. He said Keith did a tremendous job. And we know he did, because Keith was satisfied with his performance, and when he is, then he indeed has done well.

Keith competed in the Mid-Winter meet as usual and won the three-meter by a whopping 53.40 points, with 523.55. Win Young finished second with 470.15.[165]

Keith won the one-meter by a significant 28.75 points, with 492.50, to Win's 463.75. His worst dive, a reverse one-and-a-half pike somersault, took two 6s and a 6.5. His best dive, his inward one-and-a-half pike somersault, took two 8s and an 8.5.

Lurline wrote of her surprise at Keith's superior performance despite lack of preparation and her hopes for upcoming major international meets in her last 1966 journal entry:

> [Keith] entered the mid winter meet at the last minute. I didn't want him to. I didn't think he would do well because he hadn't really worked out for it. But he did fine. Won both boards and got good points.[166]
>
> Dick [Smith] called last night and said he wanted Keith to start working hard. The indoor nationals might be put ahead one week and from the indoors are three trips—the Pan Ams, a Russian trip, and a Japanese trip. So I'm hoping he will make one—the Japanese one. Only he wants the Russia one. I was thinking of Vernon and Norma [Keith's uncle and aunt in Japan] getting to see him. Oh well, if he wants to go to Russia, I hope he makes it.

The *Arizona Republic* reported on Keith's inspiring showing at the Mid-Winter Aquatic Festival:

> Both Russell and [Ann] Peterson displayed superior prowess in their optional diving to easily outscore all opposition, mostly provided by Californians.
>
> Russell annexed the men's 3-meter title with some fancy twisting in his closing four dives to defeat Win Young. Russell scored a sensational 523.55 on his 11-dive routine, while Young finished runner-up with 370.15.

The Mesa lad overtook his Hoosier rival on the third dive and steadily increased his lead through the optionals. Russell's highest single-dive score came on a superbly-executed reverse 2½ somersault that attracted the judges to award him 64.40 points. Russell iced the title with a difficult 1½ somersault with a triple twist that netted 60.90 for the 2.9-degree of difficulty dive.[167]

Chapter 8: World University Games and National Champion

Keith finally reaped the fruits of his labors at the AAU 1967 National Indoor Championships at the University of Texas in March.

The college freshman became the national champion on three-meter.[168] The competition was tight among the future 1968 U.S. Men's Olympic Team. Going into finals, Bernie Wrightson was in first with 317.65, followed by Ken Sitzberger in second with 301.10. Future Olympic bronze medalists Jim Henry followed 2.3 points behind in third with 298.80 and Win Young was 1.7 points behind that in fourth with 297.10. Keith trailed by only 0.2 of a point with 296.90, and Rick Gilbert followed 5.5 points behind in sixth, with 291.40.

Keith nailed his final dive, a forward one-and-a-half somersault with three twists, which took between an 8.5 and a 10 for 81.20 points. The extraordinary triple twister not only obliterated Bernie Wrightson's sixteen-point lead, it gave Keith the coveted national title.[169] One reporter observed, "He came on strong in the finals with exceptional execution powering him to victory."[170]

Keith called his family that night with the exciting news. Lurline wrote about their comical reaction to Cy's dead-on intuition:

> Earlier that day when Cy and I and the two little boys [Rory, 4, and Ric, 2] were out looking for campers, Cy said he was expecting a phone call from Keith. I asked why—Keith never calls. But Cy said he expected him to win this one and he would call. That night every time the phone rang, which was quite often, we both ran to answer it. It never got to ring twice. And sure enough, around 10 p.m. there he was. What a thrill.

The win qualified Keith for the Pan-American Games in Winnipeg, Canada. The Pan-Am Games have been called "the Olympics of the Western Hemisphere," which suggests their significance.[171] They are held every four years the year before the Olympics.

The Pan-Ams first took place in 1951 in Buenos Aires, Argentina. The prestigious games have since been held in Mexico City, Chicago, Brazil, Colombia, Puerto Rico, Venezuela, Cuba, and the Dominican Republic.

Indiana University divers swept the one-meter competition with Luis Nino de Rivera winning, freshman Jim Henry taking second, Indiana senior Ken Sitzberger taking third, and Indiana alumni Rick Gilbert finishing fourth. Ohio State University junior Chuck Knorr finished fifth and Keith took sixth.

Keith's friends and future Olympic teammates dominated the women's national three-meter competition. Future Olympic champion Sue Gossick, nineteen, won the title. Another future Olympic champion, Micki King, the leading figure in U.S. women's diving from 1965 to 1972, took second. Olympic champion and Keith's teammate, Lesley Bush, placed third. Future Olympic bronze medalist Keala O'Sullivan took fifth, and Olympic bronze medalist and Dick Smith teammate Patsy Willard finished seventh.[172]

Keith became a two-time national champion when he won the platform by 17.65 points, with 548.90. Going into his final four dives, Keith was 21.55 points behind Bernie Wrightson.[173] But his last dive won him the title.[174] Bernie finished second with 531.25 and Win Young took third with 512.30. It was a Dick Smith Swim Gym reunion on the podium. Their future Olympic teammate Rick Gilbert finished fourth with 499.15.

Lurline wrote about the family's rave reactions to the magnificent results:

> Then Keith won again on the tower. That was almost too much to expect. We were ecstatic. Bernie came in 2nd on both [three-meter and platform]. Two of their dives were televised for *Wide World of Sports*. That was neat to see him on that program. Lots of people saw him. Betty [Cy's sister] and family saw him in Springville [Utah]. Melvin Ray saw him in Falls Church, Virginia. Now he will get his way paid to the trials for the [Pan-Am Games] platform diving. Will be in [Santa Clara] Calif.

Keith's friends also dominated the women's platform. Lesley Bush finished second behind Patty Simms of California and ahead of Air Force Lieutenant Micki King of Michigan, in third. Dick Smith teammates Patsy Willard took fourth, Theresa Brookbank placed sixth, and future Olympic bronze medalist Ann Peterson finished seventh.

At the Pan-Am platform trials, a strained neck and back affected Keith's performance. Win Young qualified in first and Chuck Knorr qualified in second for the Pan-American Games. Rick Gilbert placed third, Bernie Wrightson was fourth, and Keith finished fifth.

The fifth Pan-American Games opened ceremoniously on July 23, 1967 in Winnipeg, Manitoba, bordered by Ontario to the east and Saskatchewan to the west.[175] This capital and largest city of Manitoba hosted 2,400 athletes from twenty-eight nations in twenty sports in games patterned after the Olympics. Queen Elizabeth's husband, Prince Philip, opened the games.

Four Arizonans, including Keith and two of his friends, took top honors. Bernie won three-meter with 837.75, but Keith nearly overtook him in the final three dives. Instead, Keith finished second, with 818.05. His friend and teammate, Kendis Moore, swam on the winning four-hundred-meter medley relay team, in a world record time of 4:30. Ed Caruthers, a University of Arizona student, was the fourth Arizonan to take top honors when he broke a Pan-Am record with a high jump of 7' 2.25" for gold.[176]

Lurline wrote about Keith's feelings, travels, and exceptional diving:

> Aug. 7, 1967 – He just got home from the Pan Ams and is leaving for Chicago in an hour to the outdoor Nationals.
>
> He had a wonderful time in Canada at the Pan Americans. He got 2nd place a few points behind Bernie. They both dived very well and Keith felt he had done a good job. Bernie agreed. He told us Keith wasn't looking good in the workouts prior to the meet, but really dived well.
>
> Keith got over $200.00 worth of luggage and clothes—two neat outfits and all kinds of suits, sweat outfits, robe etc. He is having fantastic experiences with all these trips.

The National AAU Outdoor Championships took place in Oak Park, Illinois, nine miles from Lake Michigan, near downtown Chicago. The top twelve finishers were:

1. Jim Henry 489.85 (Indiana)
2. Chuck Knorr 488.25 (Cincinnati)
3. Bernie Wrightson 484.40 (Dick Smith)
4. Ken Sitzberger 462.65 (Indiana)

5. Keith Russell 458.65 (Dick Smith)
6. Bill Main 454.90 (Santa Clara)
7. John Hahnfeldt 442.90 (Indiana)
8. Win Young 442.50 (Indiana)
9. Don McAlister 428.40 (unattached from California)
10. Julian Kru g425.55 (Santa Clara)
11. Rick Gilbert 416.25 (Indiana)
12. Bruce McManaman 406.20 (Brandon)[177]

Keith won his third National title when he took the three-meter with four strong final dives and 557.10 points. Bernie led going into finals but finished 17.45 points behind in second with 539.65. The other finalists demonstrated that Indiana and California dominated diving:

3. Jim Henry 528.10 (Indiana)
4. Rick Gilbert 484.20 (Indiana)
5. Win Young 470.50 (Indiana)
6. Ken Sitzberger 470.10 (Indiana)
7. Bill Main 464.10 (Santa Clara)
8. Don Dunfield 455.60 (Santa Clara)
9. Luis Nino De Rivera 447.80 (Mexico)
10. Julian Krug 429.15 (Santa Clara)
11. Jose Robinson 407.20 (Mexico)
12. Don McAlister 389.35 (California)[178]

Keith got a pleasant surprise when he won his fourth national title on the platform after compiling 576.95 points.[179] His Dick Smith teammates joined him at the stand. Nearly half the finalists later became major players in college coaching.

2. Win Young 567.60 (Arizona coach)
3. Bernie Wrightson 534.50 (Navy coach)
4. Chuck Knorr 531.50
5. Dick Rydze 486.05
6. Luis Nino De Rivera 478.85
7. Jim Henry 478.45

8. Julian Krug 459.70 (Pittsburgh coach)
9. Mike Brown 442.70 (Hawaii coach)
10. Robert Wilhite 441.10
11. Mike Finneran 429.40 (North Carolina State coach)
12. Jim Henderson 394.10[180]

A mistake in filling out his diving form almost cost Keith his national title.[181] Keith failed to declare an optional dive in the preliminaries. This made his overall scores lower because the optional dives always have a higher degree of difficulty. He was fifteenth after the preliminaries, with sixteenth being the cutoff to advance to the semifinals.

For the semifinals, Keith listed two optional dives instead of the required one. After the semifinals, the AAU Diving Committee conducted a heated discussion over Keith's status for failure to follow prescribed dives in the first two rounds, but they voted nine to three to let him continue to finals.[182]

Lurline wrote about the dazzling diving Keith and his buddies did at nationals and the consequential prestigious international competitions awarded him:

> [Keith] called Friday to ask me to send his passport. He didn't call to tell us how he had come in—5th. But this was on 1 meter, and it couldn't matter less.
>
> On Sat. Patsy [Willard] called. Her boyfriend, Norris, had been back there and saw the diving. He said you just couldn't believe how well Keith dived. Win put in a good triple twister—pulling down 7½s. Then Keith did the same dive and got straight 9s, and the same thing on his [forward] 3½ [somersault]. He was in 2nd going into the [three-meter] finals. Bernie ended up in that spot.
>
> Sunday I called the paper and they said Keith Russell was the winner. We were so thankful. Win was 2nd on tower and Bernie 3rd, but [Bernie] was still 2nd overall, so he and Keith will make

the Tokyo trip together. They leave Aug. 21st and the [World University] Games are between Aug. 25th and Sept. 5th. We are hoping they get to spend time with Vernon and Norma [Cy's sister]. Norma has said they will take him any place he wants to go.

Keith, Bernie, and the other World University Games swimmers stayed in San Francisco a couple days before flying to Japan via Anchorage, Alaska. Although Tokyo is 2,400 miles from Vietnam, where Keith's brother Gary was fighting on the front lines, Keith wanted to go there and give an exhibition for the troops and see Gary.

He wrote his parents from San Francisco of the discouraging outcome:

> I found out from Mr. Ruskis that it would be an impossibility to send us to Viet Nam for an exhibition. Since we are under the Cultural Affairs program of the State Dept., which has nothing to do with the entertainment program of our troops, it would be impossible to be sent in the capacity I am in.

But Keith's mother, a comical little spitfire of a woman, was determined to get her sons together as long as they were on the same continent. It didn't matter that they were at either end of the largest one. Keith's uncle Vernon Tipton later wrote about how it all came together:

> Gary and Keith Russell spent a few days with us. Gary [a marine private first class] was in Vietnam. Their mother, a very resourceful woman, called the Commandant of the Marine Corps and informed him that she wanted her marine son to be in Tokyo when her diving son participated in the World Games. After several telephone calls, she wrote to the President [of the United

> States]. Gary didn't know what was going on when a helicopter came to the front line to ferry him to an airfield for a flight to Japan.

President Lyndon B. Johnson referred Lurline to the commandant of the navy, who authorized a weeklong R&R for Gary.

Keith saw his Uncle Vernon and Aunt Norma and their family his first Sunday in Tokyo. After church and lunch with them, he hurried back for the opening ceremonies. Vernon, who received his PhD in parasitology at Berkeley, was a lieutenant colonel in the Medical Service Corps. He did medical research on epidemic hemorrhagic fever, which had been a major threat to the health of troops in Korea.

Keith wrote his family about the first day of competition and how he and his friends did. It took place at the National Olympic Pool, the scene of the 1964 Olympics:[183]

> I was happy to win [three-meter] but I felt bad about Bernie getting fourth and missing four of his final five dives. Luis Nino was second and a Swede was third. A Finish [*sic*] diver was fifth and Julio was sixth (Italian).
>
> Both Aunt Norma and Uncle Vernon came to the finals (Norma also came to the prelims) and after the finals I sat with them and watched a little swimming (saw Charlie [Hickcox] break his 200 [meter] world record).
>
> Lesley Bush won, a Japanese girl was second and Micki [King] was third. I think Inga Pertmyr, from Austria, was fourth. The first three girls were close all the way and it was a good meet. I think Micki would've won but she came out a little short on her reverse 2½; she bent her knees some—they really nail ya for that!

Keith didn't know Gary was at the platform competition and

Gary didn't want him to. The loudest applause of the day came when a Japanese diver, Yosuke Arimitsu, put a stop to U.S. domination of the games by winning the platform and Japan's first gold medal of the meet. He compiled 798.15 points to best Keith's 756.20.[184] Bernie Wrightson took fourth.

Lurline wrote in Keith's journal about that day and of her satisfaction in bringing her two sons together from opposite sides of Asia:

> A red-letter day in the life of Keith and one of the happiest in his life. Gary came from Vietnam to Tokyo to see him. I wish I could have seen those two brothers greet each other.
>
> This morning started out as any other ordinary day—no one very happy or at least especially happy. Then the phone rang. Keith was at the other end. My immediate reaction was some terrible thing had happened. Keith wouldn't call from Japan to tell me how he fared no matter how good or bad it had been. He said he was fine, but Vernon and Norma insisted he call and Vernon wanted to talk to us.
>
> The next voice on the phone was Gary's. He got a 6-day leave and watched Keith in his tower diving. Keith didn't know he was there until it was over. Keith felt bad when he didn't see Gary in San Diego.
>
> That night Rory [almost five] wanted to say the prayer and he thanked Heavenly Father that Gary got to go to Tokyo "and got out of that icky place." It was so cute. So Gary and Keith got to spend a few days together in the home of Vernon and Norma.
>
> Keith's win on the springboard was a big one—about 80 points ahead of the next diver and 100 points more than Bernie's. Bernie lost his twisting dives. Just found out Bernie has joined the navy but will get to continue his diving.

Gary and Norma went to the pressroom after the games where Keith was giving interviews. All of a sudden the reporters noticed Keith's face light up, his eyes get big, and excitement fill the air as he blurted out "Gary!" in shock. "Who is this guy?" the reporters wondered as they began interviewing him too.

Vernon recalled later, "Keith was mobbed by reporters and autograph seekers. When Gary made his appearance, the two brothers embraced and the press wanted to know what was going on. They sensed a great human-interest story. They were a very popular pair." Everyone wanted the springboard champion's picture. Japanese girls crowded around him like he was a star. He hadn't fallen from the sky, but three meters was high enough. When he arrived home, the fan mail started pouring in. Like any well-grounded young man, Keith took it all in stride.

Keith went to his second "Little Olympics" in Mexico City in much better shape than the first time. The games, nicknamed the Third International Sports Week, or Pre-Olympics, opened October 14, 1967. Fifty-seven countries participated, including both East and West Germany, North and South Korea, and Nationalist and Communist China, in eighteen Olympic events. Except for the opening and closing ceremonies, it acted as a full dress rehearsal for the 1968 Olympic Games.[185]

One newspaper article discussed Keith's key qualifications:

> Russell, who won four U.S. titles this year along with the World Student Games in Japan, will be the only U.S. [male] diver in the meet.
>
> Wrightson was rated No. 1 diver in the world the past two seasons. Russell looms as his successor off 3 and 10-meter titles in both indoor and outdoor U.S. championships, victor in the Student Games and a second in the Pan American Games.[186]

After winning four national titles and medaling in some of the world's most distinguished competitions, Keith was acknowledged as the world's best diver after beating the previous world's best diver five consecutive times in both national and international competition.

Future five-time Italian Olympian and two-time Olympic silver medalist Giorgio Franco Cagnotto won the Little Olympics three-meter competition and Keith took silver. Dick Smith noted, "Keith had a little trouble on one dive and that was enough to drop him into second, but he did some magnificent diving."

One newspaper article beautifully illustrated the men's platform competition:

> European champion Klaus Dibiasi of Italy, diving with meticulous consistency, won the gold medal in men's platform.
>
> Dibiasi took a narrow lead over Alvaro Gaxiola, 109.23 points to 108.24, during the seven compulsory dives in the morning while his real contenders—Keith Russell and Japan's [Yosuke Arimitsu]—were wallowing in seventh and eighth place.
>
> With only three free dives to worry about in the afternoon session, Dibiasi coolly lived up to a statement he made after the morning's action. "I'm mad about my standing in the points [being only .99 of a point ahead of second place] and I'm going to do something about it," said the student of engineering.
>
> What he did to rectify the situation was execute three fine dives, none as superb as Russell's final performance, but good enough to end the competition with 168.46.
>
> Russell scored only 17.28 on that opening effort and it turned out to be the difference between gold or silver. Russell scored 21.06 on his next to last dive [forward three-and-a-half somersault], which was at that time the best of the day. But he climaxed the afternoon with a [forward] one-and-a-half with three turns—good

> for 24.65—on his last try and brought down the house. With one stroke, he vaulted from fifth to second, barely edging out Japan's Yasuke, 164.70 to 163.71.[187]

Dick Smith and Hobie Billingsley expressed their frustration at the judging afterward. Dick commented that the diving was superb, but the scores failed to reflect it. He added, "I've been around diving as long as anybody and if this is any indication of judging in world competition, everyone should take steps to clean up judging."

Hobie faulted the composition of the judging panel with five Mexican judges, a Russian, and an East German. Dick pointed out that the East German and Russian judges actively coached the divers they judged. The Pre-Olympics served as a grim preview of the judging at the Olympics the following year.

Executing complicated maneuvers and subjecting the quality of those complex moves to the judgment of human beings with a personal agenda demands the ability to deal with adversity. Judges, when plagued with favoritism, do their job poorly by overrating bad dives and underrating good dives. This has also been the case in gymnastics, in which many of the same skills are left to biased people to determine how well they are performed. As late as the 1988 Seoul Olympics, *Sports Illustrated* noted, "International gymnastics was exposed as a flawed, even corrupt, sport, in which performances take a back seat to politics." The same could be said of diving. One author cited a harsh judging example at the 1988 Olympics in gymnastics:

> The East German judges were notorious for favoring their own athletes over others, especially Americans [sound familiar? They didn't just cause problems in diving]. During the 1988 Olympics, Kelly Garrison-Steves of the United States jumped off the springboard to begin her uneven bars routine.
>
> When Garrison-Steves finished her routine, the East German

judge slapped a .5 penalty on the U.S., citing a little-known rule that prohibited coaches from being on the podium during a performance. The United States protested, but it was no use.

As it turned out, the United States finished fourth—by .3. And who won the bronze medal? The East German team.[188]

Lurline focused on the good of those games in her last journal entry of 1967:

> Keith is home from Mexico City and the Little Olympics. He brought me a nice bag and himself a guitar. And he is learning to play it. Keith had a good trip. Dived well, especially on platform. Got 2 second places, but felt he should have won that one, and would have but for one dive.
>
> Both winners were Italians and had been working out at the hole [Olympic Diving Complex in Mesa]. He brought home a few [news]papers which had news about the meet and pictures. It was interesting what the paper had to say about Keith. Something about his intentness, but he broke out in a wide grin upon his last dive when he was awarded the highest points of the entire meet.

Keith received some fabulous Christmas gifts that year: a tie, a watchband, and a doorknob. That's right, a knob for his door so he could more conveniently open and close it. Only in the Russell family could one receive gifts so high-end and extravagant.

Chapter 9: World's Best Diver at His Second Olympic Trials

In January 1968, Keith was named to the AAU All-American Swimming Team on both the three-meter and ten-meter. Jim Henry received the honor on the one-meter. Keith's friend Charles Hickcox was named for the one-hundred-meter and two-hundred-meter backstroke. Several of Keith's female friends made the AAU All-American Women's Swimming Team: Micki King for the one-meter, Lesley Bush for the platform, and Kendis Moore for both the one-hundred-meter and two-hundred-meter backstroke. *Swimming World Magazine* named Keith "Most Outstanding Springboard Diver in the World" and Italy's Klaus Dibiasi "Most Outstanding Platform Diver in the World" that year as well.[189] One newspaper journalist, discussing the award, stated that Keith had also once been among the finest swimming prospects in the country and as a ten-year-old, set national age-group records in the freestyle, butterfly, and backstroke.

Russell is the premier diver in the world, with a four-for-four performance in 1967 national championship events and an even more prestigious gold medal in the World Student Games. At 20, he is the youngest diver ever to be honored as the world's best by an international poll of coaches.[190]

Lurline wrote in Keith's journal about her vision of him becoming the best diver on the planet and the possibility that he would be considered Arizona's top athlete:

> I told Keith I knew when he was 13 years old that someday he would be the top diver in the world. I know fame is fleeting—here today gone tomorrow—but nice for a little while. He has been nominated as outstanding amateur athlete of the year for Arizona. My bets are on Charles Hickcox who has had much more publicity than Keith.

Keith also received impressive publicity in Arizona State University's newspaper:

> Nine thousand hours of practice is a springboard to becoming a national and world diving champion. That's how much time 19-year-old Keith Russell has logged on diving boards, in the air, and underwater.
>
> In return he reaped four national titles last year and was recently named the world's outstanding springboard diver by the International Diving Federation. His immediate ambitions are to win the WAC [Western Athletic Conference] diving crown [which he did], the NCAA diving title [which he did], and a gold medal at the Mexico City Olympics this fall.
>
> "Keith is a self-disciplined athlete," said [Dick] Smith. "As good as

any in the United States. His goals are high, his attitude is perfect, his habits are beyond reproach, and he is a willing worker."

His long-range plans include acquiring a degree in physical education. He also hopes to participate in the 1972 Olympics and then become a diving coach [which he did].[191]

Keith was unbeatable in college diving. He won both boards against California State University–Long Beach. His family drove up with him to meets against the University of Utah and Brigham Young University. He won everything. At the Western Athletic Conference Championships at the University of New Mexico in Albuquerque, Keith competed against divers from the Universities of Arizona, New Mexico, Utah, and Wyoming, and BYU.[192] ASU won its first conference championship, and Keith became conference champion.

Keith went on to the NCAAs at Dartmouth in New Hampshire, where he achieved his goal of becoming an NCAA champion.[193] Two years earlier, Bernie Wrightson had become Arizona State University's first NCAA champion.[194] Win Young followed in second on the three-meter.

Keith's future Olympic teammate, Jim Henry, won his first of three NCAA one-meter titles. Keith won bronze and Win placed fourth, helping Indiana win its first NCAA Championship in the sport previously dominated by the University of Michigan, Ohio State, and the University of Southern California. Arizona State placed sixteenth behind

2. Yale
3. Southern California
4. Stanford
5. Southern Methodist
6. Michigan
7. Texas-Arlington

8. UCLA
9. Colorado State
10. Wisconsin
11. Dartmouth and Long Beach State (tie)
12. Michigan State
13. Princeton

The 1968 National AAU Indoor One-Meter Diving Championships took place in North Carolina at East Carolina State University. It wasn't one of Keith's better meets. The results:

1. Jim Henry 484.05 (Indiana)
2. Chuck Knorr 471.51 (Cincinnati)
3. Rick Gilbert 470.55 (Indiana)
4. Win Young 470.07 (Indiana)
5. Bryan Robbins 434.79 (unattached from Texas)
6. Luis Nino de Rivera 424.59 (Indiana)
7. Don Dunfield 420.36 (unattached from Wisconsin)
8. John Hahnfeldt 416.64 (Indiana)
9. Larry Andreasen 415.17 (unattached from California)
10. Bill Main 414.63 (Santa Clara)
11. Keith Russell 413.45 (Dick Smith)
12. Jay Meaden 411.99 (unattached from Michigan)

Future Olympians Mike Finneran took sixteenth, Tord Anderson of Sweden was seventeenth, Dick Rydze was twenty-fifth, and Jose Robinson of Mexico was twenty-seventh.

The National AAU Indoor Three-Meter and Ten-Meter Championships took place in Pittsburgh a week later.[195] Although not his best, they were better. The ten-meter results:

1. Larry Andreasen (1964 Olympic bronze medalist)
2. Win Young (1968 Olympic bronze medalist)
3. Keith Russell (predicted 1968 Olympic champion)
4. Jim Henry (1968 Olympic bronze medalist)
5. Chuck Knorr (1968 Olympic alternate)
6. Rick Gilbert (1968 Olympian and future Cornell coach)

7. Jose Robinson (1968 Mexican Olympian)
8. Tord Anderson (1968 Swedish Olympian)
9. Mike Brown (Dartmouth College diver)
10. Dick Rydze (1972 Olympic silver medalist)
11. Vic Laughlin (Future University of Northern Iowa coach)
12. Luis Nino de Rivera (1968 Mexican Olympian)

The top four on ten-meter remained the top four on three-meter:

1. Win Young, 456.15, Indiana
2. Rick Gilbert, 453.90, Indiana
3. Chuck Knorr, 446.67, Ohio State
4. Keith Russell, 441.84, Arizona State
5. Jay Meaden, 415.89, Michigan
6. Luis Nino de Rivera, 403.26, Indiana
7. Jose Robinson, 394.74, Mexico
8. Bryan Robbins, 394.44, Texas
9. Tord Anderson, 392.64, Sweden
10. Julian Krug, 384.96, Santa Clara
11. Nick Carlton, 381.30, Indiana
12. Jim Henderson, 360.90, Michigan State
13. Mike Finneran, 252.66, Santa Clara
14. Jim Henry, 251.97, Indiana
15. John Huffstutler, 248.25, Princeton
16. Don Dunfield, 244.38, Wisconsin
17. Bruce McManaman, 243.93, Michigan
18. Larry Andreasen, 242.04, California
19. Mike Brown, 239.76, Dartmouth
20. Todd Smith, 238.62, Minnesota

Lurline wrote in Keith's journal that spring about his engagement to his girlfriend of four years and how she felt about it:

> ABOUT A WEEK AGO A VERY IMPORTANT HAPPENING OCCURRED. Keith gave Marsha her diamond and they became officially engaged. They had gone out with Judy and Dave to a baseball game. When they arrived home they went directly to

the temple and got engaged. I was asleep when they came back; he came in, woke me up and told me the good news. I'm really happy about it because Marsha is a lovely girl, so talented, and sweet. It is a beautiful diamond—solitaire in yellow gold.

Coach George Haines of the famed Santa Clara Swim Club in California paid Keith's way to the Santa Clara Invitational that summer. George Haines served as the U.S. Olympic swimming coach in every Olympics between 1960 and 1980.[196] Between 1960 and 1984, he developed forty-three national champions and fifty-three Olympians who won forty-four Olympic gold medals, fourteen Olympic silver medals, and ten Olympic bronze.[197] His club swimmers include four-time Olympic champion Don Schollander and nine-time Olympic champion Mark Spitz. He also coached at UCLA and Stanford.

The diving was really a contest between Colorado native Bernie Wrightson, Texas native Jim Henry, and Arizona native Keith Russell. Bernie won the three-meter with Keith in second and Jim Henry in third. Jim then showed great form in his optional dives on platform and came from behind to win, for a flip-flop of the top-three placings. Bernie was third while Keith stayed second.[198]

The 1968 National AAU Outdoor Diving Championships were in Lincoln, Nebraska. Keith took the top odd spots except first. The platform was his best event and Bernie's worst. The results surrounded Keith with Indiana divers and future Olympians:

1. Win Young, Indiana, 1968 Olympian
2. Jim Henry, Indiana, 1968 Olympian
3. Keith Russell, Arizona State, 1968 Olympian
4. Chuck Knorr, Ohio State, 1968 Olympic alternate
5. Rick Gilbert, Indiana, 1968 Olympian
6. John Hahnfeldt, Indiana
7. Rick Earley, Army, 1972 Olympian
8. Mike Brown, Dartmouth
9. Jose Robinson, Mexico, 1968 Olympian

10. Dick Rydze, Michigan, 1972 Olympian
11. Jim Henderson, Michigan State
12. Luis Nino de Rivera, Indiana, 1968 Olympian
13. Alvaro Gaxiola, Mexico, 1968 Olympian
14. Luis Cervantes, Mexico
15. Mike Finneran, Ohio State, 1972 Olympian
16. Bernie Wrightson, Arizona State, 1968 Olympian
17. David Bush, Wisconsin, 1972 Olympian

Hobie Billingsley's Indiana divers, George Haines' Santa Clara, California divers, and Dick Smith's Arizona divers dominated the three-meter finals:

1. Bernie Wrightson, Dick Smith
2. Rick Gilbert, Indiana
3. Jim Henry, Indiana
4. Win Young, Indiana
5. Keith Russell, Dick Smith
6. Bryan Robbins, Brandon
7. Don Dunfield, Santa Clara
8. David Bush, unattached from New Jersey
9. Julian Krug, Santa Clara
10. Luis Nino de Rivera, Indiana
11. Mike Finneran, Santa Clara

With a third on ten-meter and a fifth on three-meter, Keith took seventh on one-meter. The lower the meter, the lower his finish. The results kept his future Olympic teammates in the top four:

1. Jim Henry
2. Bernie Wrightson
3. Win Young
4. Rick Gilbert
5. Julian Krug
6. John Hahnfeldt
7. Keith Russell
8. Don Dunfield
9. Chuck Knorr

10. Doug Todd
11. Luis Nino de Rivera
12. Bruce McManaman

Keith drove to the Olympic Trials in Long Beach, California that month. The Russell family took their camper to California and parked it right at the pool. This was the day they had waited so long for. It was a family affair to watch the world's best diver, their son and brother, make the 1968 U.S. Men's Olympic Team. They took their seats. Lurline got situated with pen and paper in hand, ready to record each score of the six best divers: her son of course, Bernie Wrightson, Win Young, Jim Henry, Rick Gilbert, and Larry Andreasen.

The sixth round of dives belonged to the Dick Smith divers. With Keith and Bernie each taking straight eights on their inward two-and-a-half, it was their best yet, and it shot Keith to the top. The seventh round just got better. Keith's forward three-and-a-half garnered a sparkling 8.5 and two 8s to reinforce his top spot going into finals with 318.39. Jim Henry followed in second with 315.25. Win Young went into finals with 306.56 for third while Bernie Wrightson had 302.46 for fourth. When the final scores of the preliminary round came in and the Russells saw Keith's name at number one, it just defies description what they felt – excited, elated, ecstatic, just don't fit the bill. They were screaming and yelling and laughing and hugging each other tight. But he still had three dives to go before it was a sure thing.

This was it. The last dive determined the 1968 U.S. Men's Olympic Springboard Team. The Russells sat on the edge of their seats in intense anticipation as they awaited Keith's final dive. Jim Henry's straight nines on his forward three-and-a-half somersault shot him to the top. One thing about the Russells—they are loud. So when Keith's signature forward one-and-a-half somersault with three twists took an 8.5 and two 8s for the second spot on the Olympic Team, all heaven broke loose. Family, friends, and fans the world over could feel and hear the celebratory, earth-shattering screams.

Bernie Wrightson took the third spot after his reverse one-and-a-half somersault with two-and-a-half twists gave him 506.10. Rick Gilbert finished fourth after receiving an 8.5 and two 7.5s on his reverse two-and-a-half somersault, for 477. Chuck Knorr finished in fifth with 474.72. Win Young's back one-and-a-half with two-and-a-half twists for 453.42 put him in sixth. Larry Andreasen stayed in seventh.[199]

Jim Henry finished with 511.23 points, 0.54 of a point ahead of Keith, with 510.69. Bernie Wrightson followed 4.59 points behind for the final men's Olympic springboard spot. Rick Gilbert missed a spot on the Olympic springboard team by 29.10 points.

As a new member of the 1968 U.S. Men's Olympic Diving Team, Keith knew his strongest competition at the Olympics would be his own teammates and the Italians, specifically Klaus Dibiasi and Georgio Cagnotto. At a press conference, Keith told reporters, "I'm going to work hard on mental attitude between now and the Olympics. It's going to take a lot to withstand the pressure."[200] Keith's body could just as easily execute an exceptional dive in Mexico at the Olympics as it could in the United States at practice. But his mind would know the difference. Without the scrutiny of the judges or the emotion of the audience, training was relaxed compared to the world's most watched and extreme competition. Could he perform as well as he did when he was free of the stress of such a contest? Whether he felt tense or loose, it was all in his head.

Bernie admitted to reporters that he was nervous, not because of the competition but because he had just received news that he was a new father.[201] Dick Smith put in his two cents when he told reporters,

> We are putting the strongest team together the U.S. has ever had. They have the hardest job in Mexico that any U.S. team has ever had because of the improvement of the Germans, Poles, Soviets, Italians, Mexicans and even Asians. Diving on the world level is definitely improving. The foreign nations had further to go and

have gone faster because of the enthusiasm and support of their country. Diving is a big sport in these countries and the divers are heralded as national heroes. Due to this fact alone, they may be better prepared mentally for competition than we are. We have the divers and we have the ability. We will work on mental preparation and consistency.[202]

The Russells celebrated Keith's colossal accomplishment with a trip to Knotts Berry Farm and the beach, where they witnessed a hippie revival and got in a little surfing time.

As exhilarating as the Olympic springboard trials were, the platform trials proved even more so for Keith and his family. As before, Lurline sat alert with pen and paper in hand, meticulously recording each score that each judge gave each of the top six divers. She wanted to record everything for posterity and the world.

The anticipation begins as the diver ascends the tower. It builds as he stands in position and prepares for takeoff. It peaks when he is airborne, at every twist and turn. And finally, he straightens out and goes vertical, hoping for a clean entry, with minimal splash and pointed toes. If the diver goes in clean, the result is ardent cheering from his rooting section and high scores. But if he balks, or messes up, the result is regret and poor points.

Keith entered the platform finals in second place after receiving straight eights or better on four of his seven preliminary dives. His second dive of finals, a reverse two-and-a-half, proved his best yet, receiving straight nines (and a dropped ten). With 20.81 points separating him from third place going into the final dive, the electric energy that permeated the air was palpable. One dive left. Hearts were pounding, blood was rushing, hands were gripped, waiting for that final decisive dive.

Nothing could compare with what Keith came up with on his tenth dive. In the highlight of the trials, Keith took the top spot on his forward one-and-a-half somersault with three twists, which garnered two 9s and an 8.5 (plus a dropped 10), for the highest score of 77.43 to win with 516.15. Win Young took a 9 and two 8.5s on his three-and-a-half somersault for second place, 511.41, and a trip to the Olympic Games. Rick Gilbert's forward three-and-a-half somersault gave him 486.90 and the final spot on the Olympic team. Jim Henry received two 8s and a 7.5 on his forward one-and-a-half with three twists, for 486.04 and fourth. Bernie Wrightson received an 8.5 and two 8s on his forward three-and-a-half somersault, for 485.07 and fifth. Mike Brown took two eights and a 7.5 for 467.46 and sixth. Future Olympic silver medalist Dick Rydze finished seventh with 464.58 and Chuck Knorr was eighth.

Keith had made *both* the Olympic springboard and platform teams! He had fulfilled his coach's decade-old prediction. It was a rush like no other—the Olympics was now a reality. California may have experienced a minor earthquake that day as the Russell family jumped and cheered in untempered emotion.

Swimming World magazine summed up the Olympic trials this way:

> In one of the most incredible finishes ever seen, Russell went on to win the Olympic platform Trials. The 20-year old Arizonan hit his last dive, forward 1½ somersault, with three twists for 77.43. To give an idea of the greatness of the dive, the judges scored a 10, two 9.5s; two 9s, and two 8.5s.

The *Arizona Republic* was just as laudatory about Keith:

> Keith Russell, a muscular 20-year-old, brought a packed house to its feet with a spectacular final dive to capture first place on the U.S. platform diving team headed for the Olympic Games. His

> victory in the platform competition was impressive. He scored the two highest scores with his final two dives.[203]

The *Los Angeles Times* quoted the world's most decorated Olympic diver:

> The judges awarded Russell 77.43 for his closing effort, the highest scored in four days of trials for the United States team. "This was the greatest diving I've ever seen," said Dr. Sammy Lee, twice an Olympic gold medal winner.[204]

Meanwhile, Lurline offered a behind-the-scenes glance at Keith's stellar diving:

> Keith told us that on the platform—his reverse 2½ [ninth dive]—he had no idea where he was, so he decided to come out, and it was exactly right. He got a 10 by Dr. Sammy Lee and 9s from the other judges. Then on his last dive—the triple twister, he got another 10 by Tom Gompf, and that won the meet for him. He didn't miss a single dive. I never was so tied up in knots in my life. Donetta said she never prayed so much in her entire 15 years. It was a thrill that you can get in no other way.

Following the trials, *Sports Illustrated* made some predictions. They named Keith Russell to be the Olympic springboard champion, Jim Henry to win silver, and Giorgio Cagnotto of Italy to win bronze, predicting that the "U.S. and Italy dominate." They named Klaus Dibiasi of Italy to be the Olympic platform champion, Keith to be the Olympic silver medalist, and Win Young to win bronze.[205]

Keith's best friend's sister, Bette Sue Driggs, competed in the 1968 Olympic Trials also. She was also Keith's sister's best friend. Bette Sue finished third in the first heat of the four hundred-meter freestyle and didn't make the team. Forty years later she gained fame when she starred in *The Biggest Loser* with her daughter and first female winner, Ali Vincent.

Duncan Scott, who lived on the Russells' block and was once voted "Best Swimmer" by *Swimming World* magazine, placed sixth in the heats for both the two-hundred-meter individual medley and one-hundred-meter backstroke.[206] The three-time national record breaker didn't make the Olympics either.

Swimming World magazine reviewed each member of the 1968 Olympic Diving Team and made predictions:

> The United States Olympic Trials definitely selected, by far, our greatest Olympic Diving Team. Everyone of the divers has been a United States National Champion.
>
> The Men's Tower Diving: Keith Russell will have double duty at the Olympics because he was selected as our number one platform diver. However, with Keith's disposition and competitiveness, he could very well win two gold medals in Mexico City.
>
> Chuck Knorr was selected as alternate on the basis of points scored overall. These people are the greatest group, very determined and dedicated. I feel they will be fine representatives of the United States in Mexico City.[207]

After a couple days at his fiancée's cabin near Prescott, Arizona, Keith took off for high-altitude training in Colorado Springs.[208] One of the main concerns with having the Olympic Games in Mexico City was its altitude. At 7,349 feet, it might hinder the performance of athletes not used to the high elevation, since the air contains thirty percent less oxygen. (Colorado Springs, at 6,035 feet, has the highest elevation in the United States.[209])

The Olympic Games are the athletic equivalent of attaining a doctoral degree in that it is the farthest an athlete can go. There is no greater or higher achievement in the field of sports. Focus is critical, yet that October, two things at home could have distracted Keith from that necessary concentration.

First, Keith received a call from his church to serve a two-year mission in Chile. Second, the draft board sent him a notice to come in on October 25 for his physical. The draft board had apparently not followed the Olympic Diving Trials and therefore did not know that Keith had another appearance to make as a representative of his country. Well, Lurline took care of that. Nothing was going to get in the way of her son's final preparations for Olympic gold.

Cy Russell family circa 1964
Standing: Alan, Raylene, Keith, Gary, Judy, Donetta
Sitting: Lurline, Cy holding Rory, Kathy

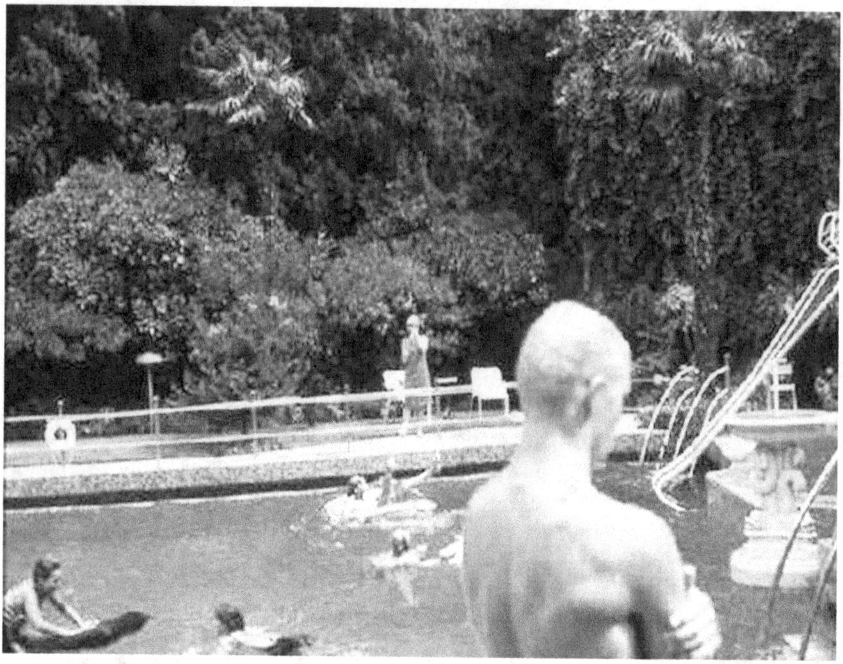

Keith in foreground with Grace Kelly in background taking home movies at the Royal Pool in Monaco in 1965. Photo courtesy of Tom Gompf.

Keith Russell, Jim Henry, guide, and Bernie Wrightson at the Air Force Academy in Colorado. Next stop: the Olympics. Photo courtesy of Rick Gilbert.

1968 U.S. Olympic diving team arriving in Mexico: Keith Russell, Win Young, Chuck Knorr, Rick Gilbert, Micki King (holding flag), Bernie Wrightson, Barbara Talmage, Keala O'Sullivan, Jim Henry, Ann Peterson, Sue Gossick, and Lesley Bush (holding camera). Photo courtesy of Rick Gilbert.

1968 U.S. Olympic diving team. Back row: Jim Henry, Chuck Knorr, Win Young, Keith Russell, Rick Gilbert, Bernie Wrightson. Front row: Ann Peterson, Micki King, Sue Gossick, Barbara Talmage, Lesley Bush, Keala O'Sullivan, Ohio State coach Ron O'Brien, Indiana University coach Hobie Billingsley, Arizona State coach Dick Smith. Photo courtesy of Rick Gilbert.

Mike Brown, Keith Russell, unknown African diver in Africa in 1971. Photo courtesy of Rick Gilbert.

Keith at the 1972 Olympic trials in Chicago. Photo courtesy of Rick Gilbert.

Keith Russell family in 2005.
Back row: Rex Russell, Ben Keller, Leah Russell, Rand Russell holding Owen, Aaron Russell, Keith, Kerri Deshler, Todd Deshler
Front row: Mindy Russell holding Braxton, Ashlyn Keller, Mindy Keller holding Claire, Michelle Russell, Regan Russell, Marsha Russell

Chapter 10: The 1968 Mexico City Olympics and Scandals

Not wanting to miss possibly the most memorable moments of their son's life, Cy and Lurline drove 1,240 miles to Mexico City with their best friends, Gene and LaVieve Swenson. When they arrived, they went to the Olympic Village to find Keith. They found it tough getting around with the tight security. Lurline wrote about their first day in Mexico City, what she thought about seeing him, and how she felt being with him:

> When we found him, he looked so thin. He got almost all the tickets we would need. We were so happy for them. He took us on a mini tour of the village which was fabulous. He got another piece of luggage and all kinds of neat clothes. It was such a wonderful thing to be with Keith. We were so proud of him.

Lurline also expressed her feelings of being the mother of an Olympian and watching him live at the Olympics:

> It is a very special thing to see your own son dive in the Olympics. We were so proud of him and our country. My heart never beat at hearing the Star Spangled Banner like it did in Mexico City. Keith had lots of people there rooting for him. Marsha, her father and mother, plus grandmother, uncle and aunt were all there.

Keith watched his friend Micki King make springboard finals, leading by 0.85 of a point with 98.17 after nailing her inward one-and-a-half pike somersault. The USSR was second, with 97.50. Sue Gossick followed 0.18 of a point behind in third with 97.32, and Keala O'Sullivan of Hawaii was fourth with 95.58.

But Sue Gossick became the new springboard Olympic champion with 150.77 points. Micki King hit the board with her forearm on her ninth dive and dropped to second place. The hit fractured her left arm, causing her to blow her last dive. She finished fourth with 137.38 points, 1.56 ahead of three-time Olympic champion Ingrid Kramer, in fifth. Tamara Pogozheva won the silver medal for the highest Soviet springboard finish in Olympic history. Keala O'Sullivan won the bronze, just 0.07 of a point behind silver.

In the men's springboard, Keith finished the first dive in first place with 12.32 points to nobody's surprise. Klaus Dibiasi of Italy, competing in his second of four Olympics, tied Keith. Jim Henry followed 0.16 of a point behind with 12.16, for the second highest score awarded. Franco Cagnotto, also of Italy, and Bernie Wrightson both followed 0.16 of a point behind, with 12.00, for the third highest awarded.

Keith received 12.41 on his second dive and dropped to fourth, just 0.01 of a point behind Jim Henry, in third. Klaus Dibiasi took the highest points again, with 13.60, to stay in first. Bernie Wrightson received the second highest points, with 13.09, and moved up to second. Mikhail Safonov of the USSR, in his second Olympics, tied with Jim Henry for the third highest points, 12.58, and moved up to sixth.

Keith's worst dive was his third. He over-rotated and dropped to fifteenth, with 34.61. Bernie Wrightson took the highest score with 15.96, to stay second with 41.05. Klaus Dibiasi received the second highest score, with 15.39, and stayed in first with 41.31. Franco Cagnotto received the third highest score, 15.01, for fifth. Jim Henry got the fourth highest score, 14.82, and stayed in third.

Bernie Wrightson took the highest score on the fourth dive, 13.12, and moved up to first. Luis Nino de Rivera, a recent Indiana University graduate representing Mexico, took the second highest score, 12.48, just 0.16 of a point more than Keith, and moved up to fifth. Keith got the third highest score, 12.32, and moved up to twelfth place, just 0.04 of a point behind eleventh. Jim Henry did his worst dive and fell to fourth. Klaus Dibiasi also did his worst dive and fell to second.

Bernie Wrightson took the highest score on the fifth dive, 15.96, to stay in first with 70.13. Klaus Dibiasi received the second highest score of 15.20 to stay in second with 66.91. Keith took the third highest score, 14.44, and moved up another three spots to ninth, with 61.37, just 0.03 of a point behind eighth. Luis Nino de Rivera tied with Keith and received 14.44 points to stay in fifth with 63.76. Jim Henry remained fourth with 64.15.

Jim Henry received the highest score on the sixth dive, 20.80, and moved up to third. Bernie Wrightson stayed first with 17.16 on his inward two-and-a-half somersault, for 87.29. Klaus Dibiasi stayed second with 18.27 for 85.18. Keith received the third highest score of 18.72 on his inward two-and-a-half somersault and moved up to seventh with 80.09.

Keith nailed his forward three-and-a-half for the highest awarded on the seventh dive, 20.52. He rose three spots to fourth. Jim Henry tied that on his back one-and-a-half somersault with two-and-a-half twists and moved up to first, with 105.47. Klaus Dibiasi took the third highest points, 19.50, and stayed in second with 104.68. Bernie Wrightson did his worst dive, a forward three-and-a-half, and fell to third with 102.95.

Bernie Wrightson's eighth dive, a reverse two-and-a-half somersault with two twists, received 22.96 for 125.93 and the gold spot. Klaus Dibiasi stayed second with 17.82, for 122.50. Jim Henry fell to third with 15.12 on his back two-and-a-half somersault for 120.59. Keith fell three spots to seventh after his back two-and-a-half somersault.

Jim Henry got the best score on the ninth dive, 21.84, on his reverse two-and-a-half, and moved up to second with 142.43. Bernie Wrightson received the second highest score, 21.28, on his back two-and-a-half somersault. Klaus Dibiasi fell to third with 139.86. Of twelve finalists, only one scored worse than Keith. His reverse two-and-a-half somersault dropped him to eighth with 130.29.

While Keith didn't know exactly where he stood going into the last dive of the Olympic springboard competition, he knew he wasn't at the top, or even close. The question now was "How high can I go?" Even with the weight of disappointment that he wasn't in the medals gripping him, he forced himself to believe that something good could happen to him. Even if it was just moving up a couple spots to the top half of the finals.

Bernie Wrightson's reverse one-and-a-half somersault with two-and-a-half twists received the highest score of the final dive, 22.96, for the title of new Olympic champion.[210] Klaus Dibiasi received 19.88 on his final effort, giving him 159.74 for the silver medal. Although only one person scored worse than Jim Henry, he won the bronze with 158.09 points.

Luis Nino de Rivera took 20.16 on his last dive and finished in fourth place with 155.71. Keith took the third highest score, 21.46, on his forward one-and-a-half somersault with three twists, but it only bumped him up two spots, and he finished in sixth place with 151.75.

The new Olympic champion spoke afterwards about his new diving style, how it won him the gold, and how luck mixed with preparation to produce the results:

> I've been doing the same dives for the last six years but now I communicate more with the audience. It's something I learned from the Russians. You smile and the audience gets with you and you get with the audience, and most important of all, it relaxes the judges because the judges are very apprehensive. If you seem relaxed, they relax. Diving is an unstable sport. Jim beat me in the Olympic Trials and I won here. We could do this again tomorrow and the results would be different. My best dive depends on the day.[211]

Keith was crushed. He couldn't believe it. He hadn't imagined this. Sixth place? Lurline wrote about that awful day for Keith:

> During the 3 meter he dived well—but not his greatest—and he got 6th. What a terrific disappointment for him. He was heartsick. We got permission to take him home with us that night—against the rules, but Dick arranged it. Marsha rode home with us in the car. We tried to joke around and had some ice cream and it really did make him feel better. We were glad we could be with him during this dark hour to ease in a small way his disappointment. We were proud of him.

One American journalist later expressed his thoughts from watching Keith dive in the Olympic springboard competition. He described the disappointment he shared with others that Keith didn't place higher, as well as the massive support for Keith:

> The first time I saw Keith Russell was from a distance. He was participating in the 3-meter dive. He came in sixth—there were those of us who thought he did better than that. The winner was Bernie Wrightson, with whom Russell had trained in the Dick Smith Swim Gym in Phoenix.
>
> Both men seemed to get more applause from one section of the hall than from all the rest. There was good reason. Half of Phoenix and Mesa was there, maybe not half—but a good cut of the crowd. I learned later from some of Keith's relatives (the Dr. Vernon Tiptons of BYU) that Keith's girlfriend, parents, and other relatives and friends had come to Mexico to see him win the gold medal.[212]

That day, Keith's friend Charles Hickcox won the two-hundred-meter individual medley. Two days later, he won the four-hundred-meter individual medley and Sharon Wichman became the first American woman to win the two-hundred-meter breaststroke.[213]

That day, Milena Duchkova, the first Czechoslovakian to compete in Olympic diving, won the women's platform with 109.59. Natalia Lobanova of the USSR led going into finals but took the silver medal with 105.14. She told reporters afterwards, "I didn't dive well. I thought I would place higher. I didn't know who of the three of us [Duchkova, Ann Peterson, or herself] would win the final. The other two are both good." Keith's Dick Smith teammate Ann Peterson won the bronze medal with 101.11. The other two American divers were also Keith's teammates. Barbara Talmage, in her second Olympics, was seventh going into finals but finished tenth. Olympic champion Lesley Bush missed her opening dive and finished twentieth.

The drama started all over again the following day in the men's platform, on October 24. Keith could live with his sixth on springboard if he could get gold on platform. In fact, the loss whetted his appetite all the more for the highest potential he could reach within himself. He just had to accentuate every positive emotion he could stimulate to improve his tower performance.

With a Russian judge favoring him, Russian diver Mikhail Safonov took the highest score of the first dive, 13.32, for first. His teammate Viktor Pogozhev took the third highest of 12.42. Keith took the fourth highest, 12.30, less than a quarter of a point behind Canadian Bob Eaton, in second with 12.54. Klaus Dibiasi took 12.16 for fifth and Win Young took 11.85 for seventh. Even with a Mexican judge favoring them, Alvaro Gaxiola received 11.70 for eighth; Luis Nino de Rivera received 11.38 for ninth; and Jose Robinson received 10.35 for twenty-fifth place. Rick Gilbert finished last of thirty-one divers.

Luis Nino de Rivera took the highest score on the second dive, 13.87, for the top spot. With a West German judge favoring him, Klaus Konzorr took the second highest score, 13.49. Win Young jumped five spots up to second place after taking the third highest score of 13.32. Alvaro Gaxiola jumped five spots to third after receiving the fourth highest score of 13.30 points. Klaus Dibiasi moved up to fourth with 24.48. Keith moved down to fifth with 24.46, just 0.02 of a point behind Dibiasi. Klaus Konzorr of West Germany was sixth with 24.37, Mikhail Safonov fell to seventh with 24.30, and his teammate, Viktor Pogozhev, fell to fifteenth. Rick Gilbert moved up to thirtieth.

Klaus Dibiasi received the highest score on the third dive with 15.68 for first with 40.06. Keith and Mexican diver Alvaro Gaxiola took the third highest score of 14.06, which moved Gaxiola up to second with 39.06 and Keith up to fourth with 38.52, just 0.51 of a point behind Win Young, in third, with 39.03. Luis Nino de Rivera dropped to fifth. Rick Gilbert moved up three spots to twenty-seventh and Mikhail Safonov fell seven spots to fourteenth.

Alvaro Gaxiola, the Mexican favorite, took the highest score, 18.98, on the fourth dive, raising him to first according to plan, with 58.04. Klaus Dibiasi fell to second place with 55.07. Win Young remained in third with 52.90. Lothar Matthes of East Germany moved into fourth with 52.03. Keith fell to fifth with 51.84 and Rick Gilbert dropped to twenty-eighth.

Rick Gilbert received the highest score on the fifth dive, 17.16, to jump to eighteenth. Luis Nino de Rivera took the second highest score, 16.10, and shot up from thirteenth to third with 66.71. Alvaro Gaxiola stayed in first with 71.36. Klaus Dibiasi stayed in second with 68.75. Keith moved up to fourth with 64.98. Win Young did his worst dive and dropped to sixth.

Klaus Dibiasi took the highest score of the sixth dive, 17.25, to reclaim first with 86. Keith received the second highest score of 16.90 on his back one-and-a-half somersault with two-and-a-half twists, to move up to third with 81.88. Win Young took the third highest, 16.20, on the same dive and moved up to fourth, with 80.46. Alvaro Gaxiola fell to second with 82.16. Luis Nino de Rivera fell to fifth with 78.07 and Rick Gilbert moved up to seventeenth.

Klaus Dibiasi also took the highest score on the seventh dive, 22.04, to stay in first. Alvaro Gaxiola took the second highest, 21.17, to stay in second. Keith took the third highest, 19.50, on his inward two-and-a-half somersault to stay in third. Win Young received 17.52 on the same dive and remained in fourth. Rick Gilbert stayed in seventeenth.

The twelve platform finalists stood as follows:

1. Klaus Dibiasi, Italy, 108.04
2. Alvaro Gaxiola, Mexico, 103.33
3. Keith Russell, United States, 101.38
4. Win Young, United States, 99.98
5. Franco Cognotto, Italy, 94.73
6. Luis Nino de Rivera, Mexico, 93.66
7. Lothar Matthes, East Germany, 92.19
8. Tord Anderson, Sweden, 92.06
9. Vladimir Vasin, Soviet Union, 91.91
10. Mikhail Safonov, Soviet Union, 91.43
11. Jose Robinson, Mexico, 91.16
12. Bernd Wucherpfenning, West Germany, 89.66

With Keith not only in the finals, but in the medals, the Russells and Lofgreens could breathe a bit easier. He was so close to that Olympic gold medal—two spots. The last three dives could definitely take him to that top position on the podium where the precious medal would be draped around his neck while the world listened to the emotion-evoking "Star-Spangled Banner" and tears swelled on the faces of his family and friends. Electricity filled the air as the platform finals concluded the 1968 Olympic Games.

Unaware that the three most important dives of his life would be the most difficult of his career, Keith climbed ten meters up to the platform. "Forward three-and-a-half," he's thinking, "Swing arms up to takeoff position. Jump hips up to take off. Rotate. Point toes on press out." In the time allotted, he practices the approach from the edge of the platform back, so he knows where to begin. He prepares his body for a dive it has successfully completed thousands of times. He prepares his mind to masterfully maneuver every move, from start to a splashless finish.

But things are stewing on the ground. Unbeknownst to Keith, before him sit ten thousand passionate Mexican spectators who are rooting hard core for their favorite diver, Alvaro Gaxiola, and who view Keith as a threat to him in his current silver medal position. Going into finals, Keith followed Alvaro by merely 1.95 points, too close for their liking, and now they had to do something about it. Klaus Dibiasi pretty much had the gold medal secured, receiving 19.92, the highest for the eighth dive, and nearly two points more than the next best (Jose Robinson). Alvaro Gaxiola's unflattering 16.08 score was too much for his fans to bear. Win Young, the other American finalist, didn't pose a threat. Fourth going into finals, his eighth dive only posted 15.38, so he wasn't a problem. The Mexicans assessed the situation and uniformly seemed to determine what needed to be done to keep their diver in the silver.

All is quiet ten meters above the crowd of ten thousand. This is standard meet conduct. Divers premeditate the precise movements for every step, rotation, and vertical water entry. Timing is crucial, and concentration necessitates silence in order to get their rhythm just right. The crowd knows this too. So, amidst this last-minute physical and mental fine-tuning, the moment when Keith's body prepares for takeoff and his mind prepares to take over, in the midst of these last few critical seconds Keith has before he has to wow the judges, the crowd explodes into a deafening blast of noise. It jerks Keith's insides, catching him off guard. The racket painfully snaps Keith out of his mode of concentration. The transition from "ready to go" to "what's that noise?" is almost excruciating. No. It *is* excruciating. He looks out to see what they are screaming at. It's him.

His mind goes blank. This instantaneous shift shocks his system. He doesn't get it. His mind is jolted into a whirl of confusion. What is going on? What are they doing? Is this for real? Keith has absolutely no idea why they are going crazy when he is about to do the dive of his life. It doesn't make sense. Keith looks down at the officials, but nobody tries to stop it. No official gets up and goes to the microphone and tells them to stop.

With a loss of concentration, Keith feels a loss of rhythm. It is that rhythm that beats at every rotation. It is that rhythm that thrusts his body at the precise pace it requires to complete three and a half revolutions in ten meters before straightening out for entry. What is he supposed to do? How is he supposed to handle this unprecedented situation? Is there any type of protocol for a diver in this awkward position? He considers his options. If he climbs down in protest, he blows his dive. If he dives amidst the outrage, he could blow points and possibly hurt himself. But he can't just stand there. That won't solve anything. He decides to go for it. But first, refocus. Keith must get back into his head. He shoves the rage out of his mind and talks his way through the dive again: "Swing arms up to takeoff position. Jump hips up to take off. Rotate. Point toes on press out." He jumps.

One, two, three and a half flips and he's in. The Russells, Swensons, and Lofgreens jumped up in wild applause and cheering, thrilled at that unbelievable dive. He did it! The ten thousand taunting spectators didn't touch him. He triumphed the opposition masterfully. He was one step closer to the prize.

Despite low points awarded by a few judges—who incidentally dropped high points on their own divers for poorly executed dives—Keith received the second highest score of 18.72. This was 2.64 more than the Mexican favorite, Alvaro Gaxiola, and the crowd was not amused. It put Keith in the silver medal spot, with 120.10, 0.69 of a point ahead of Alvaro with 119.41.

Gary watched the games and saw that first dive on television at Camp Pendleton in California. He wrote in his journal more about what he heard than what he saw: "He went from 3rd to 2nd place. And I heard what I swear was Mom gasping in disbelief that her son is capable of such a dramatic performance."

As Keith climbed on the platform for dive number nine, he had no idea where he placed. He didn't want to know. He didn't compete to be the best; he competed to do his best. Concerning himself over the placings was just an extra thought he didn't need in his head.

As he stood on the platform, he mentally rehearsed his dive—a reverse two-and-a-half. Like the previous dive, he practiced his approach from the front end of the platform, back. "Don't throw head back," he told himself while thinking through it. Although divers did not receive training on how to handle an unruly, disruptive crowd, since this was never a problem, Keith had enough discipline not to focus on what they had just tried to do to him. He had to move on. He was closer than ever to the ultimate reward. Klaus Dibiasi had taken the highest score again, 20.02, over two more than the next highest, awarded to Jose Robinson, with 17.82. Since Keith could make no sense of the crowd's behavior and could do nothing about it, he blew it off. Their outrageous conduct had been so senseless, he didn't consider they might do it again.

With mind focused and body prepared, Keith got ready for takeoff. Then they announced his name and his dive. And the crowd let loose, screaming, yelling, shouting, throwing things, whatever they could to mess Keith up. Although it surprised him, it didn't as much as at first. Trying to execute a difficult dive while ten thousand people are screaming at you might feel as if you are diving into a bed of nails. It certainly wouldn't have a calming effect. But when Keith failed to make a vertical entrance and go in cleanly, he blamed only himself. He had thrown his head back upon takeoff, which caused him to overestimate his rotations. He came out early, not fully completing the two-and-a-half flips, and went in at an angle. Certain judges took advantage of the situation and awarded him especially low marks. Keith received the lowest score awarded. It knocked him out of the medals. Klaus Dibiasi had 147.98, Alvaro Gaxiola had 135.51, Win Young had 133.04, and Keith had 131.17. But the crowd wasn't satisfied. And by now, Keith knew it.

Although he hadn't done a good reverse, Keith still felt he had a chance. Although he still didn't know why the crowd always went insane when he dove, he knew that this time he had to be prepared for the abuse. The competition became more than just the typical battle against other divers; it was a combat against irrational judges and a ruthless, out-of-control crowd. In this unfamiliar territory of "anything goes," Keith felt he'd entered no man's land.

On his trip to the top of the platform for his last dive of the 1968 Olympics, Keith knew what he was up against. And this time, it was especially bad. Keith's last dive was his ace in the hole. The forward one-and-a-half somersault with three twists, his signature dive, was a sure thing for a high score. Apparently the judges failed to award Alvaro Gaxiola high enough points for the crowd to feel safe from Keith. They snapped. It was unlike anything anyone had ever seen. After "at least twenty minutes" of chaos according to one reporter, Keith again had to center his mind so he could to fling his body into that body of protests and hope he got it right. When you bust your butt day after day, year after year, ten thousand angry Mexicans aren't going to make you forget it, no matter how hard they try. The funny thing is, the same ten thousand people who spent the day booing him on every dive, cheered for him after his last dive. It was that good.

Keith got the highest score of the last dive, 21.17, but it wasn't good enough for a medal. Win Young took the second highest score, 20.88, and a bronze medal. Alvaro Gaxiola received the third highest, 18.98, for the silver. Klaus Dibiasi won Italy its first Olympic gold medal in swimming and diving.

The final results were as follows:

1. Klaus Dibiasi, Italy, 164.18
2. Alvaro Gaxiola, Mexico, 154.49
3. Win Young, United States, 153.93
4. Keith Russell, United States, 152.34
5. Jose Robinson, Mexico, 143.62
6. Lothar Matthes, East Germany, 141.75
7. Luis Nino de Rivera, Mexico, 141.16
8. Franco Cagnotto, Italy, 138.89
9. Mikhail Safonov, Soviet Union, 138.77
10. Vladimir Vasin, Soviet Union, 138.40
11. Tord Anderson, Sweden, 131.21
12. Bernd Wucherpfennig, West Germany, 129.49

Swimming World magazine offered this version of Keith's last efforts to win Olympic gold and the crowd's last efforts to thwart his pursuit:

> The final round of dives was more a contest between the judges and the vociferous crowd of Mexican spectators, whose sportsmanship must have been developed at the bullring.
>
> The spectators, lacking any knowledge of how diving is scored, not only intimidated the judges into high scores for their countrymen,

> but their hoots, whistling and jeers affected other competitors. The most disgraceful outburst occurred after Gaxiola's ninth dive when the unruly mob of partisan fans, angered by what they believed was too low a score, brought the competitions to a complete stop for at least 20 minutes by their boos and whistles.
>
> Russell was forced to stand on the platform during this outburst, and when it somewhat subsided he attempted to execute his dive. Needless to say, the crowd achieved its purpose, as he dove poorly on a dive that is one of his best. It cost him a medal.[214]

Lurline's description of the horrific situation is more detailed, with a flavor of stardom in the end:

> At the end of three dives, Keith was in first place. He started out with his handstand dive, as did most of the divers, and Keith's was superb—the best in the entire meet. He was diving flawlessly with the exception of his reverse 2½. And he was certainly better than what the judges awarded him. He was second in the competition, no matter how you look at it. Dick told him he was a champion.
>
> The judges just couldn't give Win or Keith low enough [scores]. Keith dived the entire meet behind Gaxiola—the Spanish favorite. Keith had to go through boos throughout all his diving, but before the last dive it was horrendous. He had to stand there on the platform before 10,000 people—waiting while the catcalls were going on and paper and programs being thrown at the judges and whistles all being blown to try to quiet the crowd who ignored the officials and kept up the catcalls and whistling.
>
> Keith, when the noise would not abate, dived in the midst of the turmoil, a beautiful triple twister, which if he had got decent points on even that dive he could have got 1st or 2nd. Keith we couldn't have been more proud of you—in those circumstances you were truly a champion. Ken Sitzberger, who was broadcasting

> for CBS TV and who has never been for Keith (too busy competing against him) said on camera it was lousy judging.
>
> The papers were full of the raw deal Keith got—Sammy Lee, Hack Miller of *Salt Lake Tribune*, *Swimming World* Magazine—all had articles in papers and magazines of the unfairness. But nothing could be done. With the non-Communist judges (none of which were [from] the U.S.) Keith would have received a medal—but the greater no. of judges judged him so much lower that he came in 4th. So Keith has received letters from all over the U.S. congratulating him on his diving.

Lurline also wrote about how well her son handled the unforeseen issue:

> Keith dived superbly off platform. He got 4th. The judging was not fair. There were many magazine articles and newspaper clippings about the judging in Mexico City. [The audience] booed for 15 minutes until nothing could be heard even over the loud speaker. They had to stop the contest trying to quiet the crowd. Of course Keith had to stand there on the board all this time waiting for them to announce the dive. But he took it like a man. He knew he had done a good job. He performed so fantastic.

One Arizona newspaper said of the scandal, "Keith Russell of Mesa was the chief victim of what Dick Smith, coach of the U.S. Olympic diving team, termed as a "conspiracy" to defeat the U.S. divers in Mexico City at any costs."[215]

The judging was still a hot topic of discussion months later when *Swimming World* published an article titled "A Critical View on the Judging in Mexico" by the West German judge, Hans Sandofen:

Certainly every newspaper in countries interested in diving have written detailed accounts about the judging at Mexico's Olympiad. Unfortunately there were low scores and national bias. It should be mentioned that the partial judges who wanted to see their favorite divers win, influenced several scorings.

Looking to the Olympic Games in Munich, serious consideration must be made to reduce the judging problem to a tolerable measure. One thing certainly will not happen, that is the judge behaving in such a manner.

In my opinion, the biggest mistakes by the judges were in the cases of the Russian Tamara Pogoskeva in the Ladies' Springboard diving and even more so to the U.S. diver, Keith Russell who deserved a medal under all circumstances.

The most important winner will not be an individual person, but the sport of diving itself, which is a hobby among us all. It is very interesting to see that four of the seven judges have placed silver medal winner Gaxiola in fourth place where he belongs.

Because of over judging their own diver, the judges Kinast and Severin have lost the overall picture and therefore contributed to Gaxiola's second place. Just as grotesque is the judging of Capilla who placed his countrymen only 3.75 points behind Dibiasi.

The seven judges included,

	Name of judge	Country	Olympics	Award
1	Joaquin Capilla	Mexico	1948 1952 1956	Bronze - platform Silver - platform Gold - platform

2	Peter Heatly	Great Britain	1948 1948 1952	Fifth - platform Thirteenth - springboard Twelfth - platform
3	Tsuneo Shibahara	Japan	1936 1936	Fourth - springboard Sixth - platform
4	Gosta Olander	Sweden	1936	Twenty-third - platform
5	Mr. Kanuast	East Germany		
6	Mr. Severin	USSR		
7	Hans Sandofen	West Germany		

It is interesting to note how many total points each judge awarded each diver and thus where each diver ranked with each judge:

1. Klaus Dibiasi of Italy

Judge	Points	Ranked diver
Russian	507.15	1
East German	504.65	1
Swedish	501.40	1
Mexican	497.85	1
Japanese	496.90	2
West German	490.65	1
British	477.30	2

So in Klaus's case, five of seven judges awarded him the most points while two judges gave him the second most total points.

2. Alvaro Gaxiola of Mexico

Mexican	494.10	2
Russian	483.65	2
East German	472.00	2
Japanese	461.55	4
British	458.25	4
Swedish	423.50	4
West German	411.75	4

Interestingly, the problematic judges all awarded Alvaro Gaxiola higher points than the judges who just tried to do their job and give points based on performance. These judges ranked Alvaro second best while the other four rated him fourth best.

3. Win Young of the United States

Japanese	501.30	1
British	479.65	1
West German	463.95	2
East German	455.35	4
Swedish	452.85	3
Mexican	439.55	6
Russian	438.50	7

The same judges who gave Alvaro Gaxiola the most points gave Win the least. The Russian judge gave his divers Mikhail Safonov 11.45 more and Vladimir Vasin 7.40 more. The East German judge gave his diver, Lothar Matthes, 13.85 more than he gave Win, and the Mexican judge gave his divers Alvaro Gaxiola an absurd 54.55 more points, Luis Nino de Rivera 31.40 more, and Jose Robinson 27.70 more than he awarded Win.

4. Keith Russell

Japanese	484.95	3
Swedish	467.10	2
British	460.65	3
Mexican	455.10	5
East German	451.05	5
Russian	449.10	4
West German	443.20	3

While the four competent judges ranked Keith third best or better, the fraudulent ones had their own diver in that spot, giving them more points than Keith. The East German judge awarded his diver 18.15 more points while the Mexican judge gave Alvaro Gaxiola 39 more, Luis Nino de Rivera 16.05 more, and Jose Robinson 12.15 more.

5. Jose Robinson of Mexico

Mexican	467.25	4
Japanese	444.75	5
East German	436.20	7
Russian	429.15	8
Swedish	422.70	6
British	407.10	9
West German	394.55	7

The Mexican judge appears to have tried to get Jose into the medals, awarding him 22.50 more points than the next most total points awarded to Jose. While this judge considered only a few divers better, the British judge considered only a few divers worse than Jose.

6. Lothar Matthes of East Germany

East German	469.20	3
Russian	422.65	6
Japanese	440.25	6
Mexican	422.85	7
Swedish	421.35	7
British	405.30	10
West German	403.20	5

While the Russian, Mexican, and Swedish judges awarded this East German diver almost exactly the same amount of total points (within 1.5), and the British and West German judges awarded within 2.10 total points of each other, the East German judge gave him 28.95 more than the most any other judge gave him.

7. Luis Nino de Rivera of Mexico

Mexican	471.15	3
Russian	426.75	9
British	425.70	7
East German	424.80	9
Japanese	422.70	6
Swedish	417.90	9
West German	375.75	11

The Mexican judge gave his diver 44.4 points more than the next highest-scoring judge and 95.40 points more than the lowest, in this case. He also placed Luis *six* spots higher than half the judges, just to try to get him into the medals.

8. Franco Cognotto of Italy

Japanese	429.90	7
Swedish	425.85	5
Russian	421.20	10
British	420.00	8
East German	410.40	10
Mexican	408.15	9
West German	396.45	6

Except for the West German judge, who almost always awarded the lowest points, the judges scored this Italian fairly consistently.

9. Mikhail Safonov of Russia

Russian	449.95	3
East German	436.90	6
British	435.25	5
Swedish	420.60	8
Mexican	417.75	8
Japanese	402.75	11
West German	388.80	9

While the Russian judge ranked the Russian diver third best, the Japanese judge ranked him second worst.

10. Vladimir Vasin of Russia

Russian	445.80	5
East German	433.90	8
British	429.40	6
Swedish	412.25	10
Mexican	403.40	10
Japanese	395.00	12
West German	376.40	10

The Russian judge rated this Russian diver twice as good as most of the other judges.

11. Tord Anderson of Sweden

Japanese	410.25	9
Swedish	406.60	11
West German	391.05	8
British	389.40	11
East German	384.45	11
Russian	382.80	12
Mexican	374.85	12

Two judges actually rated the Swedish diver higher than the Swedish judge here. The judges all awarded him a similar amount of total points, indicating credible judging.

12. Bernd Wucherpfennig of West Germany

Japanese	404.10	10
Swedish	389.10	12
Mexican	384.50	11
Russian	384.00	11
East German	382.96	12
British	377.70	12
West German	341.80	12

Here, the West German judge awarded the West German diver as consistently as he did the other divers, with the lowest points.

Ward O'Connell coached at Yale University at the time. He also served as diving editor for *Swimming World* magazine and talked about the judging in Mexico:

> The judging of diving at the XIX Olympiad in Mexico City in 1968 left the sport of diving in such shambles that the ramifications are still stirring up the waters.
>
> Certain discrepancies in the awarding of dives brought a wry eye to the sport from unbiased spectators and large abuse from the Mexican spectators who witnessed the Olympico fiasco.
>
> Until now, U.S. Olympic Diving Coach, Dick Smith, has remained silent. He was unavailable for comment after the men's platform diving, the most controversial of the oddly judged diving events. But now Smith has given the judges their just due with a release to the press concerning the irrational judging.
>
> Smith accused Olympic Officials of a conspiracy "to beat the United States divers at any costs." He said recently that the principle target of the Europeans and Mexicans, was Keith Russell.
>
> Smith said the judges met before the meet to discuss competitors.

> "The West German judge was giving Keith what he deserved," said Smith, "and the others tried to get him off the panel on the basis of being biased."
>
> "Russell (who was the last diver) had a chance at a gold medal, if he had gotten some 8s and 9s. He knew he was not in favor of the judges," said Smith.
>
> Russell, with great courage, responded with a forward one-and-a-half with three twists, which changed the catcalls he had been getting from the mob of spectators to an ovation. The crowd, which had been booing and whistling during Russell's earlier dives, turned its wrath on the judges when they announced the scores.
>
> "Win [Young] really dove well and deserved his medal," said Smith, "But they weren't worried about Win. They were worried about Keith." According to Smith, Young all but offered Russell his medal after seeing the judging, and Gaxiola told Russell he deserved a medal.
>
> The real story will never be known, but it was the general opinion of those who saw the Games that one of the real sore points of the Games was the judging of the diving.[216]

The consensus among authorities, fellow competitors, witnesses, reputable judges, journalists, and commentators alike was that Keith had earned a medal, but a few discriminatory judges blatantly gave preferential treatment to their own country's divers. That has been proven by the scorings of the Mexican, Russian, and East German judges, each of whom scored his own diver to medal.

If diving awarded an all-around medal for total points on both platform and springboard, like gymnastics does for its events, Keith would have at least won silver, with 304.09 total points (151.75 on springboard and 152.34 on platform), 19.83 points behind Klaus Dibiasi with 323.92. Had the Olympic Committee awarded team medals, Keith would have won gold and enjoyed the satisfaction of knowing that he had made the most significant contribution to the team title.

The United States accumulated 872.96 points from both the springboard and platform (304.09 from Keith, 170.15 from Bernie Wrightson, 158.09 from Jim Henry, 153.93 from Win Young, and 86.70 from Rick Gilbert). Mexico, 95.85 points behind with 777.11, would have taken silver, and Italy, with 606.37, would have won bronze.

Keith's brother Gary noted a friend's observation of the Mexican audience in his journal: "Dave [Wilson] said the Mexicans fouled Keith's diving up by applauding when he was going into it."

Two-time Olympic champion Sammy Lee (who coached Greg Louganis) later wrote Keith, offering his sincerest condolences for not being awarded a well-deserved medal "not by your own shortcomings but due to the short-sighted diving judges who judge from emotions rather than objectively. If anyone is a champion it is you, Keith Russell."

Sammy Lee stated in his letter to Keith that he was "upset after the way the Mexican audience tried to upset you during the Olympic Games just for a lousy silver or bronze medal. Even to win a gold medal by narrow-minded judges isn't worth it."

The world's greatest diver up to that time also told Keith how highly he regarded him: "When Dick Smith called and said you made both the springboard and tower for the U.S. team, I was happy once more for the world of diving. You are the kind of man our country needs to display what America is all about."

The *Salt Lake Tribune* recalled years later how the Mexican audience forced the medal onto their diver's neck:

When Keith Russell stood on the platform for his final dive in the

1968 Olympics in Mexico City, the crowd was in an uproar and he had to wait before he could dive.

The diver just before Russell was the Mexican star and his point total put him in second. The crowd wanted his total to be high enough for the gold medal and the fans were noisy and demonstrative, showing their displeasure.

When the noise abated to the point where he could concentrate, Russell went into his dive. It was a good one, but was a point behind the Mexican star's total and that was enough to drop Russell to fourth place.

"In diving, it is easy to psych yourself either out of a win or into a win. When I went to the Olympic Games in 1968, I was fighting a massive problem that was frustrating my ambitions and threatening to ruin my diving," he said.[217]

Decades later, one major university newspaper discussed the crowd's effort to thwart Keith's attempts at gold:

Thirty years later, Keith Russell still remembers the 1968 Olympics in Mexico City and his fourth place finish there.

Russell, BYU's diving coach, was predicted to win the 1968 Olympic diving competition after a college career that included national and NCAA championships.

When it came down to the last three dives in the finals, Russell was still a contender for the gold medal. The crowd, knowing Russell could upset the victory for a Mexican diver, made noise in an attempt to distract him.

The pressure, combined with the crowd's distraction, was just enough to upset Russell's pursuit of the gold, putting him in fourth place, just behind the medals.[218]

Keith's Olympic experience thus bore good news and bad news. The bad news, of course, was that he didn't medal due to corrupt judging. The good news was that he dove beautifully and still ranked highly, winning more total points for his country than any other American diver. Plus, he was young and still had a chance to become an Olympic champion. He would be twenty-four at the 1972 games and twenty-eight at the 1976 games. Silver medalist Alvaro Gaxiola was thirty-one. While the title of Olympic champion may have been stripped from him by distorted judging, no one could take away his title of Olympian or the rare experience of competing in the world's most prestigious athletic competition.

One astute reporter praised the Americans for diving so phenomenally in such antagonistic circumstances:

> The U.S. divers went into the Games well-coached and in good condition. Several suffered from the usual Mexican "indigestion" problems. While the U.S. divers earned 50% of the medals (2 gold and 4 bronze), they also placed 4th twice, despite adverse circumstances, including emotional audience demonstrations.
>
> U.S.'s Win Young and Keith Russell, who placed 3rd and 4th, dove consistently well, under extremely tense conditions. These young men are clearly top-medal caliber and will undoubtedly reach their peak during the next Olympiad.[219]

Keith and Marsha rode the train home together from Mexico, a three-day trip. Keith had two weeks before he had to report to Utah for his mission, so he spent as much time with Marsha as he could. He also gave talks to youth in his church on goal setting and challenging themselves. He told his audience that they could go a lot farther with big goals than with small ones.

ASU gave Keith tickets to the presidential box for a football game. He had fun with that.

Lurline wrote in Keith's journal after he left for Utah as a way to cope with missing him:

> It didn't seem like he was going away for 2 whole years—it seemed like another trip and he would be coming back soon. But when I started going through his things and putting them away, it hit me, and I parted with a number of tears. I can't stand to have him gone for 2 years, and yet I wouldn't have it any other way. His is such a wonderful son, and I miss him so.
>
> Keith went to ASU and picked up his letter jacket which is real sharp and which he must have left with Marsha because it isn't in his closet.

So ended 1968—an amazing yet devastating year for Keith. Amazing in that he went to the Olympics as America's favorite to win gold. Devastating in that he didn't. But now he was off on another adventure.

Chapter 11: Third Olympic Trials and Eerie Experiences in Eastern Europe

The weekend before Keith left Chile to return home from his church mission, the Russells scrambled to prepare for his arrival and subsequent marriage. Keith left Chile on November 3, 1970. He stopped in Panama and visited the Panama Canal. Keith told his family he expected to fly in Friday, November 6, but he arrived earlier. Lurline described what really happened:

> We had it all planned just how we were going to meet Keith at the airport. Take along the movie camera and do all these things. Then I got woke up early one morning a day before Keith was suppose to be home and there when I opened my eyes was my very own Keith. I almost past out with shock. We were so happy to have him home. Just fantastic.

Gary had his own comical version:

> Tonight we all received a surprise, Keith came walking in—didn't expect him until Fri. When he 1st came in mom's room, I was in Alan's and jumped up to see him. I ran in, was about to shake his hand when I fell flat on my face. Marsha's coming in tonight [from Utah]—she's in for a big surprise.

On the flight, Arizona legislator Delos Ellsworth recognized Keith as a missionary and offered him a ride home. Keith accepted, since his only other option was to call his parents in the middle of the night to pick him up at the airport.

Marsha had graduated from Arizona State University in elementary education. BYU then offered her a teaching position in their dance department without her applying, as a way to entice Keith to transfer up. She accepted, knowing BYU wanted Keith and Keith wanted BYU, since Dick Smith no longer coached at ASU. Marsha taught ballet at BYU that fall of 1970 while planning their November wedding.

Keith experienced uncharacteristic trepidation before calling his girlfriend of seven years. Lurline documented a few things about that initial phone conversation, including her own feelings: "For a couple hours, he was scared to phone her. But once he did, he never got away. (And he better not ever, ever!)" They married in the Mesa Temple, a block north of Keith's parents.

During his mission, Keith decided to change his major from education to business. He wanted a more comfortable living for his family than teaching could provide. He also felt a business degree could give him a more well-rounded education and better job opportunities.

Keith had a little run-in with the three-meter soon after arriving at BYU. While executing an inward two-and-a-half somersault for the first time in two years, he hit his forehead on his second rotation.[220] Although he made it sound like nothing to his mother, it took forty stitches to close that nasty gash. He took a week off to recover, then was back at it again. One BYU newspaper article discussed Keith's indomitable spirit and tenacity:

> Keith Russell, BYU's premier diver, is proving himself to be one fellow who just doesn't give up. Now on the threshold of re-entering collegiate competition, Russell has accomplished what many would have called the impossible.
>
> To complicate matters, Russell hit the board in practice last year while attempting a dive. The cut took 40 stitches to close and you would expect most divers to wait for the wound to heal. Not so with Keith. After one week and the doctors permission, he bandaged the wound, put on a swimming cap and resumed diving.
>
> Said Coach Rollie Bester, "To come back after two years away from diving and pick up your old diving form is hard to do. But Keith made up his mind to do that. No one expected him to jump back into action after that injury, but that's what he did. He's a remarkable competitor."
>
> While the injury slowed down his timetable, Keith was still able to compete in the Pan American trials last spring. He placed 4th, 6th, and 10th in three events, but just missed a berth on the team.[221]

Five months after he started diving again, Keith competed in his first competition in over two years, the 1971 AAU Indoor National Championships, which served as the Pan-American Trials. They took place at West Point in New York where Keith's friend Win Young coached.

Future Olympians Mike Finneran and Craig Lincoln made the Pan-American team.[222] After Keith's lengthy time off, his coach felt his showing at Nationals was satisfactory, even though he didn't make finals.[223] Just qualifying for Nationals after so much time away was an extraordinary feat and spoke volumes of Keith's talent, passion, fortitude, and quest to achieve his best.

Keith went to San Pablo, California, north of Oakland, for the qualifying meet for the 1971 Outdoor Nationals in July. He won the one-meter by an extraordinary 38.73 points, with 468.99, and the three-meter by 38.31, with 569.85 against eighty divers.[224] A meet review in *Swimming World* magazine commented on Keith's superior diving: "The most outstanding performance was undoubtedly that of Keith Russell, who won both men's events with 38 points separating him from his nearest contender in each."[225]

Keith proved he hadn't lost his touch at the 1971 AAU Outdoor National Championships in Houston. In all three events, Keith not only made finals, but was the only diver west of the Mississippi to do so. The one-meter finalists dove for a greater variety of colleges than the previous decade:

1. Mike Brown, Dartmouth University
2. Mike Finneran, Ohio State University
3. Don Dunfield, University of Wisconsin
4. Jim Henry, Indiana University
5. Randy Horton, North Carolina State University
6. Tim Moore, Ohio State University
7. Steve Skilken, Ohio State University
8. Larry More, Cornell University
9. Craig Lincoln, University of Minnesota
10. Alan Ross, Louisiana State University
11. Keith Russell, Brigham Young University
12. Julian Krug, University of Wisconsin

Keith placed highest on the three-meter:

1. Jim Henry (1968 Olympic bronze medalist)
2. Craig Lincoln (1972 Olympic bronze medalist)
3. Larry More (Keith's teammate that year at meets in Germany and Russia)
4. Don Dunfield (1970 national three-meter silver medalist)

5. Keith Russell (missed fourth place by 1.20 points)
6. Mike Brown (Keith's teammate that year at meets in Africa)
7. Julian Krug (Future University of Pittsburgh diving coach)
8. Joseph Crawford (University of Michigan)
9. Dick Rydze (1972 Olympic silver medalist)
10. Phil Boggs (1976 Olympic champion)
11. Todd Smith (1972 NCAA one-meter champion)
12. Steve Skilken
13. David Bush (1972 Olympian)
14. Randy Horton (five-time Atlantic Coast Conference champion)
15. Billy Heinz (Princeton University)

Larry More, a sophomore at Cornell University, could credit Keith with much of his diving ability. He explains:

> I saw [Keith] dive in a number of competitions when I was younger. In particular, I went to the 1967 outdoor nationals in Chicago, dove in the pre-qualifying meet, didn't make it, but stayed to watch and took movies on my 8-mm camera. I took Keith and Bernie Wrightson, because I liked the style of their diving; and I watched those movies for years to see how it ought to be done.

The ten-meter results were just as colorful, but mostly featured guys with short names:

1. Dick Rydze
2. Jim Henry
3. David Bush
4. Rick Earley
5. Larry More
6. Todd Smith
7. Mike Finneran
8. Keith Russell
9. Mike Brown

Keith, Larry More, and Jim Henry went to East Germany and Russia the next month as the U.S. men's team, or the "American Pre-Olympic Team," for dual meets. Cynthia Potter, future Olympic champion Micki King, and Keith's friend Janet Ely represented the U.S. women. Larry More explains the significance of those meets:

> International meet/trips were very rare in those days, maybe one every two years or so, an honor that only the really elite senior divers went on. This was before TV was such a financial factor in the sport, not like it was only a few (maybe 5–6) years after, when there started to be many opportunities for international competition.

After stopping in Dublin, the American team flew to Munich, where they saw the Olympic site under construction and ate at the Olympiaturn, a revolving needle restaurant. From West Berlin, they crossed the Berlin Wall at Checkpoint Charlie into East Berlin. Although they enjoyed special treatment, a feeling of eeriness crept over them as they entered East Germany. Larry More recalls, "We took a bus through East Berlin. Things looked gray, desolate, ruins still left from WWII, grim, plain, project-type apartment buildings, not much going on." They were also the first team to cross the Iron Curtain in over twenty-five years.

They first competed in Leipzig, Germany, the largest city in the state of Saxony. Keith placed third on springboard and fourth on platform.[226] As usual, East German judges favored East German divers, especially future Olympic champion Falk Hoffman, which understandably upset American coach Hobie Billingsley.

The American divers then flew from East Berlin a thousand miles to Moscow, where they saw the Kremlin, Red Square, Lenin's Tomb, and more eerie, empty streets. After a couple days of sightseeing and shopping, they flew 470 miles south to Kiev for the "All-Soviet Games," equivalent to the western hemisphere's Pan-American Games.[227] Keith placed third on platform, won by Larry More.

The Americans had several interesting experiences in the Ukraine, which is bordered by Russia to the east, Belarus to the north, Poland and Hungary to the west, and Romania and the Black Sea to the south. For one, it was about 55°F, which translates to freezing when you're wet. As Larry More recalls, "There was a hot shower under the 3-M we tried to stay in, but the water temperature was so hot, we got scalded. We ran out, did our dive, and ran back under the water."

Then there was the time they were stalked by the KGB, equivalent to the CIA or FBI. This while face to face with mummies and sarcophagi in one-thousand-year-old underground passageways and cemeteries in Kiev's famous Lavra Monastery catacombs. It wasn't enough that above ground was spooky, they had to delve into dark places with dead people and be followed by scarier people. Larry More called the experience "cloak and dagger stuff."

Ten seconds after their Pan American flight took off for home, the American team broke out into "applause, hooting, and cheering that we were on our way home." Keith especially had a good reason to cheer. He had a child to welcome to the world.

Keith and Marsha welcomed their first child, Rex Trevor, into their home on October 30. Rex wanted his daddy there for the big day, so he delayed his birth for two weeks until Keith came home.

Keith competed in the South African Cup in Pretoria, the capital of South Africa, a month later. One-meter National Champion Mike Brown, British Springboard Champion Chris Walls, Pan-American Champion Liz Carruthers of Canada, future Olympian Mariette Dommers of Holland, and Cynthia Potter also competed.

One Pretoria newspaper discussed the significance of the December event:

What is regarded to be the most difficult maneouvre in diving—an inward two-and-a-half pike—may be performed in the Republic for the first time during the inaugural South Africa Cup international contest tomorrow.

The inward two-and-a-half pike—which can be executed with precision by only a handful of divers throughout the world—may be attempted by the eight Olympic-class overseas divers in the contest.

For different people, the meeting has a different significance.

For South African sportsman, in general, it marks another major breakthrough in the wall of isolation.

For the organizer, Pretoria's Ernst de Jong, chairman of South African Diving Board of Control, it marks an important milestone in his efforts to keep open the door of international contact and competition to South Africa, and, perhaps even closer to his heart, to put diving on the Republic's sporting map.

He has done much at diplomatic level for South African sport.

For local divers, it will provide the incentive to improve themselves. It will be the first time in many years that they have had the opportunity to watch and to pit their skills against some of the finest divers in the world, and, although our chosen divers are not expected to finish among the leaders, they will benefit greatly from the knowledge that they must practice even harder to attain the standard of Olympic competition.

For the overseas divers, the competition will be an important part of their build-up for the Olympic Games in Munich, West Germany, next year. Russell has the most experience.[228]

Keith's Olympic teammate, Cornell coach Rick Gilbert, went as the

American coach. The divers stayed in homes for a maximum integration experience. They toured cities, visited a village of the Ndebele natives of Zimbabwe, and toured Kruger National Park, the largest game reserve in South Africa, covering 7,330 square miles, where Keith saw baboons.[229]

Keith not only won all three events—one-meter, three-meter, and ten-meter, but he amassed 592.70 points, the second highest total ever scored.[230] Mike Brown followed 48.25 behind in second, with 544.45.[231]

The South African International followed a week later in Cape Town, 900 miles southwest of Pretoria, on Africa's southern tip. *The Cape Times* called the event an "Olympic '72 Preview." It also stated, "Russell, short, blond, and well-muscled is the favourite to win the men's event. He must be after his brilliant display at Pretoria."

Besides doing triple flips, triple twisters, and the most difficult inward dive, Keith polished off a reverse one-and-a-half somersault with two-and-a-half twists.[232]

The Cape Times article featured a large photograph of Keith doing a back dive.

It discussed his dazzling display of diving feats:

> With superb diving skill, Keith Russell of the United States won the men's section of the South African International diving competition when he amassed 591.65 points—the third highest total ever gathered by one man in the world. There was a big gap between Russell and his colleague Mike Brown.

Of the three highest scores ever accumulated in a single competition, Keith had two.

Again, Keith won all three titles and established himself as a leading contender for the 1972 Olympics that summer.[233] One Utah newspaper noted of his victories, "The South African showing shot him to the head of the list of Olympic hopefuls for '72."[234] Another newspaper discussed the likelihood of Keith making the 1972 Munich Olympics:

> If goal-setting and goal-achieving are part of the Olympic deal, BYU diver Keith Russell will be representing the USA in the 1972 Olympics.
>
> There is no guarantee that the senior will make the team. But as far as his coaches are concerned, Keith is a very strong contender for a berth on the team.
>
> "He is very definitely a world-class diver," says Cougar swimming coach Walt Cryer. "Right now I would rank him among the top three in the country in both springboard and platform."
>
> "Keith may be approaching the finest form of his career," reports BYU coach Rollie Bestor. "Rick Gilbert, who coached the U.S. divers on the [African] tour, was very much impressed with his performance at both meets."[235]

BYU competed against ASU in February 1972 and won 71-42. Keith won the one-meter by a massive 38.15 points with 302.85 and the three-meter by an ever more impressive 40.60 with 309.50, setting a six-dive record. Keith's teammates completed a sweep of the one-meter: Stan Curnow took second with 264.70, and Jim Whytlaw placed third with 245.20. Stan Curnow also took second on three-meter with 268.90.[236]

One BYU newspaper article discussed the powerful presence Keith possessed on campus and in the pool after his first college competition:

> When diving is mentioned around BYU, the first name that comes to mind is Keith Russell. The former ASU great returned to competition Friday night against his old teammates and coolly demolished all pretenders to his crown, winning the 3-meter event by a 40-point margin. Keith topped off a masterfully controlled performance with a forward one-and-a-half somersault, three twist plunge that garnered the night's highest marks. Russell's return has obscured the accomplishments of two nationally ranked divers.[237]

Competing against the University of Utah, Keith broke all kinds of school diving records. He set an eleven-dive record on the one-meter by a staggering 80.65 points, with 542.60 points. He set an eleven-dive record on the three-meter by an overwhelming 94.15 points with 567.15, (Stan Curnow held the old record of 473.0), and a six-dive record on three-meter by 37.10 points, with 372.20. Keith now owned all four BYU diving records, setting them his first month of collegiate competition.

The 1972 Western Athletic Conference Championships took place in Fort Collins, Colorado. Rollie Bestor explained why he expected BYU divers to do well: "Our divers have been impressive this year, mainly on the strength of technique and consistency. Few teams can match our divers in these two areas. Some of our divers should be strong in the nationals later this year." Those divers included Jim Whytlaw, defending WAC champion on one-meter and runner-up on three-meter, and Stan Curnow, defending WAC champion on three-meter and runner-up on one-meter. One newspaper, discussing the upcoming conference championships, predicted Keith's success: "A third Cougar could well be one of the finest in America this year."[238]

Keith not only won the three-meter conference title, he set a new WAC record by a colossal 86.85 points with 559.85. His teammates, Stan Curnow and Jim Whytlaw, took second and third on the high board. ASU Sun Devils, coached by Keith's Pan-American Games coach Ward O'Connell, took fourth and fifth.[239] Keith also won the one-meter conference title with a record total.[240]

The 1972 NCAAs were at the United States Military Academy in West Point, New York. Known as "Army" for collegiate athletic purposes, it is both the oldest military post and the oldest military academy in the United States. Thomas Jefferson established the academy. Occupying 16,000 acres, it is one of the world's largest campuses. The academy is located on the Hudson River, fifty miles north of New York City.

Besides being an educational experience for Keith, the NCAAs tested his ability to keep a positive attitude amid adversity, both in and out of his control. First, he lost the one-meter title, not because he missed a dive but because his dive was announced as an inward two-and-a-half and he did what should have been listed, according to his friend Jack Romine, "one of the best forward two-and-a-half pike somersaults I'd ever seen." The scores started coming in—9, 9.5, 9—when one judge pointed out that Keith did not do the dive announced, so he received a zero, which dropped him from first place to forty-ninth.[241] It must have felt like a punch in the stomach, but Keith knew he couldn't fight the system, so he accepted the situation.

In the three-meter event, it looked as if Keith might take it. Going into finals, he had the top spot, 9.39 points ahead of two-time national champion and future Olympic bronze medalist Craig Lincoln in second. One-meter champion Todd Smith followed another 16.56 points behind in third.

Keith missed his first dive, a reverse two-and-a-half somersault, dropping him to second. His next dive, a back two-and-a-half somersault, dropped him to third. He took 63.00 on his reverse one-and-a-half somersault with two-and-a-half twists but ended up fourth with 498.63.[242] Sixty-nine divers started the national collegiate championships. The three-meter results, accompanied by the divers' results on one-meter:

1. Craig Lincoln, Minnesota, second on one-meter
2. Larry More, Cornell, fourth
3. Tim Moore, Ohio State, third
4. Keith, BYU, first in spirit
5. Todd Smith, Ohio State, first in real life
6. Steve Skilken, Ohio State, sixth
7. Joseph Crawford, Michigan
8. Don Muir, Indiana
9. Randy Horton, North Carolina State, twelfth
10. Gary James, Indiana, fifth
11. Stan Curnow, BYU
12. Donnie Vick, Texas[243]

Indiana University won its fourth straight NCAA swimming and diving championship. Ohio State University, winning half the six diving medals, placed ninth. BYU placed twentieth ahead of Johns Hopkins in twenty-second, the University of Pennsylvania in twenty-fourth, and Harvard in twenty-eighth.

Keith went to the 1972 Indoor National Championships in Dallas and came away a more colorful man. First, going into the one-meter finals, he led by 10.05 points.[244] But Don Dunfield stole the national title with 531.18, followed closely by

1. Mike Finneran 522.84
2. Jim Henry 516.61
3. Tim Moore 506.52
4. Keith Russell 505.14[245]

Keith's trial by fire came when he came out of his forward three-and-a-half somersault exactly one-quarter of a rotation short off platform and landed flat as a pancake during practice. This is like jumping three stories off a bridge and doing a belly flop. He came out of his tuck early when he thought he saw the water and lined up his entry accordingly. His college buddy Jack Romine recalled, "I remember the sound; it was as though a mighty tree had been felled and landed in the water … It was as though everyone stopped breathing." Except for the blood that percolated from his cracked eyelids and that he coughed up, he was fine. His stomach turned blistery red, his eyes turned black and blue, and he hurt for a week. But he showed his true colors by going back at it after his body lost its various colors.

Keith had better luck at the 1972 AAU National Outdoor Championships in Lincoln, Nebraska.[246] Future Olympic champion Phil Boggs led in the three-meter preliminaries. [247] The Ohio native trained at Keith's old stomping grounds in east Mesa. Keith trailed Phil by six points going into finals, which ended up like this:[248]

1. Mike Finneran, future Olympian
2. Keith Russell, future University of Utah coach
3. Phil Boggs, future Olympic champion
4. Don Dunfield, national indoor one-meter champion
5. Jim Henry, Olympic bronze medalist
6. Dennis Hartman, 1969 Pac-10 three-meter champion
7. Mike Brown, future University of Hawaii coach
8. Stan Curnow, future Air Force Academy coach
9. Tim Moore, future Olympian
10. Todd Smith, future University of Tennessee coach
11. Dick Rydze, future Olympic silver medalist
12. John Vogel, 1961 NCAA champion

The platform competition was tight among the top eight finalists:

1. Rick Earley 490.74
2. Mike Brown 488.25 (2.49 from first)
3. Dick Rydze 478.77 (9.48 from second)
4. Joe Crawford 465.30 (13.47 from third)
5. Keith Russell 464.52 (0.78 from fourth)
6. Mike Finneran 462.28 (2.24 from fifth)
7. Phil Boggs 460.47 (1.81 from sixth)
8. Jim Henry 460.41 (0.06 from seventh)
9. Todd Smith 435.90 (24.51 from eighth)
10. Julian Krug 432.93 (2.97 from ninth)[249]

Keith hosted President Richard M. Nixon's daughter, Tricia Nixon Cox, during the women's nationals.[250] Keith's friends took everything.

Future Olympian Janet Ely won the national women's platform title. Future Olympic champion Micki King was runner-up on platform and third on one-meter.[251] And future Olympic bronze medalist Cynthia Potter won both national one-meter and three-meter titles.

Keith went to Chicago for his third Olympic trials, a trip he'd waited four years to make. His parents watched him on television and babysat Rex so Marsha could go too. The trials made history when Mike Finneran's next-to-last platform dive got the only perfect dive score awarded in major meet history. His forward one-and-a-half somersault with two-and-a-half twists garnered a perfect ten from each of the seven judges. However, Michigan star Dick Rydze finished first.

If the 1972 U.S. Men's Olympic Platform Diving Team had been picked based on performance rather than preference, Keith would have made it. But again, fans and judges manipulated the situation to get what they wanted, and they wanted Rick Earley.

The twenty-seven-year-old was both national champion and Pan-Am Games champion on platform, but only Keith executed a successful list of dives. Rick blew one dive when he hit his feet on the platform, but the judges didn't count it against him.[252] He made the final spot on the Olympic team with 540.42, while Keith finished less than a point away in fourth. One witness recalled the tense moments that determined that last Olympic spot:

> The platform event was one of the strangest scored I ever witnessed. The last dives of Rick Early and Keith would determine the outcome. As in Mexico City, both the crowd and the judges seemed to have chosen their "pick" before Early did his final dive. He had a forward 3½ pike and Keith had his trademark forward 1½ with three twists.
>
> Early dove first and received all 9½s. That really put the pressure on [Keith]. But he always performed well under pressure. Early's dive was good, but his knees were "soft" in the pike, and the entry

> wasn't vertical and a little heavy on [the] splash. The crowd and judges were cheering for him. They had basically given the last slot on the Olympic team to him, even before Keith dove.
>
> Everyone knew how [Keith] performed the dive, it had been his signature dive for over six years. He performed the dive as expected, flawless. It was clearly better than the dive Early had done. He would have to score 9½s to beat him. He scored mostly 9s and maybe two 9½s. He missed qualifying for that Olympic team by less than a point.

Keith placed fifth in the springboard trials against thirty-three other male competitors. University of Minnesota graduate Craig Lincoln finished first, Ohio State University graduate Mike Finneran placed second, and University of Wisconsin graduate David Bush, brother of Olympic champion Lesley Bush, took third. Keith lost another spot on the 1972 Olympic team.

It was like wham! Five male divers going to the Olympics and he wasn't one. He'd never considered *that* possibility. He felt he was an Olympic champion waiting to happen. He knew he had it in him. And maybe that's where it would have to stay. At least for another four years. Keith consulted his mentor, Olympic champion Dr. Sammy Lee, who confirmed that he indeed had received unjust treatment. Keith took comfort in knowing that another Olympics would come along before he hit thirty. Maybe that's when he would make his date with destiny and stand on the Olympic podium. Technically though, he had made the Olympics, as an alternate. That was better than nothing. If one of the springboard divers couldn't compete, he would.

Keith's friends dominated the women's Olympic trials. Future University of Arizona and Southern Methodist University coach Cynthia Potter, future Mission Viejo Nadadores coach Janet Ely, and future Air Force Academy coach Micki King all made both the U.S. Women's Olympic springboard and platform diving teams.

Janet Ely grew up studying Keith's diving and partially credited him with her ascent to the top:

> The "first time" I "met" Keith Russell was on film—one of my childhood coaches filmed all the great divers in the world and would have me study "the greats"—one of whom was Keith. I was so mesmerized by his boardwork and his effortless way of making the most difficult dives look easy.
>
> The "second" time I met Keith was in person at Dick Smith's Swim Gym. I was 12 and my parents sent me for two weeks of training. Everyday between my diving workouts, I would stay and watch Keith, Bernie Wrightson, and Patsy Willard, incredible to me that I was watching the world's best and being coached by their coach!
>
> The following year, 1967, I returned to Dick Smith's. Just as on film, Keith, in person struck me—not just in his mechanics, but in his demeanor. He seemed to possess more emotional control than most, very calm, focused. Keith seemed incredibly tolerant, patient, determined.

The 1972 Munich Olympics were intended to present a new, democratic, and optimistic Germany to the world.[253] The capital of Bavaria is in southern Germany. Keith wrote his parents about his feelings of watching his friends compete in the world's greatest diving competition:

> Have been watching a lot of the Olympics. I've enjoyed watching but wish I were there, especially when David Bush didn't make [springboard] finals. Craig Lincoln dove well and was happy he got a [bronze] medal. Micki King came through on 3 mtr. Poor Cindy Potter!

Vladimir Vasin of the Soviet Union, platform and springboard finalist in 1968, won springboard. Franco Cagnotto of Italy, also a 1968 platform and springboard finalist, won the silver. Italy's Klaus Dibiasi, 1968 Olympic champion, placed fourth. Future Alabama and North Carolina State coach Mike Finneran took fifth, and David Bush finished twentieth of thirty-two divers.

On platform, Klaus Dibiasi won his second Olympic gold. Dick Rydze, in first place after the semifinals, scored the silver. Franco Cagnotto claimed the bronze. Rick Earley, second after the semifinals, took sixth, and Mike Finneran finished ninth.

Micki King became Olympic Champion in the women's springboard. Janet Ely placed fourth and Cynthia Potter finished seventh. Janet Ely also took fourth on platform, Micki King took fifth, and Cynthia Potter came in at number twenty-one of twenty-seven.

Keith loved jokes. After the Olympics, he wrote his parents one:

> What did the Polock do after he won his Olympic gold medal? He went home and bronzed it! They have me helping the BYU divers. When is Gary having the baby? I'm anxious to hear it's a boy. Rex needs another boy cousin.

Keith demonstrated more wit when he wrote his parents about Rex's first birthday:

> Rex told me to thank you on his behalf for his birthday card. He got a real laugh out of his grandpa's remark. One year ago I took Marsha to the hospital, Rex being born on a cold early morning. I told Rex we were going to wake him up tomorrow morning (about 3:30 AM) just like he did to us. That announcement didn't scare him none.

Keith received another invitation to compete in Africa that December. This time he competed in Pietersburg and Durban on South Africa's east coast. He won the first meet and placed second in the second meet. Mike Finneran also represented the United States. Lurline wrote about Keith's showing: "He beat those divers who made the Olympics and had shown up so poorly in Munich. I know Keith would have done much better."

Keith thought Durban was the most beautiful place he'd ever visited. It was the first time he realized what a resort looked like. With plush vegetation and colorful flowers, he liked its arrangement on the ocean. The third largest city in South Africa, it is Africa's busiest port. It is most comparable to Los Angeles in population, although geographically, it is almost twice the size.

Although Keith did not reach his goal of making the 1972 United States Olympic Team, he had still accomplished more in the last four years than most people do in a lifetime; he had personally escorted the United States President's daughter at a major national event, broke college conference records, nearly broke world records, traveled the world, saw places forbidden by most to go, got married, and started making babies. Life was good, it wasn't fair, but it delivered some worthwhile compensation.

Chapter 12: Fourth Olympic Trials and a Surprise

Keith began 1973 with some good news and some bad news. First, he announced to his parents, "We found out, happily, that Marsha is about two months along and is due next September. Rex is excited too." The bad news was that Arizona's only ten-meter platform was being torn down. This didn't fly with Keith's plans of making the 1976 Olympic Team. If he wanted to compete on platform, he needed one to practice on.

By age twenty-five, Keith had accomplished a lot: broken national records in swimming, competed in three Olympic diving trials and one Olympics, won four national championships, traveled five continents, and graduated from college. And he was just getting started.

After college, Keith began managing the Dick Smith Swim Gym. That summer, he didn't let lack of money or platform practice stop him from going to the 1973 National Championships in Louisville, Kentucky. And his determination to get where he wanted to go paid off handsomely.

Keith proved he was still a force to be reckoned with when he won silver on both the three-meter and ten-meter. Former Dick Smith diver and future Olympic champion Phil Boggs won the national three-meter title by a mere 3.03 points, with 578.73 to Keith's 575.70. Olympian David Bush followed 17.49 points behind Keith for bronze. Dick Smith, who at one time coached all three medalists, noted how America and Arizona stood in the sport afterwards, "Our diving looks good at this point on the world level. This will put us back on the map for diving in Arizona."[254]

Keith was the biggest name at the time in the platform finals:

1. Tim Moore (1976 Olympian)
2. Keith Russell (two-time Olympian)
3. Mike Brown (future Olympic coach)
4. Todd Smith (future CEO of USA Diving)
5. Phil Boggs (future Olympic champion)
6. Billy Heinz (ranked fourth nationally in 1974)
7. Greg Garlich (coached by Keith's friend, Tom Gompf)
8. Don Craine (future University of Florida coach)
9. Julian Krug (future University of Pittsburgh coach)
10. Peter Agnew (1970 Illinois state champion)
11. Dick Quint (Michigan teammate of Peter Agnew and Don Craine)
12. Mike Motter (Ohio State University diver)
13. Tom Kenyon (1970, 1972, 1973 Missouri state champion)
14. David Bush (1972 Olympian)[255]

Although Keith could only afford a one-way ticket to Kentucky, his second-place finishes at these national championships paid his way home via Yugoslavia, where he qualified to compete in the first World Championships. This without any platform practice.

Swimming World magazine discussed the upcoming World Championships and recalled what happened to Keith five years earlier at the 1968 Olympics:

> The men's team for the World Championships will be a veteran group, with Keith Russell, 25, a member of the 1968 Olympic team, qualifying for both the three-meter and the ten-meter.
>
> Russell, who lost third place in the '68 platform at Mexico City due to highly questionable scoring, placed second in the [national] championship.
>
> The double [qualification] by Russell permitted the AAU Diving Committee to name an alternate, and David Bush was added to the team. Unless Russell withdraws from one of his events, Bush will accompany the team as a tourist, since only two entries per country are permitted in each event.[256]

Before the World Championships, a newspaper article discussed Dick Smith's return to coaching in Arizona and his unparalleled influence in the diving community. It also reported a forgivable untruth about Keith:

> Smith has won about every accolade available in his profession. Only a few short months after returning to the [Phoenix] Valley after his tenure with the Air Force Academy, Smith seems intent on regaining this area's claim to being the diving capital of the world.
>
> Smith just came back from the U.S. swimming and diving championships in Louisville where four of his protégés qualified for the world championships in Belgrade, Yugoslavia.
>
> Following a gold medal at the Mexico City Olympics in '68, Russell has graduated from Brigham Young University and hopes to keep active in his sport in the Valley until the '76 Olympics.[257]

The first FINA (Federation Internationale de Natation) World Championships took place September 1–9, 1973. Yugoslavia, made up of six socialist republics (Slovenia, Croatia, Bosnia, Montenegro,

Serbia, and Macedonia) was bordered by Albania and Greece to the south, Bulgaria to the southeast, Romania to the east, Hungary to the northeast, and Austria to the north. The Adriatic Sea was its western boundary. Belgrade, then the capital of Yugoslavia, is now the capital of Serbia.

Keith's favorite required dive, the reverse layout, received two nines and three eights. Because he nailed that dive ninety-nine times out of one hundred, he made a good leadoff man. His reverse two-and-a-half somersault, not always his best dive, received straight eights.[258]

Swimming World magazine analyzed the poor judging that failed Keith yet again in a review of the World Championships: "Keith Russell had 4 fine dives, one receiving the highest total for any one dive. He was second only to Phil but had to settle for third because Dibiasi, who missed 3 dives, received only one score below 7 on any of them."[259]

Keith beat two Olympic champions (as he often did) at the first World Championships. "Keith Russell took the bronze as Olympic gold and silver medalists Vladimir Vasin of Russia and Franco Cagnotto of Italy were unable to repeat their Munich form."[260] Phil Boggs won by 0.84 of a point.[261] Franco Cagnotto, 1972 Olympic silver and bronze medalist, finished fourth. Vyeceslav Strahov, 1972 Olympic finalist, took fifth, and Olympic Champion Vladimir Vasin finished sixth.

Keith wrote his family about his feelings on his and his teammate's performance:

> My optional dives in the finals weren't that great but no one could do better except Phil and Dibiassi. I feel bad I missed a rev. 2½. Phil Boggs did a fantastic job. He averaged 8.3 pts. on each dive! Klaus Dibiasi was only 3 pts behind Phil where I was 40 pts behind—how embarrassing. Dick was happy though.

Keith really shined on platform, where he won silver with 523.74

behind Klaus Dibiasi. Falk Hoffman of East Germany, 1972 Olympic finalist in both events, followed 31.59 points behind Keith, in third, with 492.13.[262] Torino native Franco Cagnotto finished fourth again and Tim Moore finished sixth.[263]

Swimming World commented on the top two divers:

> Russell came back to perform beautifully on tower and was a solid second behind the always highly scored Dibiasi. Dibiasi was superb for the first half of his list on tower, building up an insurmountable lead. His faulty performance in the last half of the contest only served to cut his margin of victory.[264]

Keith shared his thoughts and feelings on the greatest meet of his life:

> I never dived more consistently in my life. I never dived better. I was diving sharply. Every dive was just boom, boom, boom, boom.
>
> It was the funniest thing, because I got there, and the very first thing I did was I got up on the springboard to do a dive, and I started to do this hurdle, and I just crashed. My legs went right out from under me and I just fell off like a rag doll. And it was so embarrassing.
>
> It was a wonderful experience on the platform. Without any practice all summer, I was doing everything right. It was a really exciting time.[265]

Medaling at the World Championships allowed Keith to feel redeemed from barely missing a medal at the 1968 Olympics. He further shared his thoughts before and after that extraordinary experience:

> It was vindication for having done so poorly in the Olympics—to dive in the World Championships against everyone there; it was the best. For me, it was more meaningful. By then, I had a little more understanding, like, "I may not do well in the World Championships, but it doesn't matter. I'm still going to do this."[266]

For his stellar performance at the first World Championships, Keith made the cover of two magazines. On the December 1973 issue of *Athletic Journal*, Keith is shown in the straight position of a dive with arms out and muscles bulging, going in headfirst. On the January 1974 issue of *Swimming World*, Keith is shown with Phil Boggs. Inside reads, "The United States divers were well represented in international competition due to the successes of Air Force Lieutenant Phil Boggs, 23, and Keith Russell, 25."

Dick Smith wrote an article in that issue of *Athletic Journal* expressing the significance of the World Championships:

> Just one year after the Olympic Games in Munich, the greatest diving contest of all time was conducted.[267]
>
> The World Diving Coaches Association held its convention in Gwat, Switzerland immediately following these championships. More than 50 diving coaches from around the world were present, and more than 32 nations were represented. We were not alone in our feelings concerning the championships being the greatest diving contest ever held in the world.[268]

Dick Smith named Keith and Olympic champions Micki King, Phil Boggs, Russian Vladimir Vasin, and Italian Klaus Dibiasi, as "responsible for diving as it has developed today" and noted the sport's growth. He said that 1973 "was the most energetic and the heaviest diving year for the entire world that the sport has ever seen. From all indications, 1974 will be even more vigorous." Five years after his Olympic experience, Keith was still considered at the top of his game.

Marsha was due with their second child during the World Championships, but that baby, like his older brother, wanted his father there when he was born, so he waited for Keith to get home. On September 23, 1973, Rand Keith Russell was born in Mesa. Marsha appreciated Rand's patience. She wanted Keith there too.

In the meantime, the Dick Smith Swim Gym struggled to stay afloat, so Keith didn't always get paid. Dick received a job offer at a new development twenty-five miles north of Houston called The Woodlands. Dick accepted the job as consultant, then offered Keith a job as activities coordinator, which he accepted.

Lurline wrote in Keith's journal about some of the fancy features of the facility and how the job offer aligned perfectly with Keith's goals of training for the 1976 Olympics:

> It is a beautiful complex with indoor and outdoor pools, a platform, and a machine to soften the blow of platform diving. It sounded like something that would fit in just right for Keith's plans of working toward the '76 Olympics. All the facilities in the world. Arizona lost its platform when Western Savings bought the "hole" and developed "Leisure World." Anyway it seemed an answer to Keith's needs and he was very interested.

Keith coached the Arizona State University divers in January 1974 for Dick Smith while he trained divers in New Zealand for the Commonwealth Games, then recuperated from a fatal Pan American World Airways 707 jetliner crash in Pago Pago, Samoa.[269] One account of the deadly accident has Dick diving out of the plane, another has him kicking open a window and jumping out, and yet another has him walking out of the burning plane. One report, promoting the first and most dramatic escape scenario, reads,

> [Dick's] wife said her husband told her he had only a black eye and a bump on his head and that he was OK. He said many passengers in the plane died because they panicked, and that he survived by diving out of the burning wreckage.[270]

A *Houston Chronicle* version of the crash discussed how Dick Smith's survival affected the design of The Woodlands:

> The airliner struck a stand of palm trees. "There was no warning," said [Dick] Smith. "The first any of us knew we were in trouble is when the wing clipped off a tree. I told myself I was going to ride 'er down and when it was over I was going to get up and walk away." He did. Smith escaped the burning craft and helped rescue several other passengers, all of whom later died. The crash claimed 97 lives.
>
> "But I had the final plans for The Woodlands in my pocket at the time," said Smith. "If I had died, and the plans had burned, I'm sure there would be a different setup."[271]

Keith traveled to Minsk, Belarus for the USSR Championships in March 1974. Belarus is surrounded by Latvia to the north, Russia to the east, Ukraine to the south, and Lithuania and Poland to the west. Minsk is the capital, center, and largest city of Belarus. Keith wrote his family about what he saw and did and received at the USSR Spring Swallow Championships: "I almost made a 3½. The houses are shacks. Wait til you see this jacket they gave us. Tonight we go to the circus. The Minsk circus is one of the best of Europe."

Keith competed in the Los Angeles Invitational. Future Olympic champion Phil Boggs won the three-meter with 636.90 points, four more than his own previous world record. Six-time national champion Tim Moore took second, with 544.30. Keith scored straight 8.5s on his faithful triple twister to follow 4.40 points behind with 539.90. Mike Finneran finished fourth and BYU teammate Stan Curnow took sixth.[272] With nearly every top male diver in the nation, including 1972 Mexican Olympic finalist Carlos Giron, the invitational had the makeup and flavor of a national competition.[273]

The 1974 National AAU Outdoor Diving Championships was a memorable and momentous occasion for Keith, one he walked away from with a big fat shining grin on his face and two big fat shining gold medals around his neck. The nationals took place in August at Point Mallard Park on the Tennessee River in Decatur, Alabama.

Having not trained on platform in over eleven months, Keith made finals in seventh place and ended up national champion.[274] The big names he beat included:

2. Tim Moore (1976 Olympian)
3. Scott Cranham (1972 and 1976 Canadian Olympian)
4. Kent Vosler (1976 Olympian)
5. Steve McFarland (later named Keith 2008 Olympic judge)
6. Mike Finneran (1972 Olympian)
7. Billy Heinz (Ivy League star diver)
8. Mike Brown (future University of Texas coach)
9. Phil Boggs (1976 Olympic champion)

Defending champion Tim Moore applauded Keith's breathtaking performance, telling reporters: "Russell won the championship just as nonchalantly as you please."

One newspaper article discussed the significance of Keith's fifth national title and where he stood in the competitive world of diving:

> For a year, since Leisure World took over the property where the only tower in Arizona stood, Keith has not been able to work out on tower. His last workout on tower was a year ago in the World Championships in Belgrade where he placed second.

On his arrival at Decatur, he managed three workouts before the competition. Dick Smith, his coach, had this to say about him: "He has years of tower diving behind him and is one of the better tower divers in the world."[275]

Keith told an Alabama reporter what he had hoped to get out of the platform competition: "I just can't believe it. It was a surprise. I hadn't even been training this summer. I came to this contest just hoping to make finals so I could gain some points and maybe get enough to be selected for the Pan-American Games."[276]

The national three-meter championships proved even more exhilarating and rewarding, even though Keith felt unspectacular. He recalled later, "I really didn't feel sharp. I didn't feel particularly encouraged. The finals came along, and I just couldn't believe it. I got eights on my first dive—eights! All the judges—eight, eight, eight, eight."

His back dive, his easiest, was also his worst, for which he received 7.5s and 8s. He continues about that mind-blowing experience: "I'm going, 'Wow!' I go up there for my next dive, my reverse dive—eights! The next dive—eights! The next dive—eights! Every single dive, I couldn't believe it."

Keith dove behind reigning world champion Phil Boggs, who consistently received nines. Keith told one interviewer how he won his sixth National Championship:

> We got down to the last couple dives and he missed a dive. So if I hit my last dive, I win, because there's no way you can make up for that. Because I had not missed anything, and he had missed something, there's no way [he could win]. So I went up there, and I nailed my dive for eights and nines.

That was the most amazing thing. Maybe things fell into place because I was so relaxed having won the platform national title.[277]

Dick Smith reviewed the national championships for *Swimming World* and commented on Keith's record-breaking performance and seasoned skill:

The three-meter championship started with 47 men. As far as I can find, Keith's 625.05 for 11 dives established a new national record. Keith finished 53.85 points ahead of Phil Boggs. Keith was ahead of the field on his last three dives and with calm steadiness and nerves of steel, he increased his lead with each dive.[278]

Another reporter added about Keith's most impressive win,

He broke the American record and possibly the world record in the 3-meter with 625.05. Russell won the 3 meter by more 50 points and heads a six-member U.S. diving team which will compete in the international diving meets during the next year.[279]

The Russell family enjoyed watching Keith dive on national television. The big names that followed Keith included:

2. Phil Boggs (1976 Olympic champion)
3. Mike Finneran (1972 Olympian)
4. Tim Moore (1976 Olympian)[280]
5. Steve McFarland (future University of Miami coach)
6. Don Craine (University of Michigan star)
7. Julian Krug (University of Wisconsin's number two diver)
8. Robert Cragg (1976 Olympian)

Steve McFarland started diving with Dick Smith when he was ten. Because his family lived in Texas, he lived with Keith and his parents one summer. After competing at the University of Miami under Tom Gompf, Steve took over and coached legendary divers Greg Louganis and Phil Boggs. He also served as broadcaster at the 1988 and 1992 Olympics and judge at the 2000 Sydney and 2004 Athens Olympics.[281]

A *Swimming World* magazine article focused on Keith's spectacular double hitter when one reader asked Dick Smith, "To what do you, as Keith Russell's coach, attribute his great win on the 10-meter at the Outdoor Nationals and his comeback win on springboard?" Dick pointed out that it was more than just talent and hard work that contributed to Keith's number one national standing when he answered,

> These questions have been asked of me many times since the competition. One of the greatest compliments I have received was when divers who were competing against Keith approached me after the competition and asked me these questions.
>
> I believe that Keith Russell is without a doubt one of the finest trained and most dedicated athletes the United States has ever produced. His lifestyle and behavior are precisely those which a great athlete needs. He has developed a great awareness of the demands that sports make on the individual and the dedication required for success. Meanwhile, he has kept in balance and focus the other important aspects of life, such as family, church, and home.
>
> Though there have been many undesirable situations such as working on homemade equipment and without the use of a 10-meter, as we did this past year, we have built a relationship built on respect, confidence, and direct communication.[282]

The first international competition took place two weeks later in Concord, California, thirty miles northeast of San Francisco, at the USA–East Germany Dual Diving Meet. Keith went into springboard finals with a twelve-point lead. The other three competitors bunched up together with 370, 369, and 368. Phil Boggs executed a near-perfect forward three-and-a-half somersault for his first dive of finals and it was a fight to the finish for the American divers. But Keith won. Phil Boggs finished second and future German Olympic Champion Falk Hoffman finished third.

Swimming World magazine reported on the outcome that had the fans cheering for Keith:

> Phil was even with Keith going into the tenth round and both did outstanding dives—Bogg's reverse 2½ tuck was right on the mark and Keith's reverse 2½ twister brought a roar from the crowd. Still in a virtual tie, Bogg's 2½ with full twist scored him 74 points so Keith had to come through with a truly great triple twister to eke out a one-point victory.[283]

One newspaper commented on Keith's contribution to his country's excellent showing: "American divers Keith Russell of Mesa and Janet Ely of Albuquerque won their events to give the United States an insurmountable 148 lead in the diving."

Keith also proved to be the top American diver on platform when he finished second to Falk Hoffman. Phil Boggs finished third.

The meet, with a sellout crowd of six thousand fans, made history when John Naber, a University of Southern California student, ended German Roland Matthes' seven-year domination of the two-hundred-meter backstroke. Roland, who held the world record, hadn't lost a backstroke race since 1967. John Naber won it in 2:02.83 to Roland's 2:05.34.

The Keith Russell family moved that fall to Conroe, Texas, thirteen miles north of The Woodlands and forty miles north of Houston. Since The Woodlands was still under construction, Keith and his BYU teammate Stan Curnow, who also took a job there, held practice at the University of Houston.

Keith competed in the New Zealand Games in Christchurch in January 1975 as the only American male diver. Janet Ely, fourth at the 1972 Olympics in both events, was the only American female diver. Keith won the ten-meter after not having dived off one in three months. Aleksandr Kossenkov of the USSR, future Olympic bronze medalist, placed second. The Australians, led by Olympian Donald Wagstaff, took third, fourth, and fifth. Donald Wagstaff won the three-meter, Keith placed second, and Aleksandr Kossenkov finished third.[284]

Janet Ely was grateful for Keith after another country's coach worried her when he told her she came too close to the platform on her reverse two-and-a-halfs. She did one for Keith and asked what he thought. She recalls, "He gave me peace of mind and confidence to have a very successful platform event."

Keith traveled to Rostock, East Germany, for the DDR Championships in March.[285] Rostock, the largest city in the state of Mecklenburg, sits on the south shore of the Baltic Sea. Keith flew to West Berlin, 120 miles south, and passed through the famous Checkpoint Charlie, the only place to cross the Berlin Wall from West Germany to East Germany for foreigners. Erected in 1961, the eighty-seven mile long, twelve foot high, four foot wide wall became a symbol of the Cold War, literally separating East and West.

Not surprisingly, East German Falk Hoffman won the three-meter championships of his native country with 582.10. Phil Boggs followed just 3.8 points behind in second with 578.30. Keith took the bronze medal spot, followed by future East German Olympian Dieter Waskow in fourth, future East German Olympian Frank Taubert in fifth, and future four-time Mexican Olympian Carlos Giron in sixth.

Falk Hoffman also became the German National Champion on platform, followed by his teammate Frank Taubert. Phil Boggs took bronze, followed by Dieter Waskow in fourth, and future Olympic silver medalist Carlos Giron in fifth.

The USSR Spring Swallow Championships took place that month in Minsk. Phil Boggs won the three-meter. Pan-Am champion Carlos Giron took second and Keith won bronze with 528.69 points, 18.36 ahead of future World University Games champion Rustvam Bulatov of the USSR in fourth with 510.33.[286]

The 1975 National Indoor Diving Championships immediately followed in April at Cleveland State University. With boundless energy, Keith was one of four divers to place in the top six on both three-meter and platform. The three-meter results:

1. Phil Boggs (1976 Olympic champion)
2. Tim Moore (1976 Olympian)
3. Jim Henry (1968 Olympic bronze medalist)
4. Don Craine (future University of Arkansas coach)
5. Robert Cragg (1976 Olympian)
6. Keith Russell (two-time Olympian)
7. Billy Heinz (four-time Georgia state champion)
8. Scott Reich (future University of Arkansas coach)

The platform results:

1. Tim Moore (five-time NCAA champion)
2. Phil Boggs (three-time World champion)
3. Keith Russell (six-time national champion)
4. Kent Vosler (1976 Olympian)
5. Don Craine (future Southwestern Conference diving coach of the year)
6. Steve McFarland (two-time World University Games bronze medalist)
7. Jim Henry (five-time NCAA champion)
8. Mike Brown (Dartmouth University star)

Keith's outstanding performance scored him another all-expense-paid trip to Europe. He and national one-meter silver medalist Don Craine flew to Vienna, Austria for a meet. On both springboard and platform, Klaus Dibiasi won, his Italian teammate Franco Cagnotto took second, Keith finished third, and Don Craine took fourth in Austria.[287] Keith was so busy doing what he does best—eating, sleeping, and diving—that he didn't have time to do or see much else. From Vienna in northeastern Austria to Bolzano in northeastern Italy, the divers rented a VW bus and took two days driving through the Austrian Alps via Salzburg in western Austria. They spent a night in Zell am See, Austria, then went to the ski slopes in Kaprun, Austria, where the snow was eight feet deep.

Keith wrote his family about what he saw and thought about Italy:

> We still had our bus in Bolzano so we were able to get around better and have more time to dink around. Bolzano is a valley with at least one river that runs faster than Bob Hayes. I think the river ran so fast because the mountains still had snow on them and many of [the mountains] were close and high. I'm glad I went. Too bad I didn't try out for the World Champs.

At the Bolzano International, Keith won his third bronze medal of the trip, on springboard, behind Klaus Dibiasi and Franco Cagnotto. Don Craine took fourth on platform behind the Italians while Keith finished fifth. Keith received an award for the best front dive with a half twist.

The 1975 Outdoor National Championships took place at The Woodlands in August. They doubled as the Pan-American Games trials. Keith competed as defending champion on both three-meter and ten-meter. With the Olympics eleven months away, the pressure was on.

Keith's parents and two youngest siblings, Rory, twelve, and Ric, ten, drove out to see his new home and support him at his last Outdoor Nationals. When they arrived, no one was home, so they "went all around and tried all the windows and found one that could be open. Put in one of the boys and we were in!" To make up for breaking and entering, Cy mowed his son's huge backyard.

Lurline wrote about seeing Keith, his family, and the Woodlands, and of her opinion of "big families," which came out in a conversation with Keith's Olympic teammate:

> After our loving welcome from Marsha, Rex, and Rand, we drove to Woodlands to see Keith. What a grand place that is and how nice it was to see Keith again. We got some good hugs in and saw a number of other divers there—among them Jim Henry. He mentioned that Marsha was expecting again and Marsha asked him how many he had. He said none, but looked like they were going to have a big family. Marsha said she didn't think 3 was a big family. Jim Henry did! I told him! I told him Keith was my 4th child. What if I'd have stopped at three! I'm glad I had that 4th kid! And the other ones too.

With Cy the oldest of seven, Lurline a middle child of nine, and Keith a middle child of nine, three was just the start of something great.

When the nationals started, Lurline pulled out pen and paper and valiantly recorded each score Keith received on each dive. His scores ranged between a 6.5 (on three dives) and an 8 (on six dives). His back dive and reverse each took three 7.5s and two 8s while his inward and forward pike with a half twist each took straight 7.5s. His forward three-and-a-half somersault and reverse two-and-a-half somersault each received a 7, three 7.5s, and an 8. His best dive, his back one-and-a-half somersault with two-and-a-half twists, took two 7.5s and three

8s and his forward one-and-a-half somersault with three twists took straight sevens.

Keith missed the medals by only 1.83 points with 560.94 to Robert Cragg's 562.77 in third. The University of Pennsylvania graduate received the only perfect ten of the competition. The final three-meter results:

1. Phil Boggs (1976 Olympic champion)
2. Tim Moore (1976 Olympic fifth-place finisher on platform)
3. Robert Cragg (1976 Olympic fifth-place finisher on springboard)
4. Don Craine (future University of Florida coach)
5. Greg Louganis (future four-time Olympic champion)
6. Keith Russell (future Olympic judge)
7. Jim Henry (1968 Olympic bronze medalist)
8. Mike Finneran (1972 Olympic fifth-place finisher on springboard)[288]

When asked who might win the ten-meter title, Tim Moore answered, "Well, Boggs has to be a favorite, and guys like Russell and Finneran can't be counted out." Phil Boggs responded, "I have to go with Tim, although Russell, Finneran and others have to be top challengers."[289]

Dick Smith watched the judging of the ten-meter competition in horror. One Texas journalist documented Dick's reaction to the catastrophic fiasco they called a national meet:

> A diver comes off the 10-meter, his legs spread like a frog's. There is loud applause even before he hits the water, creating a large geyser. The seven judges score him 6½ to 8½. A very good score.
>
> Smith is appalled. "That was not even close to a good dive," Smith growls. "That hurts, it really hurts. It hurts every kid in the contest. It's sheer bias, damned bad judging."

Smith judged the dive a three-pointer. But then he doesn't think he should judge it at all. He doesn't think any coach should be a judge. There is too much room for favoritism. All the judges are coaches.

Another diver comes off the tower. Near-perfect form. He cuts the water cleanly, emerges to a smattering of polite applause. The judges score him no higher than 5½.

"See?" says Smith. "There was no applause when he came off the boards. He has no friends here. The judges don't know him. He's at a psychological disadvantage before he starts. Judging doesn't have the integrity it should have."

Smith's opinions are widely known. He is president of the American Diving Coaches Association, vice-president of the World Diving Coaches Association, a member of the United States Olympic Diving Committee and a member of the AAU Diving Committee.[290]

Both Greg Louganis and Keith dropped one spot in the platform finals and both finished in the same place they did in the three-meter. The platform results:

1. Kent Vosler (1976 Olympic fourth-place finisher)
2. Phil Boggs (1976 Olympic first-place finisher)
3. Tim Moore (1976 Olympic fifth-place finisher)
4. Jim Henry (1968 Olympic third-place finisher)
5. Greg Louganis (1976 Olympic second-place finisher)
6. Keith Russell (1968 Olympic fourth-place finisher)
7. Steve McFarland (future University of Miami coach)[291]

The competition was fierce, the judging crooked, and Keith was dethroned. Therefore, it was good he had other things to look forward to, like welcoming a new baby in January.

Lurline provided some final commentary on the national meet along with feelings, beliefs, and wishes on the last page of the journal she kept for Keith as she wrapped it up:

He was under a lot of stress. I have seen Keith dive better and I felt empathy for him. It always hurts me when disappointment comes into his life. But he's had experience dealing with this sort of thing. And in the end, this is just a passing thing in his life and not the most important thing. A big thing, but not an eternal thing.

We played rook every single minute we had a chance. Didn't have time to do a lot of brooding over the outcome. And we had fun playing. We ate ice cream and had a ball! Loved every minute of being there with them.

The hardest thing I've had to do in a long, long time was say "goodbye" to them. It really hit me about not knowing when we would see them again. And it didn't go away for a long time, that sad feeling of loss about leaving them.

But I've adjusted. And finishing up this story of Keith's life has been quite an experience. Have been proud, happy, sad, living again the experiences of the past.

I'm so proud of you, Keith, of your wife and your two little boys, and hope you get that little girl you want so much. I want you to be happy and get the very best out of life, and always keep your priorities in order and remember that your mother loves you very much—very, very much.

Lurline later reminisced about that fun visit and of her hope that having family around to support Keith cushioned the blow of not medaling in his last outdoor nationals:

Let me recall our vacations these past 5 years. The one that stands out most vividly is our visit to Keith and Marsha's in Conroe, Texas—August 1975. We were doing things every day—going

> to Houston and their famous zoo. Saw the Astrodome and the harbor and we played a lot of rook!
>
> The exciting event was the Nationals. Watching Keith dive has never ceased to be thrilling. It is such a thing of artistic beauty I never tire of it. It wasn't his best meet and he was disappointed at the outcome. But we were so proud of him. We hope we made losing a little easier on him.
>
> This dimmed his hopes of making the 1976 Olympics. This had been his goal. But striving for it has been a growing experience. He has had a lot of growth that way. But when everything is balanced out it has been worth the effort. It has taken him around the world several times, paid for his education, given him job opportunities and experience most people never dream about.

Mindy Russell was born January 17, 1976, two days after Keith turned twenty-eight. And Arizona State University inducted him into its Sports Hall of Fame one year after its establishment. Keith joined New York Yankees outfielder Reggie Jackson, Dallas Cowboy Danny White, and former teammates and Olympic medalists Patsy Willard and Bernie Wrightson. Ironically, Keith never graduated from ASU.

The 1976 National Indoor Championships, Keith's last, took place in Cleveland. While he placed higher than his last outdoor nationals, he still missed the medals. The three-meter results:

1. Tim Moore 604.59
2. Phil Boggs 599.94
3. Don Craine 567.57
4. Keith Russell 546.93
5. Brian Bungum 545.58
6. Greg Louganis 543.30
7. Jim Kennedy 510.96
8. Kent Vosler 501.63

The platform results:

1. Tim Moore 527.01
2. Greg Louganis 525.54
3. Jim Henry 506.94
4. Brian Bangum 488.34
5. Keith Russell 470.97
6. Don Craine 469.23
7. Steve McFarland 463.26
8. Patrick Bieker 450.78

Keith qualified for the Seventh Annual International Diving Meet of the Can-Am-Mex series in May in Fort Lauderdale, Florida.

Keith's humor carried over into his gardening, as he wrote his parents: "We got our garden in. We'll have tomatoes, squash, corn, onions, carrots. I'm positive about my approach. I just hope positive thoughts can grow plants."

The Fort Lauderdale International, or Can-Am-Mex (now known as the Grand Prix), attracted the best divers from Canada, America, Mexico, Italy, Russia, Brazil, and Sweden, among other places. Keith qualified to dive in it the year before but didn't go. It was held at the International Swimming Hall of Fame in southeast Florida.

Keith dove three-meter. He did well in the preliminaries, but botched his last few dives. The results showed America still dominated diving:

1. Phil Boggs, USA
2. Franco Cagnotto, Italy
3. Klaus Dibiasi, Italy
4. Tim Moore, USA
5. Don Craine, USA
6. Greg Louganis, USA
7. Keith Russell, USA
8. Jim Henry, USA
9. Carlos Giron, Mexico

10. Alexander Kosenkov, USSR
11. Porfirio Becerril, Mexico
12. Brian Bangum, USA
13. Scott Cranham, Canada
14. Ken Armstrong, Canada
15. Mathz Lindberg, Sweden
16. Milton Braga, Brazil

Keith wrote his parents afterward about his feelings and plan of attack: "I'm discouraged. I'll fight back because there's hope and because there's only a few more months to go. The trials are June 22–26."

Keith competed in the third American Cup in West Palm Beach, Florida later that month. He commented to his parents on his performance: "The weather was lousy and so was I. My two 6th place finishes were not what my plans included. My diving has been coming along until this past month, since [Nationals]."

The 1976 Olympic Trials took place in Knoxville, Tennessee in June. Keith felt his first six dives—a front, back, reverse, inward, forward with a half twist, and inward two-and-a-half—went flawlessly and was pleased with how they went down. Then came his seventh dive, a forward three-and-a-half somersault. Despite a good takeoff, he came out of his rotation early, disallowing himself to make a clean, vertical entry. He botched it, but he still had four to go and anything could happen. His next dive, a back two-and-a-half somersault, went well. His reverse two-and-a-half somersault went in nicely. Even his new dive, a back one-and-a-half somersault with two-and-a-half twists, was solid. And his final dive, his famous forward one-and-a-half with three twists, went in as expected. But he barely missed the finals. The springboard finalists included:

1. Greg Louganis, California
2. Phil Boggs, Air Force Academy
3. Robert Cragg, Pennsylvania
4. Jim Henry, Colorado
5. Tim Moore, Ohio

6. Jim Kennedy, Tennessee
7. Kent Vosler, Ohio
8. Tom Kenyon, Missouri

At that moment, Keith knew his diving days were over. He still had a chance to make the 1976 Olympic platform team, but he didn't feel that held much promise. He didn't feel on fire.

However, he felt okay with that. If he could just do his best, he would be happy.

Keith's goal on platform was consistency. And he was. His inward two-and-a-half pike brought down straight nines. He ripped every entry, going in clean. He finished his last competition just a few spots shy of a third Olympic berth. The results:

1. Greg Louganis 610.41
2. Kent Vosler 600.12
3. Tim Moore 583.89
4. Phil Boggs 550.95
5. Brian Bungum 531.12
6. Keith Russell 507.30
7. Don Craine 474.30[292]

Despite not achieving his four-year goal of making the 1976 Olympic team, Keith wrote his parents his thoughts and feelings on his Olympic Trials performance with a touch of humor:

> I missed a dive on both tower and springboard. (At least in '72 I didn't miss a dive.) To miss wouldn't have such drastic results if one would smoke the rest of one's dives. I felt I dove well but for some reason I wasn't peaked. I didn't feel bad as I was diving, just didn't smoke any. Maybe the reason is that it's against my religion to smoke.

Keith retired from twenty years of competitive diving with mixed feelings. But from the sound of a letter to his parents, he never lost his love for laughter:

> I live here in Aggie-land (Texas A&M). The jokes here are Aggie jokes. For example:
>
> Two Aggies were building a house. One would hammer then look at his nails and throw one away. This went on for sometime til the other Aggie decided to find out what was happening. "Why are you throwing those nails away?" "Some of these nails have the head on the wrong end," came the reply. "Dummy, those go on the other side of the house!"

Instead of mourning yet another loss, Keith felt a sense of relief. He felt free to try other things, to venture off into fresh territory on a new path of self-discovery. He wanted to move on and explore what other successes he might enjoy, what other talents he might uncover. What opportunities awaited him as a retired diver?

Chapter 13: Life after Competition: Giving Back

After retirement, Keith continued setting goals and listening to his mother's counsel. One day she called him and made him promise to play a game of Boggle. Lurline and her sister Kay Palmer were avid Bogglers, playing twice a week at warp speed well into their eighties. So when Keith and Marsha hosted a party, they broke it out. Keith still had a competitive edge. After finishing third, he announced his goal to become world champion Boggler.

Divers from all over the world came to The Woodlands to be coached by Keith. Particularly during summers, divers came from Brazil, Sweden, Mexico, and Germany. One diver was future University of Hawaii coach Anita Rossing. The only Swedish springboard diver at the 1984 Olympics, Anita placed eleventh. She also competed in the 1988 Seoul Olympics, finishing thirteenth, and won sixteen Swedish national championships. She married Mike Brown, Keith's teammate in Africa.

On August 14, 1978, Keith, Marsha, Rex (six), Rand (four), and

Mindy (two) welcomed Aaron Ray Russell into their family. He was born in Tomball, Texas, twenty miles south of Conroe. He followed the Russell baby tradition of arriving several weeks late.

After four years at The Woodlands, Keith felt he could contribute more to diving through college coaching. He sent resumes to UCLA, Southern California, Alabama, New Mexico State, BYU, and Utah. Only Utah responded, and he got the job. Actually, two: as diving coach, he would serve as assistant business manager for the athletic department. The Russells moved to Salt Lake City where Keith became the University of Utah's first full-time diving coach in 1979.

One University of Utah star diver had prominent college coaches tempting him to transfer to their schools. Nick Gibbs explains how Keith, without knowing, influenced his decision to stay at Utah:

> I remember [Keith] very well as a boy watching him dive for BYU and following his career. [BYU coach] Rollie Bestor used to invite me down for the home meets when I was an age-grouper.
>
> One of my favorite memories is a story that [Arizona coach] Win Young told me about the 1968 Olympics. I was competing in the Western Regional qualifying meet for the NCAA's and we had just learned that Keith would be coming to the U. of U.
>
> The coaches at Arizona and Arizona State [Ward O'Connell] were trying to convince me to leave Utah and go to their school to finish my college career. Win was coaching at the University of Arizona and I had known him for years.
>
> During the break between prelims and finals, Win was trying to talk me into coming to Arizona. For some reason he recalled the scene during the finals of the platform event in Mexico in 1968.
>
> Win had just completed his final dive and Keith was up top preparing to do his final dive. Keith was contending for a medal against Klaus Dibiasi and 3 Mexican divers.

> The last of the Mexicans finished and only Keith could knock them out of the medals. According to Win, the crowd was horrible. They booed and heckled Keith because he was an American in position to defeat the Mexican divers.
>
> Win told me he was standing next to the Mexican divers (Alvaro Gaxiola and their coach) and implored them to stop the crowd from booing. Win told me he told Alvaro, "You can stop this. How can you let this go on?" Needless to say, none of the Mexican divers responded to Win's urging and the crowd went on heckling this youngster from the USA.
>
> Win was so furious about reliving the moment that he forgot he was trying to recruit me to Arizona. I liked the story so much I decided to stay at Utah to finish my diving.

Keith's old BYU teammate, Stan Curnow, coached at Brigham Young University. In Keith's first meet as a college diving coach, his team competed against Stan's team and his diver, Doug McGregor, won three of four events for Utah.

On women's one-meter, Keith's star diver, Julie Cook, won by 7.4 points with 219.70. Stan's star diver, Lucy Wardle, took second with 212.30, and Utah's Susan Clotworthy finished third. Susan Clotworthy's father, Bob Clotworthy, was one of America's greatest divers. He won Olympic bronze in 1952 and Olympic gold in 1956.

Keith spent the last two weeks of December in Hong Kong with the University of Utah swimming and diving team. Don Reddish, Utah's athletic director, didn't want his swimmers and divers neglecting their training during the holidays, so he enticed them with exotic trips where training was part of the deal. Keith wrote his parents about an odd experience he had there:

> We saw an interesting thing the other nite. These fortunetellers

> contrived an unusual way of [fortune telling]. They train these cute little birds to pick up a card that has the person's fortune on it. It works like this. The fortuneteller shuffles these cards and then he opens up a door in which a little bird is caged. The little bird hops out, looks at the cards, then pecks and pulls out one card. The bird gets a little food then hops back into his cage. The fortuneteller explains the card to the sucker, shuffles the cards again, opens another door to a different bird which hops out and pulls out the identical card which was previously explained. That which is not explained is that the card has on its edge heroin and the bird can smell the drug because the little thing is addicted to it.

Utah traveled to Laramie for a dual meet against the University of Wyoming in January 1980. Doug McGregor won the one-meter by 45.40 with 328.15, setting a Corbett Pool record.

The Western Athletic Conference Championships were at the University of New Mexico. Keith's clan coolly creamed the competition, claiming both men's conference titles.

One-meter medals:

1. Doug McGregor, Utah
2. Nick Gibbs, Utah
3. Tom Doyle, New Mexico

Three-meter medals:

1. Doug McGregor, Utah
2. Tom Doyle, New Mexico
3. Ricardo Belarde, BYU

That year, Doug McGregor set the school record for most points on three-meter in an eleven-dive meet: 539.9.[294] Utah won the WAC championship by seventy-one points.

The following week, Keith, Doug, and Julie returned to Albuquerque for the NCAA zone-qualifying meet. Doug won one-meter but finished eighth on three-meter, so he only qualified for the NCAAs on low board. Keith thought Doug could have qualified on three-meter had he not "run out of gas."

Keith showed his true colors when another coach had his diver, Julie Cook, disqualified. Keith and his divers arrived in Albuquerque on Sunday and he wanted them to practice that day. Julie recalls how Keith kindly handled her refusal to train on the Sabbath, "I made the decision in my youth never to dive on Sunday. Keith gently encouraged me to consider just this once but supported me in my decision. I dived horribly. I was ranked fourth going into the [one-meter] meet of forty-plus divers. I didn't even make the first cut!"

Julie told Keith after that bad experience that she would not dive three-meter and embarrass herself again. But Keith persuaded her to. He filled out her entry form and they practiced hard that night. The work seemed to pay off the next day, as she made the first cut. After the next three dives, she was set to make finals when a coach stopped the competition and approached the meet officials. After a delay, they called Keith to the table. He had filled in Julie's dives incorrectly, putting her best dives first, both twisting dives. NCAA rules say a diver cannot perform two dives from the same category in the first two cuts, so they failed Julie's second twisting dive, which knocked her out of finals and bumped that coach's diver up into her place. Julie expressed her feelings of that crushing experience:

> Poor Keith! This was his 1st experience coaching at a University. It was so sad because I had had such a great year and there were some high hopes and expectations for me and I left the meet with nothing. Keith could have been frustrated that I didn't work out on Sunday and I could have been sad my sheet had been filled out wrong. But neither of us had hard feelings. No one to blame.

The 1980 NCAA Championships took place at Harvard in March. Hobie Billingsley at Indiana University and Dick Kimball at Michigan (both recruited Keith) still produced the best collegiate divers, with each getting three in finals. The Big Ten Conference clearly dominated college diving with Ohio State, Illinois, and Minnesota bringing the total to nine Big Ten divers in finals. Doug McGregor hit his feet on one-meter on his forward two-and-a-half pike and failed to place in the top thirty-three.

The one-meter finalists:

1. Greg Louganis, Miami
2. Robert Bollinger, Indiana
3. Kevin Wright, Ohio State
4. Kevin Machemer, Michigan
5. Chris Snode, Florida
6. Niki Stajkovic, Indiana
7. Ron Merriott, Michigan
8. Rick Theobald, Illinois
9. Rick Tennant, Southern Methodist
10. Doug MacAskill, Indiana
11. Brent Bordson, Minnesota
12. Ken Vigiletti, Michigan[295]

Julie Cook usually won conference dual meets, except against BYU. Keith judged her to be the best collegiate diver on one-meter in the Intermountain Area. Utah's swimming coach, Don Reddish, spoke of Utah's diving coach: "The state has two of the finest diving coaches in the country in Bob Clotworthy and [Keith] Russell. Both have been champions and are great teachers."[296]

Marsha's father offered Keith a job at his business supply store in Mesa that summer. Keith accepted the position, but had to finish the school year before taking it.

Keith spent Christmas 1980 with the University of Utah swimming and diving team in Guatemala. They didn't work out as much as planned, because it was cold, but they did make it to the beach.

Kerri Ann Russell, Keith's fifth child, was born on January 14, 1981 in Salt Lake.

Keith and BYU coach Stan Curnow went to Albuquerque with their female divers for the AIAW qualifying meet for Women's Nationals. Founded in 1971 before the NCAA supported women's sports, The Association for Intercollegiate Athletics for Women directed women's collegiate sports and administered the national championships. The AIAW closed in 1983 when the NCAA began offering women championships.

Keith shared his usual and favorite thoughts with his parents in a letter from the meet: "Can't think of much to do but eat. That's okay with me." His diver, Julie Cook, qualified on one-meter to go to the nation's most prestigious college championships.

San Diego State University hosted the 1981 Western Athletic Conference Championships. Keith's divers helped the University of Utah win the team title by 222 with 566. The University of Hawaii took second with 344.

Doug McGregor not only won the one-meter conference title by twenty-two points, he set a new conference record. He won the three-meter conference title by an even larger margin of 65.67 points.

Conference one-meter medalists:

1. Doug McGregor, Utah 500.90
2. Craig Schweiger, Hawaii 478.90
3. Tom Doyle, New Mexico 466.30

Conference three-meter medalists:

1. Doug McGregor, Utah 515.15
2. Craig Schweiger, Hawaii 449.58
3. Casey Jones, BYU 443.55

In Keith's two years at the University of Utah, he had four for four: his diver had won both boards at both conference championships.[297]

The twelfth annual AIAW Championships, or "Women's Nationals," also took place at the University of South Carolina in Columbia. From the Western Athletic Conference, Hawaii's Michele Loiseau placed the highest in twenty-third. Future Olympic silver medalist Michele Mitchell of the University of Arizona followed 0.12 of a point behind, in twenty-fourth. Julie Cook was thirty-second, ahead of chief conference rival Lucy Wardle, in thirty-fifth out of forty-one divers.[298]

The 1981 National Indoor Championships took place in Columbus. As a first-time coach at nationals, Keith did well with his diver beating future Olympians, including 1984 Olympic silver medalist Bruce Kimball in twenty-eighth. The one-meter results:

1. Greg Louganis, Miami (Olympic champion)
2. Ron Merriott, Michigan (1984 Olympic bronze medalist)
3. Dave Burgering, Michigan State (1980 Olympian)
4. Randy Ableman, Iowa (1981 NCAA champion)
5. Rick Theobald, Southern Illinois (future Auburn University coach)
6. Kevin Machemer, Michigan (1980 Olympian)
7. Matt Chelich, Michigan (1977 and 1979 NCAA champion)
8. Ron Meyer, Arkansas (1985 NCAA champion)
9. Matt Scoggin, Texas (1992 Olympian)
10. David Lindsey, Texas (1980 Texas state champion)
11. Steve Eberle, Ohio State (1981 Big West Conference champion)
12. Robbie Bollinger, Indiana (1981 and 1982 NCAA champion)
13. Doug Shaffer, UCLA (1986 NCAA champion)
14. Lenny Layland, Miami (1978 Florida state champion)
15. Doug McGregor, Utah (Western Athletic Conference champion)
16. Jesse Griffin, Michigan State (1978 Big Ten Conference champion)

17. Mike Wantuck, Ohio State (1980 Junior Olympic champion)
18. Roy Botsko, Miami, (future Masters national champion)
19. Brent Fichter, Tennessee (transferred from Florida State)
20. Mark Bradshaw, Ohio State (1988 Olympian)

Former Ohio State coach Ron O'Brien, head coach of the Mission Viejo divers in California from 1978 to 1985, placed eight divers in the top fifteen on three-meter, including Greg Louganis in gold and Dave Burgering in bronze. Michigan coach Dick Kimball placed divers in half the rest of the top fifteen spots, including Ron Merriott in silver. Doug McGreger finished twenty-seventh. After two years at Utah and six years away from Arizona, Keith moved "home" and worked at his father-in-law's printing shop in Mesa.

Chapter 14: A Diving Club of His Own: Rising Nationally

Diving was in Keith's blood. He couldn't stay away. Soon after moving back to Arizona in 1981, he began attending local diving meets organized by Mesa Parks and Recreation to scout out talented kids to join his club. Keith started the Mesa Desert Divers with Barbara Minch, who dove with him at BYU. After his brother Rory returned from his two-year church mission to the Philippines in 1983, he coached at Keith's club.

Mike Moak, who Keith coached to a state title, several college conference titles, the NCAAs, and senior nationals, became interested in diving at this time. His mother writes about the important role Keith played:

> Mike's interest in diving began at age 11 in 1982 when his mother signed him up at the Powell [Junior High] pool to take a two-week diving course with the Mesa Parks & Recreation Department. It was during those two weeks that he met Keith

Russell who later became the most significant influence in his diving career. By 1986, he was competing on the Desert Divers traveling team.

Keith found another future champion at the Mesa Junior High pool. He approached this young diver's mother and said he had a club he'd like her son to join. After he gave her his card and left, her son, Scott Turner, came up to her and asked, "Mom! Do you know who that was?!"

She replied, "Yes. That was your father's cousin's brother-in-law."

He answered "No! He's an Olympian!"

She thought that unlikely, but she signed him up and eventually found out it was true. Keith coached Scott Turner to two state titles, a Western Athletic Conference title, the NCAAs, and senior nationals.

Regan Mark Russell completed the Keith Russell family when he was born in Phoenix on September 2, 1983.

Keith and his family received an invitation from the U.S. Olympic Committee to be in a parade at Disneyland. The committee had Olympians promote the 1984 Los Angeles Olympics. This was the first Russell family trip to California. They enjoyed dinner at the Blue Bayou, which imitated a backyard dinner party on a Southern plantation. The restaurant was part of the Pirates of the Caribbean ride, the last attraction Walt Disney oversaw.

Keith and Rory drove to Los Angeles to watch the 1984 Olympic Games, and caught the women's springboard finals. Sylvie Bernier became Canada's first Olympic diving Champion. Kelly McCormick, four-time Olympic champion Pat McCormick's daughter, won the silver. By the time this Ohio State University graduate retired in 1990, she had become the first two-time Pan-American Games female springboard champion. Michigan graduate Christina Seufert won bronze. Anita Rossing, who represented Sweden and had trained with

Keith at The Woodlands, finished eleventh. The American women took the same medals on platform: Michele Mitchell won silver and Wendy Wyland got bronze.

Keith and Rory watched the men's springboard and witnessed Greg Louganis win his first Olympic gold by 92.10 points. Tan Liangde, in China's Olympic diving debut, won silver and Michigan graduate Ronald Merriott followed 0.99 of a point behind for Olympic bronze. Hongpong Li, who later coached one of Keith's Olympic divers, placed fourth. Keith's old coach, Dick Smith, coached the Egyptian divers.

Keith's best female diver, Valerie Hale, entered her freshman year of high school in 1985 and took sixth at state. She later dove for Keith at Brigham Young University.

In 1986, Keith took his top five divers, Valerie Hale, Mike Moak, Dalin Crandall, Stephanie Guariglio, and Paul Keplar, to Mission Viejo, California, for Region VIII meets. Seven states fed into Region VIII: California, Nevada, Arizona, New Mexico, Utah, Wyoming, and Colorado. Valerie finished tenth on three-meter, which disappointed her, so she promised herself she'd do better next time. Regionals qualified divers for zones, which qualified divers for Junior Nationals.

Mission Viejo is where top diving coaches like Olympic champion Sammy Lee, Olympic coach Ron O'Brien, Olympian Janet Ely, and two-time Olympian Hongping Li coached top divers like Olympic champion Greg Louganis, Olympian Matt Scoggin, Olympic silver medalist Michelle Mitchell, and Olympic champion Jennifer Chandler.

Mike Moak qualified for Junior Nationals in Orlando. After only three years of diving, he finished twelfth on one-meter in the thirteen-and-fourteen age-group.[299] Even with ten years of coaching experience, it was a phenomenal feat to place a diver that new that high at a major national competition. Future Olympic silver medalist Scott Donie won both three-meter and platform in the fifteen-seventeen division.

At the 1986 Arizona state high school meet, Valerie Hale, a sophomore, took second.[300] Mike Moak, a sophomore at Dobson High School in Mesa, won the men's state title. Keith commented on Mike's astonishing win: "Mike has fantastic potential. To come up from three or four years of diving and become a state champion … that's a pretty good statement right there. He's come a long, long way."[301]

The 1987 Region VIII Junior Olympic championships were at Arizona State University and qualified divers for the zone championships. The *Mesa Tribune* named Keith's divers Mike Moak, Valerie Hale, Devan Porter, and Stephanie Guariglio as "top Arizona entries."[302]

Mike Moak, Valerie Hale, Devan Porter, and Scott Turner all had top-two finishes. Another star, Julie Pothier, finished third in the girl's twelve-and-thirteen age-group one-meter. All five went on to dive for Keith at BYU.

The *Arizona Republic* wrote about Keith, his club, and his reasons for creating the club:

> Keith Russell, coach of Mesa's Desert Divers, never lost touch with his diving roots. And now he is giving some of the knowledge he accumulated back to the youngsters he teaches.
>
> Russell, 39, started the Desert Divers for kids 18 and under four years ago. This weekend he will take his 15-member squad to Beaverton, Ore., for a Zone Qualifying meet. The top divers advance to the Junior Olympics in Irvine, Calif.
>
> Grooming future champions is not what Russell's life is about. He only wants to give young divers the opportunity to improve in a sport they enjoy.
>
> "There's one big reason I'm doing this," said Russell, who is co-owner of Lofgreen's Printing and Office Supply Co. "I feel like I have something to give. And as long as the city of Mesa is going to

give me that opportunity then I would like to take that opportunity to the advantage of the kids.

"I get a lot of personal satisfaction from it. In 10 or 15 years to see these kids become something in the community makes it worthwhile."

The Desert Divers practice five days a week at Taylor Junior High in Mesa. Practices run from 5–7 p.m. Monday thru Friday, and twice a week the team practices from 5:30–7 a.m. Russell comes to practice straight from work.

Russell receives some compensation for his time (he charges $40 a month). But he did not form the Desert Divers for financial reasons. "It's not a moneymaking project," he said.

It is a project that takes up much of Russell's time and one that has made strides in the past year. Two members of the team—Mike Moak and Valerie Hale—placed first and second in the state high school diving meet this year.

Russell has seen his team make steady progress. Several—Mike Moak, Matt Eastin, Craig Narveson, and Devan Porter—have legitimate opportunities to reach the Junior Olympics. To do so, a diver must finish in the top five on 1-meter or 3-meter. The 16–18 age-group take the top seven.[303]

Matt Eastin's father, Hal Eastin, had been Arizona's best diver until Keith came around. At Zone Championships in Beaverton, Oregon, Mike Moak advanced to junior nationals on three-meter. Another Desert Diver, Craig Narveson, considered Arizona's top diver in the boys' fourteen-and-fifteen age-group division, won the one-meter and finished second on three-meter. Scott Turner also qualified for nationals on both boards, placing second on one-meter and third on three-meter behind Craig.

Keith said of Scott Turner's incredible performance: "He kind of came out of nowhere. That age-group isn't nearly as competitive as the

16–18 is, but for someone who's only been diving for two years, that's really good." Keith made some predictions for Craig: "He should make it to the finals (top twelve) at nationals and probably place in the top six."[304]

Devan Porter missed qualifying on one-meter by just a point and a half. Keith expressed his thoughts of Devon's performance and potential: "It was the first meet of that caliber he dove in and he did well. Next year I have no doubts he'll make it."[305]

Seven Arizona divers qualified for the 1987 U.S. Diving Junior Olympics. Keith had three and the Sun Devil Divers, founded in 1970 by Ward and Joel O'Connell, had four divers. Ward was Arizona State University's diving coach and Keith's Pan-American Games coach. His wife, Joel, was a nine-time national champion.

Craig Narveson finished eighth and Scott Turner sixteenth in the national one-meter. On three-meter, Craig finished ninth, Scott twenty-first, and Mike Moak twenty-fifth of thirty-seven of America's best young divers.[306] Keith guessed right about Craig: he made finals.

At the 1987 Arizona State High School Championships at ASU, Keith's divers took the top four spots in the men's diving. Matt Eastin won, Mike Moak followed 0.60 of a point behind in second, Scott Turner followed 3.70 points behind in third, and Dalin Crandall took fourth.

Keith had two divers in the top four in women's diving. Valerie Hale finished third and Marlo Lenox took fourth. Marlo graduated valedictorian from Dobson High in 1988 and got accepted to Stanford University, where she continued diving. Stanford's diving program is one of the nation's best. In fact, Stanford was the reigning NCAA Champion in swimming and diving for the third consecutive year.

The 1988 Region VIII Junior Olympic Championships took place at UC San Diego. While no Arizona divers won, Keith's divers took top spots:

Devan Porter finished second on both boards in the twelve-and-thirteen age-group. Mike Moak was third in the sixteen-to-eighteen three-meter of twenty-nine entrants and fourth on one-meter out of thirty. Scott Turner followed in fifth on one-meter.

Stephanie Guariglio was the highest-placing female Arizona diver in the twelve-and-thirteen division three-meter, at sixth out of twenty-four. Julie Pothier was the highest-placing female Arizona diver in the fourteen-and-fifteen one-meter, at seventh, also out of twenty-four. Valerie Hale finished sixth out of fifty-four entrants in the girls' sixteen-to-eighteen one-meter and ninth out of forty-six on three-meter.

The *Arizona Republic* featured one of Keith's best divers, Scott Turner, who had shown rapid growth in the sport, thanks to some excellent coaching:

> About a year ago, Scott Turner made a serious commitment toward his diving. Last year, with little competitive experience, Turner advanced to the Junior Olympics in the 14–15 age division. His progress was considered extraordinary.
>
> "He had been diving year-round for less than a year and to make it to nationals last year was just an awesome accomplishment," said Keith Russell, who coaches Turner.
>
> "I've learned a lot in the last year," said Turner. "Keith's a good coach. He taught me an entire high board (3-meter) list in one year and most of a low board (1-meter) list." Turner gets good elevation on most of his dives. "He's an amazingly strong and powerful diver," Russell said.
>
> Turner began diving four years ago with Mesa Parks and Recreation. His interest in the sport began to increase when he began seeing positive results. "When you progress it's a lot of fun," Turner said.[307]

Eleven Arizona divers qualified for the 1988 National Junior Olympic Championships, four more than the year before. Keith had four, one more than the year before. Mike Moak and Scott Turner qualified again with Devan Porter and Stephanie Guariglio. Two other qualifiers had previously been Desert Divers: Craig Narveson and Matt Eastin, of Phoenix Diving Club. The Sun Devil Divers also qualified four.[308]

The U.S. Junior Olympics took place in Orlando, Florida.

Devan Porter finished twelfth on one-meter and twentieth on three-meter. Stephanie Guariglio was fourteenth on three-meter and eighteenth on one-meter. Mike Moak finished fifteenth on platform and Scott Turner took thirty-third on one-meter.[309]

The *Arizona Republic* highlighted the Arizona divers' success at Junior Nationals:

> The success of the Arizona Diving Association can be measured by the number of youngsters who qualify for the Junior Olympics. And with that criteria, it was an extremely successful year for the ADA. Eleven Arizona divers competed at the Junior Olympics in Orlando, Fla.
>
> "This was the best showing Arizona has ever had," said Joel O'Connell, coach of the Sun Devil Divers. "We were well represented at the nationals." And the Sun Devil Divers was the top team from Arizona. The Sun Devil Divers finished 13th in the nation, their best finish ever.
>
> Mesa's Desert Divers, coached by Keith Russell, also were well-represented at nationals.[310]

At the 1988 Arizona High School State Championships, Scott Turner creamed his competition, winning by 55.90 points with 493.75. His former teammate Matt Eastin followed in second, with 437.85.

Valerie Hale won the state title for the women. Keith's male divers had won every state title for the last three years, but this was the first time both a male and female won.

After exceptional diving at the Senior Nationals in Boca Raton, Florida, Mike Moak and Sun Devil diver Amy Garner were selected by U.S. Diving to represent the United States on the Junior National Team in Germany, at the Aachen International Diving Meet in May 1989. Aachen, Germany is near Belgium and the Netherlands, which he saw. The trip was a highlight of Mike's diving career.

That year, Valerie Hale's father lost his job and couldn't pay for her diving. Because developing character was more important to Keith than making money, and because Valerie was a dedicated athlete, he offered to coach her for free. Keith had already done this with another star diver, future Western Athletic Conference champion Julie Pothier, who later said this about him:

> If it weren't for Keith, I would not have been the kind of diver I was. When I was 11, Keith talked to my parents about me joining his club team. I am the sixth child of nine, and it just was not possible for my parents to pay the monthly fees in training. My parents expressed this to Keith and he told them he would coach me without pay. If it wasn't for this selfless act, I would have never had the opportunities I had with diving. This is the type of man Keith was in all areas of his life. He was well respected by all the coaches.
>
> As a diver I felt Keith always put my needs and goals for diving ahead of his own. He was offered the BYU job when I was a senior in High School and so I only had to go one year without him as my coach. I was glad to dive with him again at BYU and I knew that is where he deserved to be.

The 1989 National Junior Olympic Championships took place at The Woodlands. Keith had five divers qualify. Mike Moak and Scott Turner qualified for the third time, Devan Porter qualified for the second time, and Valerie Hale and Melanie Mabry qualified for the first time. All five dove for Keith at Brigham Young University.

Devan Porter won one-meter at Regionals. Mike Moak qualified in second on platform and third on both boards, Scott Turner qualified in sixth on both boards and Valerie Hale qualified in seventh on both boards out of over forty divers.

At Junior Nationals, Mike Moak finished just 0.60 of a point from seventh in eighth and Scott Turner finished thirty-first on three-meter out of thirty-three. Mike finished twelfth and Scott twenty-sixth on one-meter out of thirty-two, behind future four-time NCAA champion Dean Panaro, in first.

Melanie Mabry finished eleventh on one-meter against future Pan-American Games silver medalist Jenny Lingamfelter in ninth. Valerie Hale finished sixteenth on three-meter out of thirty-five divers. Keith's effort to develop goal-oriented and motivated youth produced some of the best young divers in the nation.

Keith hosted a Dick Smith Swim Gym reunion at his house that year. Many of the world's greatest divers and coaches recalled their memories of Dick.

Olympic bronze medalist Ann Peterson moved from Seattle to train with Dick Smith. She noted that the fear factor in diving made it "a sport better than most sports." Nancy Poulson, a local, expressed the same sentiment. She turned to Dick and said, "Thank you for the trauma. Everything's been pretty easy ever since!"

Olympic silver medalist Jeanne Collier Sitzberger said, "I do owe a lot to this man, because without the training and discipline we went through, I don't think I could have gotten through a lot of things I've had to deal with in my life, so it's been nice to draw on that strength."

Earlier in the decade, Jeanne lost her husband, 1964 Olympic champion Ken Sitzberger.

Toivo Ohman, a 1956 Swedish Olympian, came from Stockholm. He noted that the diving world knew Dick Smith more than any other American coach and that he was America's finest ambassador of diving. Toivo added that for Dick, diving was not a goal, but "a means to building a complete personality."

Olympic champions Sammy Lee (1948 and 1952), Bob Clotworthy (1956), Lesley Bush (1964), and Bernie Wrightson (1968), attended along with 1964 Olympic silver medalist and Harvard graduate Frank Gorman, who credited Dick with putting him on the 1964 Olympic Team.

Perhaps one reason Keith was so highly esteemed among colleagues, teammates, divers, friends, and family is that the high caliber people that surrounded him rubbed off onto him. They were goal-setting, hard-working, high-achieving, never-quitting, fun-loving, go-getters.

The Zone Qualifying Meet for the 1990 Junior National Olympics took place in Mission Viejo, California. Of Keith's ten divers who qualified for Zones, four qualified for Nationals: Scott Turner took fourth on three-meter and sixth on one-meter to qualify for his fourth time. Devan Porter took second on one-meter and third on three-meter to qualify for the third time. Melanie Mabry was fifth on three-meter and sixth on one-meter to qualify for the second time. Jenny Rogers won one-meter and finished fourth on three-meter.[311]

The 1990 National Junior Olympic Championships took place at ASU in August. Melanie Mabry won bronze on three-meter and finished fifth on one-meter. Jenny Rogers finished eighth on one-meter and sixteenth on three-meter. Devan Porter got ninth on both one-meter and platform and tenth on three-meter. Scott Turner was nineteenth of thirty on three-meter and twenty-fifth on one-meter.

Scott Turner graduated from Mesa High School that year. After being recruited by such top universities as Yale, Dartmouth, Cornell, Fordham, and Boston University, as well as the universities of Georgia, Hawaii, Kansas, Tennessee, and Toledo, he picked BYU.

Keith was named 1991 Region VIII Coach of the Year for producing some of the best young divers in the United States. In the summer of 1992, BYU invited Keith to come up and do a diving camp. Afterwards, they offered him a job as BYU diving coach. He accepted. *Cougar World* quoted BYU athletic director Glen Tuckett about Keith: "We couldn't tailor-make a better person to fill this position. Keith has excellent qualifications."

At age forty-four, Keith took a job that would catapult him into the prestigious scene of college coaching and conference championships. It would give him a name in diving, give him the opportunity to create national champions, and send him around the world. Keith was on his way to international prominence in the world of diving.

Chapter 15: College Coaching II and Coaching National Teams

Keith had an impressive list of strong divers his first year at BYU:

Vanessa Bergman, 1988 Olympic Trials finalist and World Junior Champion

Valerie Hale Blau, two-time NCAA qualifier

Laurel Hill, 1991 Utah Summer Games champion

Lance Clark, Mesa Desert Diver

Mike Moak, Arizona state champion

Ted Everett, nationals qualifier

Keith let his presence be known from the get-go at his first meets as BYU diving coach. Against the University of New Mexico and New Mexico State University, Vanessa Bergman won both boards at both meets for the women while Mike Moak won both boards for the men.[312] Keith wrote his parents about what was important to him: "We always have to work our tails off. The good news is we eat pretty good."

BYU women ended the dual meet season with ten wins and one loss, posting 6-0 against fellow WAC teams. BYU men finished the season with seven wins and one loss.

Keith's stars won one team title, three individual titles, two silver, one bronze, and set one record in the women's one-meter at the 1993 Western Athletic Conference Championships in Las Vegas. Vanessa Thelin won two titles on the boards with Valerie Blau runner-up on both.[316] Because Keith was the winning team's coach, he got tossed into the pool as per tradition. There would be many tossings of Keith into the water in the future.

Sophomore Mike Moak won the WAC three-meter title and bronze on the one-meter. A recap stated that, "Mike Moak provided most of the diving highlights in 1992–1993. Moak placed consistently high throughout the season."

A *Daily Universe* article commented on the major contribution diving made to the conference championships:

> "We (the WAC) aren't in the same universe as the PAC-10, but we are probably the top 6th or 7th conference in the NCAA," [BYU swimming coach] Crump said. BYU has pulled ahead in the conference with outstanding diving.
>
> "We left a couple swimmers at home so we could bring more divers," Crump said. "All five of our kids (divers) did awesome."
>
> Crump said the other teams couldn't match BYU diving and that the diving won the WAC crown for the Cougars.[317]

The NCAA Zone E Diving Championships was an NCAA qualifying meet for divers from over twenty Division I schools in three college athletic conferences in the western half of the United States.

The Pac-10 schools provided some of the nation's toughest competition:

Stanford, eight-time NCAA team champions

Southern California, nine-time NCAA team champions

UCLA, 1982 NCAA team champions

California, two-time NCAA team champions

Arizona, coached by Olympic bronze medalist Cynthia Potter

Arizona State, coached by Ward O'Connell until 1997

The Western Athletic Conference schools with diving programs included:

From Colorado: Air Force Academy and Colorado State University

From Utah: Brigham Young University and University of Utah

As well as Fresno State, New Mexico, Hawaii, and Wyoming.

Big West Conference schools with diving programs included:

From California: UC-Irvine and San Jose State

From Nevada: UNLV and Nevada-Reno

New Mexico State

Keith produced two more champions at zones in March: Vanessa Thelin and Mike Moak, both on three-meter.[318] Valerie Blau finished second on one-meter and fourth on three-meter.[319]

In his first year as Brigham Young University's diving coach, Keith proved he could create not only the best divers in the western half of the United States, but in the country, by placing two female divers in the top twenty on both boards at the NCAAs in Minneapolis. Vanessa Thelin won silver and Valerie Blau finished eleventh on one-meter, behind Auburn diver Marina Smith, who won the sixth NCAA one-meter title for the Southeastern Conference in the twelve years of the Championships.

Vanessa was first in the three-meter preliminaries but finished twelfth with 456.35, while Valerie finished nineteenth, behind Stanford's defending NCAA champion, Eileen Richetelli.[320]

Two-time Olympic silver medalist and future Arizona coach Michelle Mitchell later stated, "If you get anybody into NCAAs, either one or two divers, it's huge."[321] Keith had three, with Mike Moak, who finished seventeenth on three-meter and thirtieth on one-meter. Miami's two-time NCAA champion, Dean Panaro, won both boards for the Southeastern Conference. Keith thought Mike had a chance for All-American honors, but he hit his heels on his back one-and-a-half tuck.

Season Two

Keith's son Aaron, a high school sophomore, won the 1994 Utah state high school championships. While Keith strived to help young adults realize their athletic potential, success seemed to follow him and everyone he touched seemed to turn to gold, or at least find themselves in winner's circles.

Keith's 1993 conference champions defended their titles, broke more records, and won an additional title at the 1994 Western Athletic Conference Championships in Las Vegas in March. Vanessa Thelin broke the one-meter WAC record by 41 points with 495 and the three-meter WAC record by 34.85 with 572.80. Freshman Cristina Conn followed 97.50 points behind in second on three-meter, with 475.30.

BYU women won the Western Athletic Conference team title by 126 points with 609, well ahead of chief WAC rival, Colorado State University, in second with 483. Fresno State followed 96 points behind, in third, with 387. BYU men also won.

As a three-time WAC one-meter champion and a three-time WAC three-meter champion, Vanessa Thelin was on her way to becoming America's best collegiate one-meter diver. At the NCAA Zone E Diving Championships at Southern California, Vanessa easily outdistanced the field of twenty-seven divers on one-meter to win the title. With BYU freshman Cristina Conn in seventh and her freshman teammate Julie Pothier in ninth, Keith had three in the top ten.

Vanessa led on three-meter until she missed her ninth dive, a reverse two-and-a-half pike. This allowed USC's Elena Romera to take the lead on the last three and win with 492.85 to Vanessa's 470.85. Keith commented on her performance: "Vanessa dove well; she just had the one miss. Her best dive was an inward 2½ pike. It has a difficulty of 3.0 and few women do it." Cristina Conn was eleventh and Julie Pothier was sixteenth against the powerhouse Pac-10.

The 1994 NCAAs in March in Indianapolis served as Vanessa Thelin's shining moment. She finished the one-meter preliminaries in first and won the national title with 449.80 points, the best NCAA total in three years. She nailed her forward two-and-a-half pike somersault for sixty-one points, the highest scored dive of the meet. She became BYU's eighth female athlete and second diver to win an NCAA title. BYU's Courtney Nelson took the first two NCAA platform titles in 1990 and 1991.

Just 3.25 points away from qualifying for the NCAA three-meter finals, Vanessa finished tenth, with 450.75, behind Stanford's 1993 and 1994 three-meter champion, Eileen Richetelli. Afterwards, Vanessa told Keith she was pregnant.

With Keith producing an NCAA champion, BYU took the hint that he was good and inducted him into BYU's Athletic Hall of Fame, along with Steve Young, who *Sports Illustrated* rated as the number-one college quarterback of all time; William Reed Fehlberg, 1973 NCAA runner-up wrestler, leading BYU to a national fourth-place; and NCAA record-breaking pitcher Scott Nielsen.[322]

Season Three

With Keith's winning record, four champion divers signed with BYU for 1994-1995:

Melanie Mabry, Arizona state champion

Devan Porter, two-time Arizona state champion

Nathan Cook, two-time Utah state champion

Matthew Dahl, three-time California Interscholastic Federation champion and UCLA transfer student

The first meet of the season took place in South Bend, Indiana, against Notre Dame. The Fighting Irish men didn't put up much of a fight as BYU won 191-108. Mike Moak won both boards.

Although the Fighting Irish women won 160-139, the Cougar divers smeared them like Irish cream. Julie Pothier won both boards and Cristina Conn finished second on both boards. BYU junior Emi Watabe placed third on one-meter and fellow junior teammate Courtney Taylor took third on three-meter for a complete blue-and-white sweep.[323]

The 1995 Western Athletic Conference Championships took place in Las Vegas. Keith's young crew scored the most medals. Sophomore Cristina Conn won the three-meter WAC title and silver on one-meter.[324] Sophomore Julie Pothier won bronze on both boards.[325] Sophomore Nate Cook won the conference titles on both boards. His teammates grabbed silver, bronze, and fourth on one-meter.

Keith had two female divers and five male divers qualify for the NCAA Zone E Diving Championships in Pasadena, California. Against fifty-seven divers from seventeen schools, Cristina Conn finished in the top ten on both boards.[326] Julie Pothier finished in the top fourteen on both boards.[327]

Although all five guys finished in the top ten on both boards, only Mike Moak qualified. Freshman Devan Porter's best finish was sixth on one-meter. Sophomore Matt Dahl's best finish was sixth on three-meter. Nate Cook was seventh on both boards.[328] Producing half the ten best divers in the western half of the country, with one of the most competitive conferences in diving, spoke volumes about Keith's coaching ability.

Mike Moak finished twenty-fifth out of thirty-four divers on one-meter at the NCAA's, won by Minnesota's 1993 NCAA platform champion, P.J. Bogart. Both Mike and P.J. were from Mesa, Arizona. While Mike trained with Mesa Desert Divers, P.J. trained with Sun Devil Divers.

Mike Moak dove for Keith from 1985 to 1995 and had a soft spot in his heart for him. The three-time WAC champion later recalled the positive impact Keith had on him in his youth:

> Keith was the father figure in my life. I spent more time with him since the age of 14 than my own father. I can think of no adult who has had a greater influence on my life. Myself and Valerie Hale (Blau) spent the most time with Keith; started diving with him when he first started Desert Divers after moving to Mesa.
>
> He taught me the most important lessons I have learned about how to succeed.
>
> EVERY person I have ever known who knows Keith, can't say enough about what a nice guy he is.

To his divers, Keith was more than a diving coach. He was a friend, a mentor, and a hero. He made everyone feel appreciated, comfortable, and loved. He enjoyed kicking back and eating, playing games, eating, telling jokes, eating, visiting, and eating some more. He was like a favorite warm blanket wrapped around tight. The patience, warmth, and integrity he exhibited, while cranking out champions left and right, made him an inspiration to the athletic community.

Season Four

Keith recruited more diving champions for the 1995–1996 season:

Andrew Wright, Arizona state champion

Kristin Reeder, Utah state champion and region champion

Laurel Bisk, ninth at the 1992 Junior Olympics

With his oldest son Rex finishing his senior year of college, daughter Mindy finishing her freshman year of college, and second son Rand somewhere in between, Keith had three kids at BYU. All three received academic scholarships.

The 1996 Western Athletic Conference Championships took place at Palo Alto College in San Antonio. Keith enjoyed his best season yet as his divers won every title and several medals. The most shocking win was Kristin Reeder's on three-meter. The freshman claimed the title after less than two years of diving. The *San Antonio Express* revealed her secret:

> Reeder said she handled the pressure by visualizing her dives. "I didn't have a sense that I was ahead," she said. "I just tried to concentrate and I felt confident." Reeder nailed her dives, consistently receiving sevens and eights. She felt her best dive was a reverse 2½.[329]

Women's three-meter results:

1. Kristin Reeder, BYU
2. Anji Hintze, Utah
3. Julie Pothier, BYU
4. Jennifer Noonan, Colorado State
5. Karen Jankowski, Utah

6. Emi Watabe, BYU
7. Kristy Majo, Utah
8. Erica Torgrude, Colorado State
9. Laurel Bisk, BYU
10. Courtney Stacy, BYU

Julie Pothier, leading from the start, won the one-meter title. Going into the semi-finals, BYU divers had the top four spots.[330] Julie especially benefited from Keith's encouragement. He had made it possible for her to dive in college by training her for free when he coached the Desert Divers in Arizona and her family could not afford the expenses. Julie later revealed what his selfless service meant to her, "I hold Keith up there with the best of them. He will always have a special place in my life." He had discovered her talent early, nurtured it freely from beginning to end, and took her to the top, a gift she would forever treasure. It's giving acts like that which bond coach and athlete.

The new three-meter conference champion, Kristin, had her own reasons to praise Keith for his reassuring words of comfort. She found it difficult spending so much time in a swimsuit. She had the normal concerns about her appearance, despite being a top collegiate athlete. But Keith wanted his athletes to feel good about themselves. Her story:

> He is a great man. A man of few words. He was a great coach. Something he said one time has always stood out. I was talking to one of my teammates about my frustrations with my body and how I wanted to change some things. Keith piped in telling me I looked great and I didn't need to worry about changing anything. That was very refreshing to me. Especially because previous coaches were always on my case. Keith saw the bigger picture. I have always been grateful for his comment about that.

The men saw one Cougar defend his title, another Cougar emerge as WAC champion, and a WAC record break. Senior Scott Turner dethroned teammate Nate Cook on one-meter.

The results:

1. Scott Turner, BYU
2. Nate Cook, BYU
3. Tony LaMontagne, Utah
4. Shawn Schuessler, Hawaii
5. Dan Kooyman, Utah
6. William Reid, Utah
7. Andrew Wright, BYU
8. Coby Leslie, Air Force

Nate Cook came back with a vengeance to reclaim his three-meter conference title and set a WAC conference record with 612.40 points. Scott Turner was runner-up. The *San Antonio Express* quoted Keith on Nate's third conference title: "He took his lead to the extreme and finished up as the WAC champion that he is. He gave the crowd a fantastic performance."[331]

Although five Cougar divers (Laurel Bisk, Kristin Reeder, Julie Pothier, Nathan Cook, and Scott Turner) qualified for the NCAA Zone E Diving Championships in Oregon, only one went on to the NCAAs: Scott.[332] Nathan missed qualifying by four points.[333]

The 1996 NCAA Championships took place at the University of Texas at Austin. Competing against thirty-five divers from schools like Fordham, Stanford, Louisiana State, North Carolina State, Ohio State, and Penn State, as well as Alabama, Arkansas, Arizona, Florida, Iowa, Kentucky, Minnesota, Nebraska, Tennessee, American, and Navy, Scott Turner finished twenty-eighth on both boards. Another Mesa, Arizona native, P.J. Bogart, defended his NCAA one-meter title and led going into the three-meter finals. But P.J. finished three-meter in fourth behind three Miami divers.

Keith said of the NCAAs, "It was a very fair competition. I felt we pretty much got what we deserved. We went to represent BYU well, and I think we did that." He noted that Scott didn't compete against divers with greater athletic ability, but against divers with greater commitment to the sport. Scott was happy just to reach his goal of qualifying for the NCAAs.[334]

Keith's oldest son, Rex, graduated from BYU in zoology that spring and was accepted to the University of Texas at Galveston Medical School. Another son, Aaron, seventeen, went to the U.S. Nationals in Minneapolis and won bronze on three-meter and took fourth on one-meter. Keith's children grew into accomplished adults with much to offer.

Vanessa Thelin competed in the 1996 Olympic Trials in Indianapolis. She was Keith's first diver to qualify for the Olympic trials. Her first dive looked good, but she missed her hands, which messed up her entry. Then she hit her feet on the board on her inward two-and-a-half pike. She made semifinals but finished fourteenth.

Keith, Marsha, and Aaron drove to the 1996 Atlanta Olympics. They saw the first Chinese man become Olympic springboard champion. China took the silver too. Mark Lenzi, 1992 Olympic springboard champion, won bronze. Scott Donie, 1992 Olympic platform silver medalist, finished fourth. Florida Gator Melissa Moses missed Olympic springboard bronze by 1.65 points to finish fourth, while Miami freshman Jenny Keim finished ninth.

Season Five

Keith got the golden ticket for the 1996–1997 season. His star recruits:

Rachelle Smith (later Rachelle Kunkel), Utah state champion and future Olympian

Rachel Degener, Utah State runner-up and national qualifier

Spencer Lamoreaux, 1992 Junior Olympic State Champion

Five universities joined the Western Athletic Conference in 1996, including UNLV, Rice, San Jose State, Texas Christian University, and Southern Methodist University, giving Keith's divers a run for their money. SMU spawned Olympic silver medalist Scott Donie, as well as NCAA champions Krista Wilson (1990 and 1991) and Cheril Santini (1992 and 1995) and took the 1996 NCAA runner-up team spot. Only SMU and BYU divers medaled on the boards at the 1997 WAC championships, with each school scoring six (half) medals.

Women's one-meter:

1. Jenny Lingamfelter, Southern Methodist
2. Rachelle Smith, BYU
3. Julie Parkinson, BYU
4. Christina Conn, BYU
5. Kristi Mayo, Utah

Women's three-meter:

1. Jenny Lingamfelter, Southern Methodist
2. Julie Parkinson, BYU
3. Cristina Conn, BYU
4. Kristen Link, Southern Methodist
5. Kristin Reeder, BYU

Men's one-meter:

1. Ali Al-Hasan, Southern Methodist
2. Nate Cook, BYU
3. Jason Hubbart, Southern Methodist

Men's three-meter:

1. Ali Al-Hasan, Southern Methodist
2. Jason Hubbart, Southern Methodist
3. Nate Cook, BYU

4. Shawn Patrick, Hawaii
5. Dustin Jones, Utah
6. L.J. Hill, Southern Methodist
7. Adam Knippa, TCU
8. Spencer Lamoreaux, BYU

Keith took two divers to the 1997 NCAAs: Seniors Cristina Conn and Nate Cook. Cristina finished nineteenth on three-meter and twenty-first on one-meter. Southern California won their first NCAA team championship, ending five years of domination by Stanford.

Nathan Cook qualified in first on one-meter and second on three-meter at zones. He went on to become one of Keith's highest placing divers at the NCAAs, in twelfth on three-meter and sixteenth on one-meter. Miami divers won everything: 1991 Pan-Am platform champion and 1993 Cuban national champion Rio Ramirez won his first of three NCAA one-meter titles and 1995 NCAA platform champion Tyce Routson won three-meter and platform. Auburn won its first NCAA team title.

Season Six

Keith recruited top divers with extensive accolades for the 1997–1998 season:

Justin Wilcock, Utah state championships runner-up and four-time region champion

Jessica Nye, two-time Washington state champion and three-time league champion

Jenny Rogers, two-time Arizona state champion and NCAA Zone B champion (diving for Georgia)

Georgia is in the NCAA's strongest conference for diving, the Southeastern Conference, whose schools had produced over a dozen champions since the first women's NCAAs in 1982: Auburn (1), Arkansas (1), Florida (8), Louisiana State (2), and Tennessee (1).

The 1998 Western Athletic Conference Championships mirrored the previous one for the women (two silver, two bronze), but the men really cranked out the wins.

Women's one-meter:

1. Jenny Lingamfelter, Southern Methodist
2. Rachelle Smith, BYU
3. Cristina Conn, BYU
4. Laurel Bisk, BYU
5. Sarah Crawford, Texas Christian
6. Rachel Degener, BYU
7. Erica Fleming, Fresno State
8. Kristy Mayo, Utah

Women's three-meter:

1. Jenny Lingamfelter, Southern Methodist
2. Rachelle Smith, BYU
3. Sarah Crawford, Texas Christian
4. Jenny Rogers, BYU
5. Cristina Conn, BYU
6. Rachel Degener, BYU
7. Jessica Nye, BYU
8. Erica Fleming, Fresno State

Women's platform:

1. Kristin Link, Southern Methodist
2. Sarah Crawford, Texas Christian
3. Jenny Rogers, BYU
4. Bennet Burt, Southern Methodist
5. Erica Fleming, Fresno State
6. J.P. Palmer, Hawaii
7. Laurel Bisk, BYU
8. Rachelle Smith, BYU

Men's one-meter:

1. Justin Wilcock, BYU
2. Nick Smith, Utah
3. Devan Porter, BYU
4. Matt Dahl, BYU

Men's three-meter:

1. Justin Wilcock, BYU
2. Matt Dahl, BYU
3. Adam Knippa, Texas Christian
4. Devan Porter, BYU

Men's platform:

1. Justin Wilcock, BYU
2. Adam Knippa, Texas Christian
3. Kevin Saal, Texas Christian
4. Spencer Lamoreaux, BYU

Keith qualified two divers for the 1998 Men's NCAA Championships in Auburn, Alabama. Justin Wilcock qualified in second in all three events. Matt Dahl qualified in third on one-meter. Sophomore Devan Porter finished sixth on three-meter.

At the NCAAs, Justin finished fifteenth on platform, nineteenth on three-meter and twenty-first on one-meter. Matt Dahl was thirtieth on three-meter and thirty-fourth on one-meter. Stanford won its eighth men's NCAA team title.

Cristina Conn, one of Keith's first recruits his second season, graduated that spring. The 1995 WAC champion recalled the good times, the things he taught her, and his calm demeanor: "Keith was pretty relaxed with us kids. Keith helped me learn how to deal with conflict. I had such a fun time razzling him!" For Keith, fun was a priority. It was part of being a Russell.

Season Seven

Keith champion recruits for the 1998–1999 season:

Justin Beardall, Utah State Champion

Viraj Patil, Indian National Champion

At the 1999 Western Athletic Conference Championships, BYU's last, Keith produced two champions, four runners-up, and a dozen other finalists.

Men's one-meter:

1. Nick Smith, Utah
2. Justin Beardall, BYU
3. Oscar Delgado, Wyoming
4. Matt Dahl, BYU
5. L.J. Hill, Southern Methodist
6. Devan Porter, BYU

Men's three-meter:

1. Devan Porter, BYU
2. Justin Beardall, BYU
3. Kevin Saal, Texas Christian
4. L.J. Hill, Southern Methodist
5. Nick Smith, Utah
6. Matt Dahl, BYU

Men's platform:

1. Viraj Patil, BYU
2. Oscar Delgado, Wyoming
3. Dave Devemark, Air Force
4. Kevin Saal, Texas Christian
5. Chris Van Hoose, Hawaii
6. Justin Beardall, BYU
7. Doug Hulse, Air Force
8. Devan Porter, BYU

Women's one-meter:

1. Jenny Lingamfelter, Southern Methodist
2. Rachelle Smith, BYU
3. Crystal Gregory, Utah
4. Kristin Link, Southern Methodist
5. Laurel Eldredge, BYU
6. Jessica Nye, BYU

Women's three-meter:

1. Jenny Lingamfelter, Southern Methodist
2. Kristin Link, Southern Methodist
3. Jenny Dahl, BYU
4. Rachelle Smith, BYU
5. Laurel Eldridge, BYU

Women's platform:

1. Kristin Link, Southern Methodist
2. Jenny Dahl, BYU
3. Crystal Gregory, Utah
4. Rachelle Smith, BYU
5. Laurel Eldridge, BYU
6. Jessica Nye, BYU

Rachelle Smith and Justin Beardall both qualified for the NCAAs. The women's NCAAs took place at the University of Georgia in Athens. Rachelle finished fifteenth on one-meter, won by fellow WACer Jenny Lingamfelter, and was twenty-third on three-meter, won by Miami's two-time Olympian Jenny Keim.

At the 1999 U.S. Spring National Championships in Orlando, Rachelle won silver on one-meter behind Kansas' 1996 NCAA champion, Michelle Rojohn. This qualified her for the World University Games in July in Spain and made her Keith's first BYU diver to qualify for an international competition.

At the men's NCAAs, Justin finished twenty-sixth on three-meter. Three-time Olympian and University of Texas freshman Troy Dumais won his first of four NCAA three-meter titles. Justin was twenty-ninth on one-meter and helped BYU place twelfth in the Sears Cup standings. Also known as the NACDA Directors' Cup, the National Association of Collegiate Directors of Athletics awards colleges and universities with the most success in collegiate athletics. Points for the Sears Cup are based on order of finish in NCAA-sponsored championships.

Six Zone E schools took half the top twelve spots, indicating the fierce competition in the zone:

1. Stanford (Zone E)
2. Georgia (Zone B)
3. Penn State (Zone C)
4. Florida (Zone B)
5. UCLA (Zone E)
6. Michigan (Zone C)
7. Duke (Zone B)
8. Virginia (Zone B)
9. Arizona (Zone E)
10. Southern California (Zone E)
11. Texas (Zone D)
12. Brigham Young (Zone E)

(tie) Arizona State (Zone E)

BYU joined the new Mountain West Conference in 1999 with Colorado State University, Air Force Academy, New Mexico, San Diego State, UNLV, Utah, and Wyoming.

Keith was national coach for the 1999 World University Games in Palma de Mallorca, Spain. Eleven-time national champion and Louisiana State University coach Doug Shaffer and Nebraska coach Jim Hocking joined Keith. Mallorca is an island off the east coast of Spain. Palma is its major city. Keith got in some snorkeling time, but the water was mucky. He also visited the La Seu Cathedral, started in 1229 by King James I of Aragon and finished in 1601. The French Gothic style cathedral is a commanding ornament on the Bay of Palma, on the southwest side of Mallorca.

The diving team included:

Jenny Lingamfelter, 1999 Pan-American Games silver medalist

Kathy Pesek, 1998 NCAA champion for Tennessee

Kristin Link, 1998 and 1999 Western Athletic Conference champion

Laura Wilkinson, 1999 NCAA champion and future Olympic champion

Michelle Davison, 1999 Southeastern Conference champion and future Olympian

Rachelle Smith, 1999 National champion and future Olympian

Eric Cook, future Big Twelve Conference champion for Nebraska

Justin Dumais, future Olympian and thirteen-time national champion

Mike Collier, 1999 Big Ten and Zone C champion for Indiana

Travis Niemeyer, 1996 Big Eight champion for Nebraska

Troy Dumais, 1999 NCAA champion and future Olympian

Jenny Lingamfelter won bronze on one-meter[335] while the U.S. men won team bronze.[336]

Other top placings:

Troy Dumais, fifth, three-meter

Travis Niemeyer, sixth, one-meter

Michelle Davison, seventh, three-meter

Jenny Lingamfelter, eighth, three-meter

Michelle Davison, ninth, one-meter

Kathy Pesek, tenth, ten-meter

Justin Dumais, eleventh, three-meter

Justin Dumais, twelfth, platform

Rochelle Smith, thirteenth, one-meter

At the U.S. Summer National Championships, Rachelle won her first national one-meter title. Rachelle later recalled her trip to the top and Keith's vital role on that path. She described what his encouragement, humor, sincerity, and confidence meant to her and how he inspired her to be her best:

> Keith was like a favorite uncle. I can't remember a week that went by that he didn't tell me that I was a champion, that I had what it would take to be great. His encouragement was sincere and made it easy for me to believe in myself. His confidence in me motivated and inspired me to take my talent as far as I let it. Even after I moved on to another coach, I would call and talk to Keith whenever I needed a confidence booster. He is a wonderful man and it was an honor for me to have dove for him at BYU.

Keith added more champions to the 1999–2000 roster, including:

Bryce Barrand, Colorado state champion

Scott Randal, two-time Arizona state champion

Aaron Russell, four-time Utah state champion

Aubrie Cropper, two-time Nevada state champion

Kelly Einfeldt, Utah state champion and Nationals qualifier

Tina Morrow, Mesa Desert Diver and regional champion

Anna Tutunnikova, two-time Russian National champion

By the twenty-first century, Keith had accrued ten years of college coaching experience between two Division I schools, coached divers to dozens of conference titles and several NCAA zone titles, and become a regular fixture at the NCAAs. He had coached a national team, an NCAA champion, and national champions. And that was just the success he enjoyed in his public life. He was still happily married after thirty years and loved watching his six children grow into successful adults. But his most rewarding years still lay ahead.

Chapter 16: A Different Road to the Olympics: It Feels Like Gold

Season Eight

The twenty-first century opened and the 1999–2000 season closed with Keith's divers winning both team and four individual titles at conference.

Women's one-meter:

1. Rachelle Kunkel, BYU
2. Anna Tutunnikova, BYU
3. Jill Comins, Utah
4. Kristy Mayo, Utah
5. Erica Fleming, Utah
6. Kelli Einfeldt, BYU

Women's three-meter:

1. Rachelle Kunkel, BYU
2. Crystal Gregory, Utah

3. Anna Tutunnikova, BYU
4. Kristy Mayo, Utah
5. Tina Morrow, BYU
6. Kelli Einfeldt, BYU

Women's platform:

1. Crystal Gregory, Utah
2. Rachelle Kunkel, BYU
3. Kristy Mayo, Utah
4. Wendy O'Connell, Wyoming
5. Anna Tutunnikova, BYU
6. Dominy Alderman, Wyoming

Men's one-meter:

1. Aaron Russell, BYU
2. Devan Porter, BYU
3. Viraj Patil, BYU
4. Nick Smith, Utah
5. Oscar Delgado, Wyoming
6. Scott Randall, BYU

Men's three-meter:

1. Devan Porter, BYU
2. Oscar Delgado, Wyoming
3. Scott Randall, BYU
4. Aaron Russell, BYU
5. Nick Smith, Utah
6. Viraj Patil, BYU

Men's platform:

1. Oscar Delgado, Wyoming
2. Aaron Russell, BYU
3. Viraj Patil, BYU
4. Scott Randall, BYU
5. Devan Porter, BYU
6. Doug Hulse, Air Force

The 2000 NCAA Zone E Qualifying Meet took place in Federal Way, Washington. Despite a much larger and more powerful field, Keith's divers dominated. Rachelle Kunkel won both boards (the one-meter by 59.30) and Aaron won three-meter.[337] Devan Porter finished second on one-meter and third on three-meter. With Scott Randall fifth and Viraj Patil tenth on three-meter, BYU had four of the ten best divers in the west.[338]

The 2000 Women's NCAA Championships took place in Indianapolis. Rachelle Kunkel finished the one-meter prelims in first, more than twenty points ahead of her closest competitor. But heading into her final dive, a reverse two-and-a-half somersault, she was one point behind. She came up short and came in sixth, a nine-spot improvement from the previous year's fifteenth-place finish. Only two conferences placed divers higher (Atlantic Coast and Southeastern), while Pac-10 schools took the next three spots:

1. Jamie Watkins, Louisiana State, Southeastern
2. Jenny Keim, Miami, Atlantic Coast
3. Ashley Culpepper, Louisiana State, Southeastern
4. Robyn Grimes, Florida, Southeastern
5. Emily Spychala, Miami, Atlantic Coast
6. Rachelle Kunkel, BYU, Mountain West
7. Kellie Brennan, Southern California, Pac-10
8. Katrina Pfeuffer, Arizona State, Pac-10
9. Lindsay Berryman, Arizona, Pac-10

Rachelle's twentieth place on three-meter gave BYU an NCAA finish in twenty-ninth.

Southeastern Conference schools, as well as the University of Miami, also dominated the Men's NCAAs in Minneapolis. The one-meter results:

1. Troy Dumais, Texas, Big-12 Conference
2. Shannon Roy, Tennessee, Southeastern
3. Imre Lengyel, Miami
4. Stefan Ahrens, Miami

5. Dan Croaston, Minnesota, Big-Ten
6. Jud Campbell, Georgia, Southeastern
7. Tyce Routson, Miami
8. John Eisler, Texas, Big-12
9. Ruben Vaca, Arizona, Pac-10
10. Clayton Moss, Kentucky, Southeastern
11. Kyle Prandi, Miami
12. Corey Fox, Louisiana State, Southeastern
13. Brandon Hulko, South Carolina, Southeastern
14. Aaron Russell, BYU, Mountain West

Aaron Russell finished twenty-fourth on three-meter. Devan, whose bad back prohibited warm-ups, finished thirtieth on one-meter and thirty-second on three-meter.[339]

Rachelle Kunkel graduated that spring, but dove for Keith another year. The first thing she did was win a second national title at the 2000 U.S. Indoor National Diving Championships at the University of Minnesota. Perhaps Keith's secret to success lay not only in his accurate coaching before a dive, but in his animated cheering after one. Rachelle reveals how he reinforced that great feeling of going in flawlessly:

> My favorite memory of Keith was the dancing he did when I did a good dive. The feeling of knowing you did a great dive is terrific, but coming up out of the water and seeing Keith doing a jig on the deck made that feeling even better. It meant the dive must have been near perfect or maybe he had been eating too many gummy bears. Either way it always livened up our practices and put everyone in a good mood.

Season Nine

Keith looked forward to the next season: "Led by All-Americans Justin Wilcock and Aaron Russell, we will be well represented at all our meets, including the NCAA Nationals."[340]

Keith added two star divers to his team for the 2000–2001 season:

Tessa Dahl, Utah State Champion

Rachelle Routsong, Junior Olympic National Team member

Keith welcomed his first daughter-in-law into the family in December. Rex met Mindy, a nurse at Utah Valley Regional Medical Center in Provo, through the cardiologist she worked for. After he finished his internship, he did his residency at Johns Hopkins in Baltimore, where she worked in the surgical ICU.

BYU men finished the 2000–2001 dual-meet season ranked fifteenth in the nation with a perfect 12-0 record.[341] With his divers winning conference, zone, and national titles, Keith was "quickly asserting himself as a prominent coach in the diving community."

The 2001 Mountain West Conference Championships in Oklahoma City gave Keith four more champions, one record-breaker, and all six runner-up spots.

Men's one-meter:

1. Justin Wilcock, BYU
2. Aaron Russell, BYU
3. Oscar Delgado, Wyoming
4. Viraj Patil, BYU

Men's three-meter:

1. Aaron Russell, BYU
2. Justin Wilcock, BYU
3. Oscar Delgado, Wyoming
4. Viraj Patil, BYU

Men's platform:

1. Justin Wilcock, BYU
2. Viraj Patil, BYU
3. Aaron Russell, BYU

Women's one-meter:

1. Sarah Law, Air Force Academy
2. Kelli Einfeldt, BYU
3. Anna Tutunnikova, BYU
4. Jill Lish, Utah
5. Lauren Colaric, Wyoming
6. Lori Anderson, Colorado State
7. Lindsay Schroeder, Colorado State
8. Jessica Nye, BYU

Women's three-meter:

1. Anna Tutunnikova, BYU
2. Kelli Einfeldt, BYU
3. Sarah Law, Air Force Academy
4. Jill Lish, Utah
5. Wendy O' Connell, Wyoming
6. Tracey Berghian, New Mexico
7. Lauren Colaric, Wyoming
8. Jessica Nye, BYU

Women's platform:

1. Sarah Law, Air Force Academy
2. Tessa Clark, BYU
3. Jill Lish, Utah
4. Anna Tutunnikova, BYU
5. Tracey Berghian, New Mexico
6. Kelli Einfeldt, BYU

BYU women won the MWC Championships by 279 points with

815, followed by Colorado State University in second with 536. BYU men also won.

Keith had three top ten male and two top ten female divers west of the Rocky Mountains at Zone E Championships in Federal Way, Washington, but only two qualified for the NCAAs. Aaron Russell had the best finish in second on three-meter. Justin Wilcock finished third on both one-meter and platform and fourth on three-meter. Viraj Patil finished ninth on both three-meter and platform.[342]

At the 2001 NCAA Championships in East Meadow on Long Island, Anna Tutunnikova finished twenty-fourth on three-meter and twenty-seventh best on one-meter. Keith received a shocking call in New York from his mother. His father, diagnosed with cancer a year earlier, had passed away at home. He was eighty. Cy had always been a big, strong man, seemingly invincible to Keith. That hardy image of his dad was so deeply emblazoned in Keith's mind, he couldn't fathom the loss. Despite his age and bad leg, this man who never got sick, never took a day off from teaching grade-schoolers until he retired, didn't act old. He loved tending his roses, working in his vegetable garden, and building furniture in his shop. He never hesitated to climb on the roof of the apartment complex he owned to fix something. The news left Keith in denial for months.

The men's NCAA Championships were at Texas A&M University in College Station, later that week. Aaron Russell was the only Zone E diver in the top twenty on one-meter, in which the Southeastern Conference had a major presence. The results:

1. Troy Dumais, Texas, Big 12 Conference
2. Justin Dumais, Texas, Big 12
3. Jud Campbell, Georgia, Southeastern
4. Thomas Davidson, Indiana, Big Ten
5. Clayton Moss, Kentucky, Southeastern
6. Shannon Roy, Tennessee, Southeastern
7. Gabi Chereches, Tennessee, Southeastern
8. Mark Fichera, Columbia, Ivy League

9. Heath Knowling, Ohio State, Big Ten
10. Erik Petursson, Louisiana State, Southeastern
11. Brandon Hulko, South Carolina, Southeastern
12. Kyle Prandi, Miami, Atlantic Coast
13. Aaron Russell, Brigham Young, Mountain West
14. Corey Fox, Louisiana State, Southeastern
15. Adam Morgan, Texas A&M, Big 12
16. Dan Croaston, Minnesota, Big Ten
17. Hank Richardson, Florida, Southeastern
18. Jesse Evan, Texas A&M, Big 12
19. Chris Alderman, Penn State, Big Ten
20. Kris Daugherty, Georgia, Southeastern

Aaron Russell finished twenty-first on three-meter and twenty-fifth on platform. Arizona's Omar Ojeda won silver on three-meter and bronze on platform.

BYU tied fellow Mountain West Conference school UNLV for a thirtieth place NCAA team finish. Keith left early to attend his father's funeral. He shared his feelings about his dad with one interviewer:

> Keith says he was most affected by his father, Cyrus Russell, whom he looked up to as his hero in sports and life. "My dad, as far as I was concerned, was the best thing that ever lived," says Keith. "He could do no wrong. He had so many talents and he was humble. He played football on scholarship at ASU and broke records in track and field. Everybody around him seemed to look up to him. So I looked up to my dad more than anybody."[343]

In addition to their athletic success, BYU men ranked number one in academics, with a team GPA of 3.35.

Keith acquired a second son-in-law when Kerri, twenty, married Todd Deshler in April. Todd graduated from BYU that month in sociology and eventually taught aviation science at Utah Valley University. Kerri graduated two years later. While Keith's professional success was obvious at nearly every dual, conference, zone, and NCAA meet, his personal success showed through his children's many successes.

The "2001–2002 BYU Men's Swimming Outlook" highlighted Keith's electrifying divers:

> The BYU men's team went 12-0 in dual conference meets last year. Diving should be the strongest and most exciting event to watch this season. Highly recruited Andy Bradley, state champion from Virginia, has a bright future. "This year we have the greatest men's diving team ever assembled at BYU," said Keith Russell.[344]

Keith's second son, Rand, married Leah Fleming in Utah on July 14, 2001. Rand was in dental school at the University of Maryland in Baltimore and Leah was majoring in psychology at Towson University, just north of Baltimore. Four days later, Keith became a grandfather when his oldest daughter, Mindy, gave birth to Ashlyn.

Keith went to the 2001 World University Games in Beijing, China as the national coach. He was excited about this trip, since China dominated diving and Rachelle Kunkel went as national three-meter champion. Other team members included:

Justin Dumais, Texas star and future Olympian

Kyle Prandi, Miami star and future Olympian

Tom Davidson, Indiana star and future Berkeley coach

Dominica Fusaro, Southern California star

Danielle Stramandi, 1998 Ivy League champion

USC coach Hong Ping Li accompanied the national team to his hometown and took them to the Great Wall of China and the Forbidden City.

Kyle Prandi and Justin Dumais made platform finals, with Kyle in second, but neither medaled. Chinese Olympic champion Tian Liang won. Kyle finished tenth, and Justin twelfth. Keith expressed his confidence in his men: "I thought this was our night. We had two people in the finals who I thought would do it. The opportunity was there."[345]

Kyle and Justin finished fifth in the synchronized platform, behind China in first. The U.S. Olympic Committee commented on Rachelle's spectacular synchronized three-meter performance:

> Rachelle Kunkel (Brigham Young University) and Danielle Stramandi (Princeton) were impressive, finishing fifth [on] three-meter even though they had never paired previously and had very limited practice together. China took gold.[346]

The highlight was when the U.S. men won the team bronze medal. China took team gold. Justin Dumais, in his third World University Games, said these were by far the most competitive.

Keith shared his thoughts on his divers' exceptional performance:

> I was very pleased with the members of the team. They did a great job if for no other reason than they were willing to do whatever we asked them to do. There were several who did some diving they don't normally do.[347]

Season Ten

Keith recruited more champions for the 2001–2002 season:

Andy Bradley, Virginia state champion and Junior Pan Am Games silver medalist

Landon Trost, two-time Utah state champion and valedictorian.

On the morning of September 11, 2001, Keith had the television on as he got ready to go to the airport for a USA Diving national convention in Detroit. Although the tragedy that struck the nation that morning caught his attention, he didn't know what to make of it, except that we were now at war. Since he didn't hear otherwise, he continued preparing for his flight.

Keith stopped by BYU to get Justin Wilcock, who was going as an athlete representative. As Keith backed out of the parking spot for the hour drive to Salt Lake, the radio announced the airport closures. Keith pulled back in and went to work, still in shock over the attack.

At the 2002 Mountain West Conference Championships in Oklahoma City, Keith's men kicked butt, while "only" two female divers made finals on the boards.

Men's one-meter:

1. Justin Wilcock, BYU
2. Aaron Russell, BYU
3. Justin Beardall, BYU
4. Viraj Patil, BYU
5. Brady Lindberg, Air Force
6. Andy Bradley, BYU
7. Lucas Richmond, UNLV
8. Adam Miller, Wyoming

Justin Wilcock shattered the MWC three-meter record by 27.90 with 607.90:

1. Justin Wilcock, BYU
2. Aaron Russell, BYU
3. Andy Bradley, BYU
4. Viraj Patil, BYU
5. Justin Beardall, BYU
6. Brady Lindberg, Air Force
7. Landon Trost, BYU
8. Adam Miller, Wyoming

Men's platform:

1. Justin Wilcock, BYU
2. Viraj Patil, BYU
3. Aaron Russell, BYU
4. Brady Lindberg, Air Force
5. Justin Beardall, BYU
6. Adam Miller, Wyoming
7. Andy Bradley, BYU
8. Landon Trost, BYU

Women's one-meter:

1. Sarah Law, Air Force
2. Becca Barras, New Mexico
3. Tracey Berghian, New Mexico
4. Lori Anderson, Colorado State
5. Michelle Hager, Air Force
6. Ashlie Niederer, Wyoming
7. Kelli Einfeldt, BYU
8. Erin Shumway, Colorado State

Women's three-meter:

1. Sarah Law, Air Force
2. Becca Barras, New Mexico
3. Tracey Berghian, New Mexico
4. Kelli Einfeldt, BYU
5. Kara Crisp, Colorado State
6. Erin Shumway, Colorado State
7. Tessa Clark, BYU

BYU men won the Mountain West Conference team title by 181 points, with 931 to UNLV's 750. BYU women also won.

BYU had a solid showing at the 2002 NCAA Zone E Diving Championships at Stanford in the men's three-meter:

1. Omar Ojeda, Arizona
2. Justin Wilcock, BYU
3. Joshua Anderson, Arizona
4. Andy Bradley, BYU
5. Aaron Russell, BYU
6. Thomas McCrummen, Arizona State
7. Adam Peterson, Stanford
8. Scott Koenig, Arizona
9. Ruben Vaca, Arizona
10. Gordon Blukis, Arizona State
11. Mike Gowdy, Hawaii
12. Justin Beardall, BYU

Arizona showcased the best divers in the western half of the United States on platform, followed by BYU:

1. Ruben Vaca, Arizona
2. Justin Wilcock, BYU
3. Scott Koenig, Arizona
4. Joshua Anderson, Arizona
5. Adam Peterson, Stanford
6. Viraj Patil, BYU
7. Omar Ojeda, Arizona
8. Jesse Fonner, Stanford
9. Aaron Russell, BYU

Kelli Einfeldt was sixteenth on both boards for BYU out of forty-eight western divers.

The 2002 Men's NCAA Championships took place at the University of Georgia. BYU was among the top twenty-two schools represented in the contest of thirty-five divers. Keith was one of eight coaches with more than one diver who qualified. Andy Bradley finished sixteenth on one-meter and twenty-sixth on three-meter. Justin Wilcock finished fourteenth on one-meter and better in the rest.

Men's three-meter:

1. Troy Dumais, Texas
2. Imre Lengyel, Miami
3. Phil Jones, Tennessee
4. Justin Dumais, Texas
5. Clayton Moss, Kentucky
6. Omar Ojeda, Arizona
7. Justin Wilcock, BYU
8. Kyle Prandi, Miami
9. Miguel Velazquez, Miami
10. Stefan Ahrens, Miami

Men's platform (with Miami and Texas taking half the top twelve spots):

1. Imre Lengyel, Miami
2. Justin Dumais, Texas
3. Matthew Bricker, Auburn
4. Miguel Velazquez, Miami
5. Troy Dumais, Texas
6. Clayton Moss, Kentucky
7. Jason Coben, Michigan
8. Jonathan Linette, Texas
9. Caesar Garcia, Auburn
10. Kyle Prandi, Miami
11. Ruben Vaca, Arizona
12. Justin Wilcock, BYU

Justin Wilcock's performance was significant because it marked the first time a Cougar diver had earned first-team All-American status since Keith in 1972. BYU men's swim coach Tim Powers emphasized the magnitude of that accomplishment: "Wilcock was the only diver to score points in the platform without having the opportunity to practice on a ten-meter platform." BYU only had a five-meter.

BYU men moved up in NCAA rankings to twenty-third in the nation, with one loss after a nineteen dual-meet winning streak.

Aaron Russell practiced four hours daily and was the star of the 2002–2003 season. One BYU article showcased his athletic abilities, academic pursuits, and personality:

> Aaron's parents worked hard to make sure their children were involved in sports. Aaron and his three brothers all played football.
>
> Viraj Patil is a national champion from India and works out with Aaron. Patil said, "Aaron is fun to work with, he's pretty competitive. More than anyone else I have always tried to follow Aaron. I look up to him."
>
> Last year Aaron graduated one year early from BYU with a bachelor's degree in Portuguese and is now working on a master's degree also in Portuguese. He hopes to be accepted to law school.
>
> Yet there is one honor that has continued to elude this athlete who is one of the greatest divers to come to BYU—being named first-team All-American is one of Aaron's main goals this season. "Over the summer we went to Nationals," said Keith. "He finished in the top eight where the first team All-American would be. That showed he can do it, he can reach his goal."[348]

Season Eleven

Keith added Ohio Capital Conference Champion Aubrey Low to his winning team for the 2002–2003 season.

At the 2003 Mountain West Conference Championships in Oklahoma City, Keith's men were unstoppable, taking eight of nine medals and breaking another conference record.

Men's one-meter:

1. Aaron Russell, BYU
2. Justin Beardall, BYU
3. Scott Randall, BYU

4. Brad Lindberg, Air Force
5. Adam Miller, Wyoming
6. Ben Chapman, Air Force
7. Landon Trost, BYU
8. Tyler Wistisen, UNLV

Men's three-meter:

1. Aaron Russell, BYU
2. Justin Beardall, BYU
3. Scott Randall, BYU
4. Adam Miller, Wyoming
5. Brady Lindberg, Air Force
6. Ben Chapman, Air Force
7. Landon Trost, BYU
8. Tyler Wistisen, UNLV

Men's platform:

1. Aaron Russell, BYU (499.80 for the new record)
2. Brady Lindberg, Air Force (401.80)
3. Justin Beardall, BYU
4. Scott Randall, BYU
5. Adam Miller, Wyoming
6. Ben Chapman, Air Force
7. Doug Hulse, Air Force
8. Landon Trost, BYU

Women's one-meter:

1. Becca Barras, New Mexico
2. Kelli Einfeldt, BYU
3. Tracey Berghian, New Mexico
4. Lori Vigil, Colorado State
5. Aubrey Low, BYU

Women's three-meter:

1. Tracey Berghian, New Mexico

2. Kelli Einfeldt, BYU (First going into finals by 49.35)[349]
3. Becca Barras, New Mexico
4. Lori Vigil, Colorado State
5. Michelle Hager, Air Force
6. Nichole McLean, UNLV
7. Lydia Kimball, Wyoming
8. Rachelle Routsong, BYU

Women's platform:

1. Jessica Williams, Air Force
2. Becca Barras, New Mexico
3. Tracey Berghian, New Mexico
4. Nichole McLean, UNLV
5. Kelli Einfeldt, BYU
6. Aubrey Low, BYU

For the fourth straight year, both BYU men and women won the MWC Championships. BYU men beat Air Force, in second, by 273 with 908.

BYU men finished second on both boards at the NCAA Zone E qualifying meet: Justin Beardall on one-meter and Aaron Russell on three-meter, each behind ASU's future NCAA champion Joona Puhakka.[350] Aaron Russell finished third on one-meter behind Justin. With Scott Randall also qualifying, Keith sent the most western divers to the 2003 NCAAs.[351]

The 2003 Men's NCAA Championships took place at the University of Texas at Austin. Aaron Russell made his mark against the formidable Southeastern Conference schools.

One-meter results:

1. Joona Puhakka, Arizona State University, Pac-10
2. Andy Bradley, South Carolina, Southeastern
3. Clayton Moss, Kentucky, Southeastern
4. Aaron Russell, BYU, Mountain West

5. Zach Wilcox, Florida, Southeastern
6. Kris Daugherty, Georgia, Southeastern
7. Phil Jones, Tennessee, Southeastern
8. Todd Avery, Georgia, Southeastern
9. Caesar Garcia, Auburn, Southeastern
10. Brice Dumais, Southern Methodist, Conference USA
11. Michael Gowdy, Hawaii, Western Athletic
12. Matt Bricker, Auburn, Southeastern
13. Stewart Smith, Alabama, Southeastern
14. Jason Coben, Michigan, Big Ten
15. Josh Anderson, Arizona, Pac-10
16. Ray Vincent, Southern California, Pac-10
17. Miguel Velsquez, Miami, Atlantic Coast
18. Justin Beardall, BYU, Mountain West

Scott Randall finished twenty-fifth.

Former Cougar diver Andy Bradley finished seventh for South Carolina on three-meter. Aaron Russell followed in tenth, Justin Beardall twenty-first, and Scott Randall twenty-ninth. BYU placed twenty-second at the NCAAs.[352] Wyoming was the only other MWC school in the top forty, at twenty-eight.

Kelli Einfeldt ended her collegiate career that year as one of Keith's best female divers. She had made finals on both boards all four years and won a total of four silver at conference. She later recalled what made Keith one of America's best coaches: "I learned self-confidence, determination, patience, and integrity from him. He has a gift to see the potential of a person and help that person reach that potential. We all love Keith for his influence in our lives." Clearly Keith cared about his athletes outside the pool. He went beyond teaching them techniques of diving and taught them secrets to success and happiness, for both their sport and their life.

Season Twelve:

Keith recruited a couple winners for the 2003–2004 season:

Mindy Jones, 2003 Colorado Diver of the Year

Dallas Heal, three-time regional champion and nationals qualifier

At the 2004 Mountain West Conference Championships in Oklahoma City, both BYU men and women won their fifth straight team title.

Men's one-meter results:

1. Justin Beardall, BYU
2. Sterling Richards, Utah
3. Scott Randall, BYU

Men's three-meter results:

1. Sterling Richards, Utah
2. Scott Randall, BYU
3. Justin Beardall, BYU

Men's platform:

1. Scott Randall, BYU
2. Justin Beardall, BYU
3. John Lynch, Wyoming

A total of four female Cougars made finals.

Women's one-meter:

1. Becca Barras, New Mexico
2. Tracey Berghian, New Mexico
3. Saara Haapanen, Wyoming
4. Lori Vigil, Colorado State
5. Aubrey Low, BYU
6. Christen Boyle, Wyoming
7. Nichole McLean, UNLV
8. Mindy Jones, BYU

Women's three-meter:

1. Tracey Berghian, New Mexico
2. Becca Barras, New Mexico
3. Lori Vigil, Colorado State
4. Nichole McLean, UNLV
5. Aubrey Low, BYU
6. Saara Haapanen, Wyoming
7. Rachelle Routsong, BYU
8. Aubrey Cropper, BYU

Women's platform:

1. Becca Barras, New Mexico
2. Tracey Berghian, New Mexico
3. Nichole McLean, UNLV
4. Rachelle Routsong, BYU
5. Lori Vigil, Colorado State
6. Jessica Field, UNLV
7. Aubrey Low, BYU
8. Saara Haapanen, Wyoming

Justin Beardall competed in his third and last NCAA Championships on Long Island and finished seventeenth on three-meter and thirty-second on one-meter. At this point, an average of two Cougar divers had qualified for the NCAAs each year for twelve years since Keith arrived. Three qualified three times, one qualified three times, and two qualified six times.

Keith received the greatest thrill of his career watching the 2004 Olympic Trials. Rachelle Kunkel now trained in Los Angeles with two-time Olympian Hongping Li at the University of Southern California Trojan Dive Club while working three twelve-hour shifts weekly as a labor and delivery nurse. Justin Wilcock trained in Texas with Ken Armstrong at The Woodlands, where Keith once coached. Keith witnessed his protégés make the Olympics in St. Peters, Missouri, thirty miles northeast of St. Louis.

Rachelle Kunkel went into springboard finals second to Kimiko Soldati. Rachelle was a little off on her back two-and-a-half pike, for 7.5s and 63.90. Kimiko failed to find her way out of her inward two-and-a-half pike for 4.5s for 39, giving Rachelle a six-point lead in first. Rachelle received 8.5s for 73.40 on her reverse two-and-a-half pike to keep her six-point lead. She then was a little heavy on her inward two-and-a-half pike entry, giving Kimiko a 1.56 lead. On her last dive, Rachelle received sevens for 65.70 on her forward three-and-a-half pike, just enough to edge out 2000 Olympian Michelle Davison, and take second and a spot on the 2004 U.S. Olympic Team.[353]

Justin Wilcock went into springboard finals in third, one point from second, then scored nines on his first three dives to move up one.[354] On the third dive, Troy Dumais went short on his back two-and-a-half pike, while Justin Wilcock nailed his reverse two-and-a-half somersault with one and a half twists for 84, and first. Troy took nines on his inward two-and-a-half pike to put him back in first for good. Justin put in a forward two-and-a-half somersault with two twists for sevens and second. His last dive, an inward two-and-a-half pike somersault took good sevens. Troy Dumais and Justin Wilcock made the 2004 U.S. Men's Olympic Springboard Team.[355]

Justin Wilcock went to the Athens Olympics with a stress fracture in his fifth vertebrate, which prevented him from having the strength to push off the board. He finished last out of thirty-two divers, while Troy Dumais finished sixth.

Rachelle was the highest-placing American in the women's springboard, in ninth. Indiana's Kimiko Soldati finished twelve spots below Rachelle in twenty-first.

Justin Wilcock later talked about Keith's role in getting him to the Olympics and why Keith was one of the nation's top coaches:

> I have so many fond memories of Keith Russell. I first got to know him as a young kid going to his summer diving clinic.

> Keith was always so happy. I came to know Keith as an incredible coach, having a great sense of humor.
>
> Keith helped me go from being a small town diver to one of the top collegiate divers in the country. His knowledge of the sport and experience as a diver and coach made him one of our country's best.

After serving three years as Keith's assistant coach, Anna Tutunnikova became the diving coach at Binghamton University in Binghamton, New York. Binghamton joined the America East Conference in 2001. The first six years, Binghamton men took first or second in team conference championships to Maryland or Boston University.[356] Anna Tutunnikova's profile on Binghamton's Web site acknowledged her work with the famed Cougar coach: "While at Brigham Young, she worked with one of the country's most respected coaches, 1968 Olympian Keith Russell."[357]

Season Thirteen

Keith added a few top divers for the 2004–2005 season:

Angela Nelson, fifth on three-meter at the Junior Olympic Winter Nationals

Kristin Pitt, 2004 Colorado State Diver of the year

Ron Morris, two-time California Interscholastic Federation champion

Bryce Engstrom, ranked twenty-fifth in the nation by the National Interscholastic Swimming Coaches Association

For the first time at the Mountain West Conference Championships, neither BYU teams won. Both finished second to UNLV but Keith's divers won two titles.

Men's one-meter:

1. Scott Randall, BYU
2. Sterling Richards, Utah
3. John Lynch, Wyoming
4. Adam Miller, Wyoming
5. Andy Jones, Utah
6. Ron Morris, BYU

Men's three-meter:

1. Sterling Richards, Utah
2. Scott Randall, BYU
3. Damion Brown, Utah
4. John Lynch, Wyoming
5. Ron Morris, BYU
6. Adam Miller, Wyoming
7. Kevin Bretting, Wyoming
8. Bryce Engstrom, BYU

Men's platform

1. Ron Morris, BYU
2. Scott Randall, BYU
3. John Lynch, Wyoming
4. Andy Jones, Utah
5. Damion Brown, Utah
6. Adam Miller, Wyoming
7. Bryce Engstrom, BYU
8. Davey Greer, Air Force

Women's one-meter:

1. Becca Barras, New Mexico
2. Kelsey Patterson, Utah
3. Angela Nelson, BYU
4. Aubrey Low, BYU
5. Daryl Packard, UNLV
6. Kristin Pitt, BYU

Women's three-meter:

1. Kelsey Patterson, Utah
2. Becca Barras, New Mexico
3. Ginni van Katwijk, Wyoming
4. Angela Nelson, BYU
5. Kristin Pitt, BYU
6. Aubrey Low, BYU

Women's platform:

1. Becca Barras, New Mexico
2. Kelsey Patterson, Utah
3. Ginni van Katwijk, Wyoming
4. Jessica Field, UNLV
5. Aubrey Low, BYU
6. Nichole McLean, UNLV

Scott Randall was the only Mountain West Conference diver to qualify for the 2005 NCAAs. Keith praised Scott for that achievement, saying, "You have to dive well to beat divers from the PAC-10." Scott returned the compliment, telling one interviewer, "BYU has always had a good diving history. Coach (Keith) Russell is one of the best coaches in the nation."[358]

Scott Randall successfully finished thirty-fourth (last) on three-meter and thirty-fifth (last) on one-meter, both won by ASU's Joona Puhakka.

Season Fourteen

Keith's star recruits for the 2005–2006 season included:

Scott Thalman, Colorado State Diver of the year

Kimberly Chang, 2005 California Interscholastic Federation runner-up

Both BYU men and women took second at the 2006 Mountain West Conference Championships, although the men came undefeated with a 5-0 conference record.

Men's one-meter:

1. Sterling Richards, Utah
2. Kelly McCain, Texas Christian
3. Kevin Bretting, Wyoming
4. John Lynch, Wyoming
5. Ron Morris, BYU
6. Brady Lindberg, Air Force

Men's three-meter:

1. Sterling Richards, Utah
2. Kelly McCain, Texas Christian
3. John Lynch, Wyoming
4. Kevin Bretting, Wyoming
5. Brady Lindberg, Air Force
6. Ron Morris, BYU

Men's platform:

1. Brady Lindberg, Air Force
2. Ron Morris, BYU
3. R.J. Hesselberg, Texas Christian
4. Andrew Jones, Utah
5. Damion Brown, Utah
6. Kevin Bretting, Wyoming
7. John Lynch, Wyoming
8. Scott Thalman, BYU

Women's one-meter:

1. Kelsey Patterson, Utah
2. Kelly Seely, Texas Christian
3. Brittany Wainwright, Wyoming
4. Carrie Quinn, New Mexico

5. Emily Keefer, Wyoming
6. Karin Knudson, Colorado State
7. Angela Nelson, BYU

Women's three-meter:

1. Kelly Seely, Texas Christian
2. Kelsey Patterson, Utah
3. Saara Haapanen, Wyoming
4. Emily Keefer, Wyoming
5. Angela Nelson, BYU
6. Anna Braszkewiecz, Utah

Women's platform:

1. Kelsey Patterson, Utah
2. Danielle Dowds, Air Force
3. Kimberly Chang, BYU
4. Angela Nelson, BYU

Aaron Russell married Jamie Anderson on May 20, 2006. He was in law school in Houston and Jamie was a technical systems analyst for ExxonMobil. After passing the bar, Aaron worked for ExxonMobil as an associate land representative. He was Keith's last child to marry.

That summer, Keith and Marsha moved their daughter Mindy and her young children, Ashlyn, Claire, and baby McKay, from California to Provo. Mindy's husband, Ben, had accepted a teaching position in Utah. They lived with Keith and Marsha while their house was built.

After months of horrible headaches, a radiologist found a "small spot" in Mindy's brain. In October, a neuroradiologist noted that the lesion was too small to cause headaches, but he saw a significant Chiari malformation, a condition where brain tissue protrudes into the spinal canal.

By November, Mindy was unstable standing and by December, she was forgetting things. She had another CT scan and was told there was "something different," but wasn't told what. The next day, Marsha insisted Ben take Mindy to the ER after noticing her weakened state. There they learned that Mindy's CT scan showed the lesion had grown to the size of a grape. Another MRI showed two more. They quickly admitted her to the hospital.

Mindy had a spinal tap the following day and the doctors found no cancer cells. It broke Keith and Marsha's hearts to leave her in the hospital on Christmas Eve. Mindy had surgery on Christmas to remove the tumor on the midline of her brain. Dr. Reichman didn't remove the other two because of their precarious positions. By now, Mindy had lost twenty pounds and veered right when walking.

When Mindy came home, only her children brought her out of her unresponsive state. Dr. Reichman said the cancer was an astrocytoma, a malignant tumor of nervous tissue composed of astrocytes (star-shaped cells), either level two or three, he thought.

The final report came January 3, 2007. The cancer was level four, a glioblastoma, a malignant tumor of the central nervous system in the cerebrum, the worst-case scenario. Although Keith and Marsha were devastated, they felt thankful that Mindy remained mostly unaware. Their radiation oncologist, Dr. Clark, was optimistic because of Mindy's young age (thirty) and good health.

Marsha began educating herself on Mindy's cancer, searching for reasons to be hopeful:

> We spent the weekend reading up on cancer diets and reading about people on the internet who were still living after having level-4 glioblastoma. I printed up the stories. I read some to her, but it was hard to be optimistic because all of them had one thing in common: they had tumors that had been removed.
>
> Mindy took her first dose of chemo drugs Tuesday night. After radiation, she seemed to have renewed energy. I was in the dining

> room when she was coming down the stairs from my room with McKay in her arms. She hadn't been able to pick him up and hold him for at least two months. She took him and fed him, then got the kids ready for bed. She took the girls and read stories and sang songs. Then she wanted them to sleep with her.

Friday, January 12, Ben and Marsha took Mindy to the hospital for her treatments, but she was immediately admitted to the ER. Marsha left to get her pajamas, and when she returned, Mindy was on oxygen. Marsha noticed Mindy going a few seconds without breathing and foaming at the mouth. Marsha called in the doctor, who immediately admitted her to the ICU.

Mindy went into a coma that night. Swelling in her brain suppressed her breathing and other life processes. Mindy's sister-in-law Mindy, a nurse, flew in the next night from Maryland and talked with her nurses, who confirmed this was the end.

Keith and Marsha notified Mindy's brothers: Rex in Maryland, Rand in North Carolina, and Aaron in Texas. Kerri and Regan were in Utah. They put her on life support for two days, long enough for everyone to fly in and gather by her bedside to say their good-byes. Marsha recalls the last tender moments of Mindy's life:

> January 14, on Kerri's birthday, we all met at the hospital. Aaron called and we kept him on speakerphone so he could participate.
>
> We then went to Mindy's room and each of us had time to talk to Mindy. We then took her off of life support and she passed away at 2:30 pm.

Mindy's funeral was on her thirty-first birthday. All of Keith's brothers and sisters came, plus many other family members, including his vibrant, eighty-five year old mother, providing a tremendous support system. With the calm demeanor he is known for, Keith greeted those who attended the viewing and service. Keith's belief that he'd see Mindy in the next life gave him some sense of peace and comfort. He had taken many blows in his life and endured them with a power and grace second to none. And he took the ultimate blow of losing a child no differently.

Season Fifteen

Keith's star recruits for the 2006–2007 season included:

- Brandon Watson, Fifth at 2006 Senior Nationals and Junior World Team qualifier
- Marc Nelson, 2003 and 2004 Utah state champion
- Travis Day, three-time runner-up Utah state high school champion
- Emily Woods, 2006 Kentucky high school state champion
- Megan McGhie, 2006 Nevada state champion and regional champion
- Ava Jackman, 2006 Utah state high school champion
- Tricia Bowen, 2005 Utah state high school champion
- Tawni Jones, 2003 and 2005 Arizona state champion

The 2007 Mountain West Conference Championships belonged to Brandon Watson. He became Keith's eleventh BYU men's conference winner on both boards.

Men's one-meter:

1. Brandon Watson, BYU
2. Andrew Jones, Utah
3. Kevin Bretting, Wyoming
4. Damian Brown, Utah
5. John Lynch, Wyoming
6. Brady Lindberg, Air Force
7. R.J. Hesselberg, Texas Christian
8. Travis Day, BYU

Men's three-meter:

1. Brandon Watson, BYU
2. John Lynch, Wyoming
3. Kevin Bretting, Wyoming
4. David Arlington, Air Force
5. Andrew Jones, Utah
6. Tyler Miller, Wyoming
7. Damian Brown, Utah
8. Travis Day, BYU

Men's platform:

1. Brady Lindberg, Air Force
2. Brandon Watson, BYU
3. R.J. Hesselberg, Texas Christian
4. Andrew Jones, Utah
5. John Lynch, Wyoming

Women's one-meter:

1. Saara Haapanen, Wyoming
2. Angela Nelson, BYU
3. Kelsey Patterson, Utah
4. Tawni Jones, BYU

Women's three-meter:

1. Kelsey Patterson, Utah
2. Angela Nelson, BYU
3. Tawni Jones, BYU
4. Saara Haapanen, Wyoming
5. Emily Keefer, Wyoming
6. Carrie Quinn, New Mexico
7. Ava Jackman, BYU
8. Nicole Kelley, Colorado State

Women's platform:

1. Kelsey Patterson, Utah
2. Angela Nelson, BYU
3. Emily Woods, BYU
4. Tawni Jones, BYU

Qualifying two divers from Zone E for the 2007 NCAAs was especially impressive after all eleven female Zone E divers cleaned everyone's clock at the 2006 NCAAs, taking every top-eleven spot on one-meter and dominating American collegiate diving. No doubt BYU competed in the toughest zone at the time.

One-meter		Three-meter
1	Rui Wang, Hawaii	1
2	Qiong Jie Huang, Hawaii	2
3	Megan Farrow, Hawaii	3
4	Blythe Hartley, Southern California	4
5	Kimberley Popp, Southern California	
6	Cassidy Krug, Stanford	5
7	Tiffany Manning, Arizona	6
8	Kelsey Patterson, Utah	7
9	Erin Hobbs, Arizona State	8
10	Marisa Samaniego, UCLA	9
11	Devon Owen, Nevada-Reno	10

After missing out on the fun in 2006, Keith had one of his best NCAA showings ever. Brandon Watson finished fifth on three-meter, the highest placing freshman. After finishing the one-meter preliminaries in twelfth, he finished sixteenth after five straight Zone E divers. Freshman Tawni Jones was twenty-seventh on three-meter and thirty-sixth on three-meter.

Keith spent the summer darting all over the world, judging major meets on three major continents: to Germany in June for the German

Grand Prix; to Bangkok, Thailand in August for the World University Games, where the U.S. women won silver and the U.S. men won bronze; and to Mexico in September for the first World Series of Diving, where divers competed by invitation instead of qualification.

In a way, Keith's life had come full circle. First, he returned to the site of the 1968 Mexico City Olympics to judge the September World Series. A month later, he was named 2008 Olympic judge by Dick Smith Swim Gym teammate and one-time roommate Steve McFarland, who served on the board of trustees of USA Diving:

> I am more than relieved to announce that Keith Russell was named by the FINA Bureau as an Olympic Official. Keith, you are a terrific representative for this position and I hope you are set to judge the World Cup in China this February. I look forward to seeing you there. Best wishes, Steve.

What an honor to be the only American judge at an Olympic competition, even more rare than fighting for a spot on the team. He revealed his feelings about this privileged distinction to *LDS Living* magazine: "It's the epitome of everything that I have done. It feels as if I have won a gold medal." Another Dick Smith teammate, 1968 Olympic champion Bernie Wrightson, agreed with his selection, stating, "Wow for Keith! He, of all of us, deserves to be a judge there."

Season Sixteen

BYU women won their seventh Mountain West Conference championships in 2008.

Women's one-meter:

1. Tawni Jones, BYU
2. Stephanie Ortiz, Wyoming
3. Brittany Wainwright, Wyoming
4. Karin Knudson, Colorado State

5. Ava Jackman, BYU
6. Carrie Quinn, New Mexico

Women's three-meter:

1. Tawni Jones, BYU
2. Brittany Wainwright, Wyoming
3. Carrie Quinn, New Mexico
4. Stephanie Ortiz, Wyoming
5. Karin Knudson, Colorado State
6. Ava Jackman, BYU

Women's platform:

1. Kwan Ling Yu, Utah
2. Jennifer Ferguson, Texas Christian
3. Tawni Jones, BYU
4. Danielle Dowds, Air Force
5. Amy Freeberg, San Diego State
6. Emily Woods, BYU

Men's three-meter:

1. Raymond Hesselberg, Texas Christian
2. Mark Murdock, Wyoming
3. Joseph Callens, Texas Christian
4. Kyle Gobner, Wyoming
5. Tyler Miller, Wyoming
6. Bryce Engstrom, BYU

Tawni Jones qualified for the 2008 NCAAs, where she improved ten spots from 2007 to finish twenty-sixth on one-meter and thirteen spots on three-meter to finish fourteenth. She later expressed how fortunate she felt to dive for Keith:

> Keith Russell has been more than a coach to me during my time at BYU. He has been a father figure and someone I knew really cared about me. It has been easy diving for Keith because I

know I can trust him. He is always making jokes or saying funny comments to keep the mood at practice light and fun, but he also motivates us to work hard.

One time during my sophomore year I was very discouraged about a couple things and as I thought about what to do, Keith came into my mind. I went over to his house and asked him for a blessing. It made me realize how lucky I was, because nowhere else would I have been able to have had that experience with my coach.

Keith has always been someone I felt I could turn to for advice and someone that would just listen. Something he always would say to me was, "We'll do our best. That's all we can do." Whenever he said this, I felt better and knew it wasn't about winning or losing, it was about giving your all and that being enough. I love Keith and love diving for him. He has made diving for BYU more than I could have hoped for.

For Keith, a competition wasn't about being the best as much as it was about seeing everybody's best. It was about getting together with great athletes and putting on a great show. It was about representing his school or his country well. Of course he wanted his divers to win, but if they dove their best, that's all he could ask for, and he'd be happy with that.

Season Seventeen

Keith's star recuits for the 2008–2009 season included:

David Corless, two-time California Interscholastic Federation runner-up, recruited by Army, Brown, Columbia, Cornell, and Yale.

Sam Hatch, 2007 Arizona state champion and two-time regional champion

BYU won half the board titles at the 2009 Mountain West Conference championships.

Men's one-meter:

1. Ron Morris, BYU
2. Kyle Bogner, Wyoming
3. Tyler Miller, Wyoming
4. Kyle Callens, Texas Christian
5. David Arlington, Air Force
6. R.J. Hesselberg, Texas Christian
7. Kyle Van Valkenburg, Air Force

Men's three-meter:

1. R.J. Hesselberg, Texas Christian
2. Kyle Callens, Texas Christian
3. Mark Murdock, Wyoming
4. Ron Morris, BYU
5. Kyle Van Valkenburg, Air Force
6. Sam Hatch, BYU

Women's one-meter:

1. Ava Jackman, BYU
2. Stephanie Ortiz, Wyoming
3. Tawni Jones, BYU

Women's three-meter:

1. Stephanie Ortiz, Wyoming
2. Emily Huth, Wyoming
3. Jennifer Ferguson, Texas Christian
4. Tawni Jones, BYU
5. Ava Jackman, BYU

For only the second time in seventeen years, Keith didn't qualify a diver for the NCAAs, the ultimate competition in collegiate athletics. But it is no easy task to constantly recruit and train divers to become one of America's thirty-five best college divers. Fortunately, at this point in his life, Keith has enough fond memories in his sixty-plus years to fill a book. He has these rich memories because of what he has made his life about: giving. He has found fulfillment in helping others achieve their best, their dreams, and their goals.

Keith's success as a father is seen in his children's success. All six attended BYU, which in 2007 ranked seventieth best out of more than fourteen hundred schools in the *U.S. News and World Report* "America's Best Colleges." His oldest son is an award-winning anesthesiologist, another is a dentist, another is a law school graduate.[359]

Everyone who knows Keith always has something nice to say about him, as some the nation's best divers:

Olympian Rachelle Kunkel remembers Keith at Christmas:

> There are several memories I treasure about Keith, each time I think about them, I get a good laugh. One was watching *Three Amigos* with Keith. This was something we did as a team during Christmas-break training. It was a non-stop laugh-fest. Keith had seen the movie many times and would start laughing before each funny part and continue laughing to the next funny part, laughing through the whole movie. We would laugh at him laughing, because he couldn't stop laughing. It was a fun way to get an abdominal workout!

Olympic bronze medalist Tom Gompf watched Keith grow up and enjoyed the show. He has also observed that Keith hasn't received a lot of the credit he has deserved:

> I had the pleasure of diving with Keith and enjoyed immensely watching Keith develop into one of the best divers of the time. At the 1968 Olympic tryout in Long Beach I had the wonderful

opportunity to be a judge for the Men's 10-meter Platform where Keith qualified for the Olympic team. I will never forget Keith's forward one and a half with 3 twists. I didn't hesitate to award him a 10. Over the many years I've known Keith, I would have to say he deserved many more 10s for his performance as a diver, coach, father, and example for all of us in the diving world.

Olympic champion Bernie Wrightson spent more time with Keith than anyone in the 1960s and still remembers, in these powerful words, what a great athlete and guy he was:

> I trained with Keith almost every day starting the summer of 1962 until the end of the Olympics in 1968.
> First, there has never been a nicer guy on this planet. In those 6 years, I never saw Keith get mad—at anything! Meanwhile, I was known to bounce off the rafters on a weekly basis.
> Second, no one I have met before or after is more loyal and thoughtful of his family and friends. You want to be Keith's friend because he will never leave your side. Never.
> Third, there are few more gifted athletes, anywhere. Anytime.

Olympian Justin Wilcock paid him this honor:

> I think the greatest testament to Keith's character is his reputation. Keith is known worldwide, and if you ask any of those people about Keith, they will all tell you he is one of the nicest people.
>
> Whenever I tell people I was coached by Keith, they always express how great they think he is. He is known as a man of great integrity and has often been asked to give his opinion or be part of a committee in USA Diving because of this reputation. I am

grateful to have been influenced by this man and to be able to say that I was coached by the great Keith Russell.

Keith is an ideal example of the American dream. Through hours and years of practice at his passion, he has given himself the freedom to see where life could take him, and it has taken him far and wide, high and low, and beyond his wildest imagination. He is living proof that, in the words of his friend, Olympic champion Sammy Lee, "The last two words in American is I can."

Endnotes

1. F. Ward O'Connell, "Diving Twists: A Column on Diving," *Swimming World*, December 1968, 14.
2. Bob Crawford, "Keith and Kendis: Tale of Two Switches."
3. Dave Schulthess, "Wins Two International Diving Meets ... Keith Russell's Goal: '72 Olympics."
4. George Moore, "Presenting — The Tops of Arizona's Prep Gridders," *Arizona Republic*, date unknown, 1968, Sunday edition.
5. "Jackrabbits Bid for Class B Championship in Annual Track and Field Meet Held in Phoenix."
6. http://www.kuconnection.org/april2002/people_Glenn.asp.
7. "Mesa Swimmer Home from Coast."
8. Ted Kazy, "Mesa AC Swimmers Retain AAU Crown," *Arizona Republic*, June 23, 1957, 30.
9. Larry B. Marton, "MAC Tankers Cut National Relay Record"
10. http://www.jewishsports.net/biopages/MarilynRamenofsky.htm.
11. Jerry Eaton, "Mesa Swim Stars Win at Coronado," *Arizona Republic*, June 21, 1958, 31.
12. Hugh Harelson, "Encanto, Mesa Swim Junior Swim Titles," "Russell Sets 3 Marks; MAC Girls on Top"; and "New Records Set by Mesa Swimmers in Tucson Meet."
13. Bob Crawford, "Thirty Events Scheduled for Encanto Junior Olympics."
14. "Mesa, Encanto Win Swim Titles."
15. "Two Mesans Win Honors at Swim Meet."
16. Jerry Eaton, "Swim Gym to Host Holiday Water Festival," *Arizona Republic*, December 25, 1958.
17. http://www.ishof.org/honorees/89/89ldraves.html
18. http://www.ishof.org/honorees/89/89zolsen.html
19. http://www.ishof.org/honorees/88/88sgossick.html
20. "Russell, Willard Win Swim Events" and "Valley Divers Win Awards."
21. Biography for Tony Dow found at http://www.imdb.com/name/nm0235638/bio.
22. Biography for Esther Williams, found at http://www.esther-williams.com/bio .htm.
23. Biography for Buster Crabbe found at http://www.imdb.com/name/ nm0185568/bio.
24. Jerry Eaton, "Saguaro Swimmers Set 19 Marks," *Arizona Republic*.
25. "Age Group Sub-Teens to Swim" and "Swimmers Wind Up Age Meets."
26. "Mesa, PCC [Phoenix County Club] Aces Tops."
27. "Mesa Swimmers Capture AAU Tank Championships."
28. "Mesa, PCC [Phoenix County Club] Aces Tops," under "Other Winners—girls."
29. http://www.sptimes.com/2003/07/27/Tampabay/_Sincerely__Bruce_D_K .shtml.

30. "Mesa Mermaid Sets Rome Diving Debut," *Arizona Republic*, August 26, 1960, 45.
31. "Patsy Dives to Eighth Place: Held First Place but Optional Pick Proves Downfall," *Mesa Tribune,* August 26, 1960, front page.
32. "Patsy's Comeback Falls Short of Medal: Fights Her Way Up from Eighth to Fourth Place," *Mesa Tribune*, August 27, 1960, front page.
33. "German, Russ Get Gold; U.S. Olympians Falter," *Deseret News and Telegram*, August 30, 1960.
34. "588 Slated to Compete in LV Swimming Meet," *Las Vegas Sun*, September 9, 1960.
35. Bob Rockafield, "Aquatic Meet Opens Tuesday: Fourteen Diving Events Launch Festivities," *Arizona Republic.*
36. www.csulaathletics.com/Sports/gen/2007/HOF.asp.
37. Bob Rockafield, "Aquatic Meet Opens Tuesday: Fourteen Diving Events Launch Festivities."
38. "Russell Places Fifth in Diving."
39. "Saguaro Swim Meet Entries Up: Entry Deadline Set" and "Youthful Plungers Face Test."
40. "Mesa Deacon's President Prepares for Diving Contests in Japan."
41. Jim Chemi, "After First Aid another Record: Bump Fails to Halt Mesa Boy," *Phoenix Gazette.*
42. http://yalebulldogs.cstv.com/sports/m-swim/stats/2004-2005/olympicgames.html.
43. Chemi, "First Aid."
44. http://en.wikipedia.org/wiki/1961_Maccabiah_Games.
45. Chemi, "First Aid."
46. http://sportsillustrated.cnn.com/magazine/features/si50/states/arizona/greatest.
47. Gene Goltz, *Arizona Republic*, 28 December 1961, 47.
48. Gene Goltz, "Mesa's Russell Wins Two Diving Events in Meet," *Arizona Republic.*
49. Ibid.
50. Gene Goltz, "Poulson Win Paces Diving," *Arizona Republic.*
51. Bob Rockafield, "Smith Pupils National Leaders."
52. "Willard Regains Crown."
53. Jim Chemi, "West's Best Divers in Saguaro," *Phoenix Gazette.*
54. Rockafield, "Smith Swimmers Top Saguaro Invitational; Records Tumble," *Arizona Republic*, May 27, 1962. Section C. Page 1.
55. Jim Chemi, "Mesa Shows Swim Balance," *Phoenix Gazette.*
56. Jim Chemi, "EYES ON MEXICO: 68-Event Tank Meet Set For Sunnyslope," *Phoenix Gazette.*
57. Jim Chemi,"19 Valley Tank Stars Off For Big LA Meet," Phoenix Gazette, July, 1962.
58. "Smith Gym Pupil Wins L.A. Diving Title" and "Valley Dominates Cal Meet Diving."
59. "Tank Stars Score At L.A."
60. "Valley Divers Set For Philly Tests," *Phoenix Gazette.*

61. Jim Chemi, "19 Valley Tank Stars Off For Big LA Meet," *Phoenix Gazette.*
62. "Local Swim Gym Competitors Head For Distant Tourneys."
63. "Jay Moxley Takes NAAU Diving Title."
64. Jim Chemi, "3 National Records Fall in AJO Swim" *Phoenix Gazette* and "Swim Gym Stars Net 4 Places."
65. "Valley Tank Stars Seek More Medals."
66. "Local Swim Gym Competitors Head For Distant Tourneys."
67. "11 Valley Dive Stars In Philadelphia Meet," *Phoenix Gazette.*
68. Jim Chemi, "5 All-America Divers In Meet," *Phoenix Gazette.*
69. "Billingsley Retiring," *New York Times,* Feb. 5, 1989.
70. http://www.ishof.org/honorees/83/83hbillingsley.html.
71. Bentley Historical Library – University of Michigan Athletics History – NCAA Diving Champions. http://bentley.umich.edu/athdept///swimmen/diving.htm.
72. Courtney Lewis, "Diving Area Named For Kimball," *Michigan Daily,* Feb. 2, 2002. http://media.www.michigandaily.com/media/storage/paper851/news/2002/02/11/Sports/Diving.Area.Named.For.Kimball-1404303.shtml.
73. Michigan in the Olympics – 1964 Tokyo. http://bentley.umich.edu/bhl/olymp2/ol1964.htm
74. Michigan in the Olympics – UM Olympic Coaches and Administrators. httpport.htm://bentley.umich.edu/bhl/olymp2/olcoach.htm.
75. http://www.databaseolympics.com/games/gamess.
76. Jim Chemi, "Wrightson New Dive Star," *Phoenix Gazette.*
77. ibid.
78. "Mesan Achieves National Rating In Diving Event."
79. http://pittsburghpanthers.cstv.com/sports/c-swim/mtt/krug_julian00.html.
80. "3-Meter Title At Lorenzo."
81. "Senior Open Tank Tests At Encanto."
82. "Mesa Swimmer Shines at Encanto."
83. Jim Chemi, "New Stars Face Swimfest," *Phoenix Gazette.*
84. Dan Hafner, "Finneran in Stunning Swim Upset."
85. ibid.
86. "Mettler Shines in Jr. Olympics."
87. "Clark Sets Swim Mark in AAU Test," *Arizona Republic,* 12 August 1963.
88. ibid.
89. "Phoenicians Thwarted in AAU Diving, Swimming Meet."
90. http://www.mpsaz.org/athletic/history/hall_of_fame/teams.htm.
91. Jim Chemi, "Patsy Holds Mid-Winter Title," *Phoenix Gazette.*
92. Jim Dobkins, "DeRivera, Patsy Willard Diving Winners," *Arizona Republic.*
93. ibid.
94. "Mesa Adds New Sport."
95. "Mesa High Tops Coronado."
96. "Mesa Swimmers Beat Scottsdale By 52-34 Margin."
97. "Mesa Outsplashes Westwood 56- 30," *Mesa Tribune.*
98. "Mesa High Swimmers Win."

99. "State Swim Meet Saturday."
100. "Koski Predicts Palo Verde Win" and "Titans Capture Swimming Title."
101. "Local Tankers Place High Nationally."
102. "Club Dedicates Diving Tower."
103. "Mesans Enter Diving Meet."
104. "Club Dedicates Diving Tower."
105. "Olympic Diving Tank May Be Built Here," *Mesa Tribune*, November 8, 1963, 7.
106. "Unions Donate Labor for Olympic Tank."
107. "Mesans Place Third In Diving Meet."
108. "AAU Senior Meet: U.S. Record Smashed."
109. Ibid.
110. "More About Arizona Swimming," continued from page 1-C.
111. Ibid. Also Jim Dobkins, "AAU Senior Meet U.S. Record Smashed."
112. "Mesans Place Well In Arizona AAU Meet."
113. "Arizona Stars Shine Brightly In AAU Events."
114. "State Divers Sweep AAU Championship."
115. Jim Chemi, "[St]. . .ate Aquatic Stars Seek Olympic Berths," *Phoenix Gazette*,
116. "State Adds Six Divers To Trials."
117. www.nycgovparks.org/sub_your_park/park_of_the_month/2005_07/thml/astoria_park.html.
118. "Swimmers Competing In Trials."
119. "Patsy Willard 3rd, Olympian Again; Wrightson Fourth."
120. Ibid.
121. Harald Lechenperg, ed., *Olympic Games 1964* (New York: A.S. Barnes and Co., 1964), 176.
122. "U.S. Adds Medal."
123. Lechenperg 178.
124. Paul De Tullio, "Mesa's Mettler Swims His Way To New Haven," *Mesa Tribune.*
125. "Wrightson Finished 3rd In Diving."
126. "Indiana's Gilbert Captures . . ." rest of title cut off.
127. Jim Chemi, "Diving Honors To Wrightson," *Phoenix Gazette.*
128. Dick Smith, "Russell, Teeples Top Divers," *Arizona Republic*, Sunday, May 16, 1965.
129. ibid.
130. "Russell Wins 3-Meter Event" and "Valley Swim Stars Shine."
131. Jim Dobkins, "Tanks, Titles, Trips For Moore Family," *Arizona Republic*, July 3, 1965.
132. "Wrightson Takes AAU Title Again," *Arizona Republic*, August 12, 1965.
133. "Wrightson Now Seeks Dive Sweep."
134. "Wrightson Wins 2nd. . ."
135. Ibid.
136. "Large Field Entered In AAU Swim Meet."
137. "Phoenix Swimmers Star In AAU Test."

138. Standings. *Swimming World Magazine*, September 1965, 44.
139. "Large Field Entered In AAU Swim Meet."
140. "Mesa Diver Wins Crown," "Smith Divers Go On Tour," and "Mesans to Make European Tour."
141. http://www.cardiffcastle.com/castle.htm.
142. www.cardiffontheweb.com.
143. "Mesa Diver Wins in Spain," *Mesa Tribune*, 7 September 1964 and "Diving Win To Russell."
144. "U.S. Effort in Spain Affected by Tough Weather and Competition," *Swimming World*, Oct. 1965, 12.
145. *U.S. News and World Report* 2007 edition of America's Best Colleges.
146. "Mesan Gets Grand Slam."
147. "Russell's Diving Sparks Mid-Winter Aqua Meet."
148. "Russell, Willard Dominate Diving."
149. http://tornadoproject.com/.
150. http://www.srh.noaa.gov/mlb/132c.html.
151. *Swimming World*, May 1966, "Senior Men's National AAU Indoor Championships" meet results, 55.
152. "All-America Aquatic Team Includes Seven Arizonans."
153. "O'Connell, Gossick, & Willard Win," *Swimming World*, May 1966, 9.
154. Steve Weston, "Denslow, Russell Dive to Victories," *Arizona Republic*.
155. Steve Weston, "Margin in Prelims Leads 13-Year-Old Phoenician to National Diving Crown."
156. "Arizona's Divers in Bad Luck."
157. "Wrightson Wins Again."
158. "Wrightson Retains Diving Title; Miss Moore Poised."
159. "Injury Didn't Stop Russell."
160. "Diver's Death Draws Inquiry," *The New York Times*. January 5, 1984.
161. Bob Ottum, "Getting High in Mexico City," *Sports Illustrated*, October 25, 1965.
162. "MESA: Arizona Youth, Rates 'High Diver.'"
163. Steve Weston, "Bernie, Charlie Top: Improving Youngsters Blossoming."
164. *Swimming World* meet results, 10.
165. "Mesa Diver Sensational at Festival."
166. Steve Weston, "Bernie, Charlie Top: Improving Youngsters Blossoming."
167. "Russell, Peterson Champs: Dive Tests Open Aquatic Competition," *Arizona Republic*.
168. "Russell Grabs Honors in 3-Meter Board," *Tempe Daily*. "National Indoor Diving Championships to Open," *Arizona Republic*.
169. "Russell Nabs Two Gold Medals," *Swimming World*, May 1967, 38.
170. "Russell Grabs Honors in 3-Meter Board," *Tempe Daily*.
171. http://www.aafla.org/8saa/PanAm/winnipeg67.htm nickname on flag.
172. "Local Divers Swap Honors."
173. "Arizonans Lead Diving Contests," *Phoenix Gazette*.
174. "Patty Simms, Russell Win."

175. “Rain Mars Pan-Am Opening,” *Arizona Republic*, July 24, 1967.
176. “Arizonans Star.”
177. “World Swim Records Fall.”
178. “Hickcox, Russell Score Firsts: Schollander Rips Mark.”
179. Jerry Liska, “Russell Double Winner in AAU.”
180. “Russell Captures Platform Diving: World Records Bettered By Burton, Buckingham.”
181. Swimming World, National AAU Men’s Championships meet results, September 1967.
182. “Russell Captures Platform Diving.”
183. “Tank Forces . . . ? . . . Tour Japan.”
184. Kenneth Moriyasu, “More World Marks-But US Swim Monopoly Ends.”
185. “Pre-Games Test: No Flags In Mexico,” October 14, 1967.
186. “Russell in Pre-Olympic Diving.”
187. Jerry Megahan, “Italy’s Dibiasi, Russia’s Alexeeva Win Platform Diving,” *The News*, Oct. 25, 1967.
188. Dan Gutman, *Gymnastics*, New York: the Penguin Group, 1996, 101.
189. *Swimming World*, January 1968, 10.
190. Bob Crawford, “Keith and Kendis: Tale of 2 Switches.”
191. “9,000 Hours Reap Success,” *State Press*, February 8, 1968.
192. “Russell Awaits Olympic Diving Competition,” *State Press Weekend*, May 17, 1968, 3-B.
193. ibid.
194. http://www.ci.santa-clara.ca.us/park_recreation/pr_internat_swim.html. history.html.
195. Mike McDermott, “Keith Russell to Defend 2 Diving Titles,” *Arizona Republic*, April 7, 1968.
196. http://www.ci.santa-clara.ca.us/park_recreation/pr_internat_swim.html.
197. http://news.surfwax.com/sports/files/Mark_Spitz.html.
198. *Swimming World*, September 1968, 26.
199. “Wrightson, Russell Get Olympic Berths,” *Arizona Republic*, August 23, 1968.
200. *Swimming World*, September 1968, 20.
201. *Swimming World* says it was a boy. *Arizona Republic* says it was a girl.
202. *Swimming World*, September 1968, 20.
203. “Russell Nabs First in Platform Diving,” *Arizona Republic*, August 25, 1968.
204. Paul Zimmerman, “Russell’s Final Dive Wins Olympic Trials,” *Los Angeles Times*.
205. “The Problem Olympics,” *Sports Illustrated*, September 30, 1968.
206. *Swimming World*, September 1968.
207. F. Ward O’Connell, “Diving Twists: A Column on Diving,” *Swimming World*, Sept. 1968, 23.
208. “Bernie, Keith Both Capture Olympic Spots,” *Phoenix Gazette*, August 23, 1968.
209. http://www.experiencecoloradosprings.com/travel.asp?pageid=17%7C57%7C113%7C152.
210. R. Jackson Smith, “Another Look at XIX Olympic Diving,” *Swimming World*, 1968, 14.

211. *Swimming World*, November 1968.
212. Hack Miller, *Salt Lake Tribune* (?), "LDS Diver Seeks Gold," Week of Monday, October 21, 1968.
213. http://jordan.fortwayne.com/ns/sports/top50/wichman.php
214. "Olympic Story," *Swimming World*, November 1968, 19 and 51.
215. "Mesan Victim of Olympic 'Conspiracy', Coach Claims."
216. F. Ward O'Connell, "Diving Twists: A Column on Diving," *Swimming World*, 1968, 14.
217. Marion Dunn, "BYU Ace Diver Sets Sail For Summer Olympics," *Salt Lake Tribune.*
218. Karen Duffin, "BYU Diving Coach Leads Life of Perseverance," *The Daily Universe*, March 11, 1998.
219. R. Jackson Smith, "Another Look at XIX Olympic Diving," *Swimming World*, 1968, 14.
220. "Diver Sets Sail (For) Olympics," *Salt Lake Tribune*, Jan. 1972. No date but mentions 2 mo. old Rex.
221. "BYU Diver Eyes Olympic Spot," no date.
222. *Swimming World*, May 1971, 20.
223. "BYU Diver Eyes Olympic Spot," *Daily Herald*, January 18, 1972.
224. "National AAU Diving Champs" meet results, *Swimming World*, September 1971, 61.
225. Lew McDonald, "National Pre-Qualifying Zone III – California," *Swimming World*, October 1971, 31.
226. "Mesa Swimmer to Represent US in European Competition."
227. "U.S.A. Team Routs U.S.S.R. and Britain," *Swimming World*, October 1971, 5.
228. Denis Hands, "Top Divers in City," *Pretoria News*, December 10, 1971, 28.
229. Dick Smith, "Dick Smith's Diving," *Swimming World*, April 1972, 22.
230. Dave Schulthess, "Wins Two International Diving Meets . . . Keith Russell's Goal: '72 Olympics."
231. Dick Smith, "Dick Smith's Diving," *Swimming World*, April 1972, 22.
232. Neville Leck, "Olympic '72 Preview," *Cape Times*, December 18, 1971, 20.
233. "Diver Sets Sail (For) Olympics," *Salt Lake Tribune*, No date.
234. "BYU Diver Eyes Olympic Spot," *Daily Herald*, January 18, 1972.
235. Dave Schulthess, "Wins Two International Diving Meets . . . Keith Russell's Goal: '72 Olympics."
236. "Y Swimmers Nab Win Over ASU," *Deseret News*, February 4, 1972.
237. Dave Clemens, "Diving trio leads Aquatics."
238. "Cougars Hope to Amass Many Points in Diving," *Herald*, March 1, 1972, 6.
239. "Rams End Utah Reign."
240. "Rams Upset Utes For Swimming Title; Cougars Take Third."
241. "Divers Put BYU In NCAA Top 20."
242. NCAA results, *Swimming World*, April 1972.
243. Dick Smith, "NCAA Diving Championships," *Swimming World*, April 1972, 15.
244. Dick Smith, "Boggs, Dunfield, Rydze, King, Potter, Knape Win AAU Dive Titles," *Swimming World*, May 1972, 21.

245. "Hoosiers, Santa Clara COP AAU Indoor Combined," *Swimming World*, June 1972, 59.
246. "Five Diving Champions Crowned at Nationals," *Swimming World*, August 1972, 6.
247. "Boggs, Russell falter."
248. "Boggs, Ely in AAU diving lead."
249. "AAU National Diving Meet," results, *Swimming World*, October 1972, 72.
250. Ibid.
251. "Boggs, Russell falter."
252. "Finneran executes first perfect dive."
253. www.brainyencyclopedia.com/encyclopedia/1/19/1972_summer_olympics.html.
254. "Local Athletes Shine . . . ? . . . in AAU Title Swim," August 23, 1973.
255. "1973 Men's Senior AAU Outdoor Diving Championships" meet results, *Swimming World*, Sept. 1973.
256. "AAU Diving," *Swimming World*, September 1973, 71.
257. Verne Boatner, "Swift Can't Stay Away."
258. Dick Smith, "Diving at the First World Championships," *Athletic Journal*, December 1973, 32-34.
259. Carolyn Finneran, "Diving Championships," *Swimming World*, October 1973, 30.
260. "Boggs Wins Gold Medal."
261. "Mesa Diver Gets Bronze."
262. "U.S. Wins World Swimming Team Title: Montgomery takes 100 free for 4th gold," *Arizona Republic*, September 10, 1973.
263. United States Olympic Committee newsletter, Volume 8, Number 4, October 1973, 3.
264. Carolyn Finneran, "Diving Championships," *Swimming World*, October, 1973, 30.
265. *Winning Spirit III: An Inside Look at LDS Sports Heroes*, 74.
266. Ibid.
267. Dick Smith, "Diving at the First World Championships," *Athletic Journal*, December 1973, 32.
268. Smith 34-35.
269. "95 Killed as Jetliner Crashes and Burns Near Pago Pago."
270. "Swim Coach Dick Smith Safe in Crash."
271. Stan Redding, "Dick Smith: A restless man who is probably the best diving coach in the world and who minces no words in condemning the judges who decide which divers go to the Olympics," *Houston Chronicle*, Sunday, September 21, 1975, 7.
272. "Boggs Tops Diving; Russell Places 3rd."
273. "Boggs Highlights Los Angeles Invitational Diving Meet," *Swimming World*, September 1974, 58.
274. "Mesa Diver Wins Again," August 21, 1974.
275. ibid.
276. Janet Murphy, "Russell Wins a Big One," *Decatur Daily*, August 15, 1974, B-3.

277. *Winning Spirit III: An Inside Look at LDS Sports Heroes*. 76.
278. Dick Smith, *Swimming World*, October 1974, 33.
279. "Mesa Diver Wins Again," August 21, 1974.
280. "Russell Sacks Diving Crown on Record Total," August 18, 1974.
281. www.ishof.org/Honorees/2005/05smcfarland.html.
282. Dick Smith, "Diving," *Swimming World*, October 1974, 31.
283. Carolyn Finneran, "USA – DDR Diving," *Swimming World*, October 1974, 11.
284. "Mesa Diver Keith Russell Joins Old Coach in Texas."
285. DDR Diving Championships Results, *Swimming World*, June? 1975, 86.
286. "Diving in Review: 1975 Was No Flop," *Swimming World*, January 1976, 8.
287. "Dibiasi Wins on Platform."
288. Myron McReynolds, "Boggs, Moore Snare Pan American Spots," *Daily Courier*, August 15, 1975.
289. Myron McReynolds, "Boggs, McIngvale Snap Up Titles: Boggs, Moore Snare Pan American Spots," *Daily Courier* (Texas), August 15, 1975, 5.
290. Stan Redding, "Dick Smith: A restless man who is probably the best diving coach in the world," *Houston Chronicle*, September 21, 1975, 7.
291. Myron McReynolds, "Ely Dazzles Crowd, Judges," *Daily Courier*, Aug. 17, 1975, 6.
292. "Louganis Stars in Diving Trials," *Swimming World*, August 1976, 25.
293. William Pitchford, "Rory Russell's Diving Leads Swimmers to Wins," *Jackrabbit*, April 27, 1979, 4.
294. The University of Utah, Men's Swimming and Diving Records, PDF File found at http://graphics.fansonly.com/photos/schools/utah/sports/c-swim/auto_pdf/06-07-media-guide.pdf.
295. For the Record: 1980 NCAA Swimming and Diving Championships results, Swimming World.
296. John Mooney, "Best Woman Since Beck? Utes' Cook Diving For Olympic Spot," *Salt Lake Tribune*, February 1980.
297. For the Record: Western Athletic Conference Championships results, *Swimming World*, April 1981, 90.
298. For the Record: AIAW Championships, *Swimming World*, April 1981, 81.
299. Gary Horowitz, "Desert Divers Soaring Higher Behind Ex-Olympians Coaching," *Arizona Republic*, August 7, 1987.
300. Rob Grady, "Brophy boys, Xavier girls repeat state titles," *Mesa Tribune*, November 16, 1986.
301. Gary Horowitz, "Desert Divers Soaring Higher," *Arizona Republic*.
302. "Junior Divers Spring into Regional Meet," *Mesa Tribune*, July 23, 1987.
303. Gary Horowitz, "Desert Divers Soaring Higher Behind Ex-Olympians Coaching," *Arizona Republic*, August 7, 1987.
304. Gary Horowitz, "3 Desert Divers Reach Nationals," *Arizona Republic*, August 14, 1987.
305. Ibid.
306. Gary Horowitz, "Garner's Silver Medal Top Effort by Arizona Divers at Nationals," *Arizona Republic*, August 28, 1987.

307. Gary Horowitz, "Mesa Diver Makes Quite a Splash," *Arizona Republic*, July 27, 1988.
308. *Phoenix Gazette*, August 10, 1988.
309. Gary Horowitz, "A Great Year for Arizona Divers," *Arizona Republic*, August 1988.
310. Ibid.
311. "Seven Local Divers Qualify for Nationals in Junior Olympics," *Mesa Tribune*, August 3, 1990.
312. Brett Jewkes, "Y Women Win 2 Swim Meets, Men Split 2 in New Mexico," *Daily Universe*, November 10, 1992.
313. Untitled four-paragraph article, *Deseret News*, January 8, 1993.
314. "Three BYU Divers at Invitational," *Daily Herald*, January 5, 1993.
315. Taunya Terry, "Divers Make a Splash in Texas," *Daily Universe*, January 12, 1993.
316. Taunya Terry, "BYU Diver Sets Sights on All-America Honor," *Daily Universe*, March 10, 1993.
317. Taunya Terry, "Cougar Swimmers Win WAC Title, Prepare for NCAA Championships," *Daily Universe*, March 4, 1993.
318. "BYU Diver 1st in 3-meter Springboard," March 13, 1993.
319. "Blau 2nd at Zone E Diving Meet," *Daily Herald*, March 14, 1993.
320. "All-Americans," *Daily Herald*, March 20, 1993.
321. http://media.wildcat.arizona.edu/media/storage/paper997/news/2008/03/13/Sports/Dive-Teams.Plunge.Into.Zone.E.Regional.Champs-3267596.shtml.
322. Dick Harmon, "Young Leads Five into BYU Athletic Hall of Fame," *Daily Herald*, March 25, 1994.
323. "Cougar Men Paddle Past Notre Dame; Women Fall," *Daily Herald*, October 15, 1994.
324. "BYU Ace Sets WAC Record," *Daily Herald*, March 3, 1995.
325. Jon Mano, "Cougar Women Dominate Field, Swim to 3rd Straight WAC Title," *Daily Universe*, March 6, 1995.
326. "Cougar Divers off to Regionals," *Daily Herald*, March 9, 1995.
327. "BYU's Moak Dives into Nationals," *Deseret News*, March 12, 1995.
328. "BYU Divers Reach NCAA Meet," *Daily Herald*, March 11, 1995.
329. Marissa Silvera, "First Two Victories Go to BYU Divers," *San Antonio Express*.
330. Marissa Silvera, "Cougars Still in Command at WAC Meet," *San Antonio Express*.
331. ibid.
332. Scott Apgar, "Y Divers Hope They Hit the 'Zone' This Week," *Daily Universe*.
333. Scott Apgar, "Diver Earns NCAA Spot at Zone Competition," *Daily Universe*.
334. Scott Apgar, "Turner Ready to 'Dive' into New Phase of Life," *Daily Universe*, April 1, 1996.
335. World Student Games – swimming and diving (women) at http://www.gbrathletics.com/sport/swimwsgw.htm.
336. World Student Games – swimming and diving (men) at http://www.gbrathletics.com/sport/swimwsg.htm.
337. Tricia Garner, "Cougar Women Looking to Make a Splash at 2000 NCAA Championships," *Daily Universe*, March 14, 2000.

338. Tricia Garner, "Cougar Divers Sweep First Day of Regional Qualifying Meet," *Daily Universe,* March 10, 2000.
339. Tricia Garner, "Cougar Men Struggle in Second Day of NCAAs," *Daily Universe,* March 24, 2000.
340. Shane Bevell, "2000-2001 Men's Swimming Outlook," *Daily Universe,* October 16, 2000.
341. Shane Bevel, "Cougars Ready to Defend MWC Title," *Daily Universe,* February 12, 2001.
342. Shane Bevel, "Divers Perform Well at Qualifying Meet," *Daily Universe,* March 10, 2001.
343. *Winning Spirit: An Inside Look at LDS Sports Heroes.*
344. Joseph Evans, "2001-2002 Men's Swimming Outlook," *Daily Universe,* July 1, 2001.
345. Carla O'Connell, "2001 World University Games: Medal Quest Continues for U.S. Divers," August 27, 2001. Found at http://www.usoc.org/73_3277.htm.
346. Carla O'Connell, "2001 World University Games: U.S. Men's Team Earns Bronze Medal," August 29, 2001. Found at http://www.usoc.org/73_3311.htm.
347. Ibid.
348. Jason Wells, "Aaron Russell, All-American and Academic All-American," *Daily Universe.* October 23, 2002.
349. Jason Wells, "Men and Women Lead MWC Heading into Final Day," *Daily Universe.* February 21, 2003.
350. http://gostanford.cstv.com/sports/m-swim/recaps/031703aaa.html.
351. http://usctrojans.cstv.com/sports/m-swim/stats/032703aab.html.
352. BYU Swimming and Diving 2003-2004 Media Guide, 31.
353. Ron Kontura, www.usadiver.com/o_trails_04/w3m_finals.htm. "Soldati/Kunkel Athens Bound."
354. Kyle Cottam, "Former BYU Divers Heading to Finals in U.S. Olympic Team Trials," *Daily Universe,* June 10, 2004.
355. Ron Kontura, www.usadiver.com/o_trails_04/w3m_finals.htm. "Dumais Win 3-Meter, Wilcock Second."
356. http://www.americaeast.com/swimming.
357. http://athletics.binghamton.edu/sports/mswim/coaches.html.
358. Kyle Cottam, "Randall Fulfills Goal by Competing in the NCAAs ," *Daily Universe,* March 22, 2005.
359. Rex received the Air Force Achievement Medal on June 8, 2006 for "outstanding achievement as Anesthesiologist, Surgical Element and Mobile Field Surgical Team, 379th Expeditionary Medical Group, 379th Air Expeditionary Wing, Al Udeid Air Base, Qatar.